The Consulting Astrologer's Guidebook

Books by Donna Cunningham

Published by Samuel Weiser

Being a Lunar Type in a Solar World
Healing Pluto Problems
The Consulting Astrologer's Guidebook

From Other Publishers

An Astrological Guide to Self-Awareness
Astrology and Spiritual Development
Astrology and Vibrational Healing
Flower Remedies Handbook
Moon Signs: Key to Your Inner Life

With Andrew Ramer

Spiritual Dimensions of Healing Addictions
The Further Dimensions of Healing Addictions

The Consulting Astrologer's Guidebook

Donna Cunningham

SAMUEL WEISER, INC.

York Beach, Maine

First published in 1994 by
Samuel Weiser, Inc.
P.O. Box 612
York Beach, ME 03910-0612

Library of Congress Cataloging-in-Publication Data
Cunningham, Donna
The consulting astrologer's guidebook / by Donna Cunningham.
p. cm.
Includes bibliographical references and index.
1. Astrologers—Training of. 2. Astrology—Practice. I. Title.
BF1711.C86 1994
133.5'023—dc20 93–42845
CIP

ISBN 0–87728–790–2
MG

Charts used in this book have been calculated and printed by Astrolabe, Inc. of Brewster, MA, using its *Nova* and *Printwheels* computer programs.

Typeset in 10 point Garamond

Printed in the United States of America
99 98 97 96 95 94
10 9 8 7 6 5 4 3 2 1

The paper used in this publication meets the minimum requirements of the American National Standard for Permanence of Paper for Printed Library Materials Z39.48–1984.

This book is dedicated to my own personal A List—to the astrological forerunners and colleagues I most respect for their contributions to our field. Please forgive the Americocentricity of my vision—as an astrologer, I grew up with these people!

Evangeline Adams
Edith Custer
Doris Chase Doane
Zipporah Dobyns
Charles Emerson
Francoise Gauquelin
Michel Gauquelin
Jeff Green
Liz Greene
Rob Hand
Doris Hebel
Isabel Hickey
Richard Idemon
Jeff Jawer
Jim Lewis
Betty Lundsted
Michael Lutin
Marion March
Tracy Marks
Joan McEvers
Neil Michelsen
Buz Myers
Ingrid Naiman
Eileen Nauman
Joan Negus
Ken Negus
Alan Oaken
Maritha Pottenger
Lois Rodden
Dane Rudhyar
John Ruskell
Howard Sasportas
Erin Sullivan
Noel Tyl
Donna Van Toen

TABLE OF CONTENTS

List of Charts

Acknowledgments

To Betty Lundsted for agreeing to be my editor on this project and thus giving us the benefit of her own years of astrological practice. To Samuel Weiser, Inc., for making this text possible.

To *The Mountain Astrologer*, for permission to reprint a variety of articles from my series for professional astrologers. To the other astrological journals worldwide, too numerous to list, who also printed brief sections of this material as a way of seeding the idea of a curriculum for professional astrologers.

To Llewellyn Publications, for permission to reprint my chapters from two of their New World Astrology Series anthologies, "Updating the Tradition," from *How to Use Vocational Astrology for Success in the Workplace*, edited by Noel Tyl, and "Codependency, the Adult Child Syndrome and How They Affect Astrological Practice," from *Astrological Counseling*, edited by Joan McEvers.

To Dell Horoscope Magazine for permission to reprint my article, "What in Heaven's Name is a NORMAL Crisis?" from the 10/92 issue.

To Gail Fairfield for permission to reprint an excerpt from my foreword to her excellent book, *Choice-Centered Astrology*.

To Bill Baeckler, an excellent vocational counselor and astrological colleague, for his input into the chapter on vocational astrology, as well as his astute comments on other chapters.

INTRODUCTION

Why Can't Jenny Read?

Have you been studying astrology for a number of years and still feel ill-equipped to read a chart? Or, have you been doing readings for a while, but still feel inadequate when confronted with clients' problems? If so, you are not alone. In doing workshops for various astrological organizations around the world, it is puzzling and dismaying to see so many bright, caring students who seem to have a great deal to offer, but who are stuck at the threshold of practicing astrology. Often, they are stuck for five, six, or even ten years without being able to cross that threshold. A great many others read the occasional chart but aren't pleased with their performance or still lack the confidence to go ahead and develop a practice.

After observing this phenomenon for a while, I decided a group discussion might help, so I began leading discussions at conferences and workshops under the title, "Why Can't Jenny Read?" The rooms overflowed with advanced students and the newly professional who needed a forum to express their concerns and uncertainties. Throughout this book, we'll look at issues these groups repeatedly raised, as no doubt many of the same issues have troubled others.

What became abundantly clear in listening to them, however, is that THERE IS ONE MAIN REASON JENNY CAN'T READ—AND THAT IS BECAUSE WE AREN'T TEACHING HER HOW. Although their self-doubts are often agonizing, the lack is not so much in the students as in the curriculum. There are plenty of classes, workshops, and conferences about the various branches and techniques of astrology. Even in isolated areas where there are no groups, there are books galore on any area of interest. After five or seven or as many as ten years of study, surely these students are not lacking in knowledge of astrology.

What advanced students often lack is the knowledge of how to talk to people about what they know—the counseling dimension of astrological practice. Thankfully, for many years there have been many astrological books and workshops with a psychological bent, so that we can gain an understanding of human motivation.

Two particularly useful volumes are from the Llewellyn New World Astrology Series—*Astrological Counseling: The Path of Self-Actualization*, edited by Joan McEvers, and *How to Use Vocational Astrology for Success in the Workplace*, edited by Noel Tyl. Llewellyn was kind enough to allow me to reprint my own chapters from those two books as Chapters Five and Six in this one, so that this book will be complete.

As I surveyed the available literature, it became clear that what was missing was how to conduct an astrological reading in such a way as to further the client's self-awareness—a how-to-do-readings text for astrologers. Without a professional-level curriculum, we cannot become a full-fledged profession and earn public respect. As this important gap in the curriculum became clear, I decided it was time to share my knowledge. I have the background—a master's in social work and more than 25 years counseling experience. Rather than continue to gripe and moan about the lack of a professional curriculum, maybe it was something I needed to do. So, I got to work. It wasn't easy to articulate what to do in a chart reading, any more than it is to explain how to walk. The process forced me to think through the principles I learned in social work. I had to adjust what I knew so that it would apply to astrology readings, and I learned a great deal in the process!

The result became a series of lectures about astrological counseling. [I also went to a recording studio and did a series of professional training tapes.] As the material developed, it turned into articles for *The Mountain Astrologer* and other journals. Some of these articles are reprinted here in more detail than was possible in those space-limited articles or in the time-limited lectures and workshops they were based on.

So—what do student astrologers who don't read charts say? Their main reasons for hesitating could be summarized as follows:

"I don't know enough."
"It's too much responsibility."
"I'm overwhelmed with clients' problems."
"I don't know how to help them."
"There's so much in the chart, I don't know where to start."
"I don't know how to explain the chart to them."
"I don't feel I could charge money for it."
"I couldn't make a living that way."

The chapters in this book are designed to explore some of these issues in depth. I provide information and exercises designed to help you come to some resolutions. For instance, Chapter One explains a way of finding an effective focus for the reading, and Chapter Two is a guide for translating astrologese into plain English, so astrologers can communicate with clients. Chapter Three teaches you how to deal with crisis situations, and Chapter Four explores sources of help for the often overwhelming problems clients bring to readings. Resolving the common ambivalence about charging for readings and making a decent living as an astrologer are the focus of Chapter Eight.

In the course of this book, many questions will come up for which I do not present answers. When you are on the front lines doing readings, you need to be able to think questions like these through for yourself. It is premature, at this stage of evolution of astrology as a profession, for any of us to draw hard and fast rules. Furthermore, I don't have all the answers. Really. You won't either. The best-trained therapists and healers in the world don't have all the answers. They just get on with it, with nearly as much agonizing in the beginning as you are doing. But, hopefully this book will give you some tools so that you, too, can get on with it.

I will also present some standards that may seem daunting to carry out. Many of them are ideals to aim for, and I certainly can't claim to live up to all of them all the time, either. All of us make many mistakes in the course of learning our craft, and I derived many of these principles through the mistakes made in working with clients. We all learn by doing, but my hope is that this book will help you to avoid some unnecessary errors.

As we think through various counseling issues, many parallels to well-established professions, such as psychotherapy, will arise. What we do is not the same as what they do, but, like them, we are dealing with people's emotions and difficulties. Therefore, it can be useful to see if what they have learned, with a longer history of professional training and discipline, can clarify matters for us.

One helpful feature that well-established professions provide their students is an apprenticeship structure. The doctor-in-training completes a long internship and residency, the student nurse also rotates through various wards, the social work student spends two or three days a week in the field, and the student teacher spends a semester or more in the schools. This is a required part of their curriculum, and successfully completing it is a prerequisite for graduation.

Apprenticeships consist of a period of observation and reduced responsibility in which a teacher or mentor closely supervises the student. Under the guidance of a well-seasoned professional, the student is able to try out the techniques learned in class on a small, carefully-selected set of patients or clients. As the student gains in skill and experience, the caseload and set of responsibilities gradually increase, until the new practitioner is able to function independently.

At this writing, apprenticeship programs are nearly unheard of in astrology, with a few welcome exceptions. This, and the lack of a set of minimum standards which astrologers would have to meet in order to practice, are the main criteria of a profession which astrology has yet to meet. Without such features, it is difficult for any discipline to be recognized and accepted—and for good reason. The apprenticeship system is the hallmark of a true profession, as it protects both the student and the people the profession is designed to serve.

Why are there few apprenticeship programs to help students bridge the gap into professional practice? It is partially because we astrologers tend to be Uranian types. We are richly endowed with positive Uranian qualities like egalitarianism, inventiveness, a unique perspective on life, and humanitarianism. Unfortunately, we as a group also partake, all too richly, of other Uranian qualities which get in the way of accepting supervision and the apprenticeship system. We tend to be fiercely independent, arrogant, willful, resentful—even contemptuous—of authority, convinced we know more than anyone, and certain that the rules don't apply to us because we're so special.

This book is being written as Uranus moves through Capricorn, and it has been gratifying to see the increasing climate of receptivity to professional training materials and to the idea of standards. Although we have a long way to go, this passage of Uranus (the ruler of astrology) through Capricorn (the sign of professions, responsibility, self-discipline, and maturity), is a hopeful sign. Collectively, we are beginning to plant the seeds of a new era in astrology, seeds that will mature into a true profession and this book has been born out of my desire to contribute to that professional development.

I have a dream. My hope is that this book will rapidly be out of date or lost in a crowd of such books—that it will stimulate my many astrological colleagues with counseling backgrounds to develop training materials of their own. My wish is that twenty years from now—or even more optimistically, ten years from now—it will have a sort of historical quaintness. The first such how-to-do-readings book, to be sure, but rapidly dwarfed by such quantum leaps in training for professional astrologers that it deserves little more than a footnote. My dream is that in the distant future, students will read these words in a required History of Astrology course and say, "No apprenticeship system? How quaint! However did they manage?"

—Donna Cunningham

CHAPTER ONE

Conducting Effective Chart Readings by Beginning—and Ending—Well

What do you need to get from a book of this nature? What would help you be more comfortable and adept at reading charts? Where are you in your professional development—are you just beginning to do readings or have you been doing them for some time? What situations are hardest for you in dealing with clients? What issues could we discuss that would meet your needs as an astrologer? In sitting down to write this, I wish I could hear your answers. It would help me know what you need. Perhaps if there are still important concerns left when the book is finished, you could write to say what you'd like to see in another one in the future.

A book can't be interactive—you can't tell me what you need so that I can base the book on it—but a chart consultation *can and should be* interactive. The way this chapter began—by asking what you need to get from the book—is a good way to begin a session. Ask something like, "What do you need to get from a reading at this time?" or "Why are you wanting an astrology reading now?" Questions like these serve two purposes. First, they let clients know you are interested in hearing what they need so you can serve them better. Second, they help focus the session so you organize it around the client's most important concerns.

The old adage, "Well begun is half done," applies to astrology readings also. The way you structure your first contacts with a client sets the tone for the session. When you are focused and specific in these earliest encounters, the reading itself is more apt to be focused and specific. The more specific, the more likely it is to be effective and the more likely it is to satisfy the client. Rather than meandering for hours, you cover the defined needs in a reasonable length of time. This presumes that both you and the client will prepare for the meeting. This chapter will cover the phone call or conversation in which you make the appointment and the crucial first ten to fifteen minutes of the actual session. We will also discuss how to stay focused, and how to end the session well, providing closure for the client and setting the stage for future readings.

The Merits of Setting a Contract

In social work, which is my background, it is common to set a contract before beginning the work. What is a contract? It is an agreement between the client and the helping person about the nature of the work they will do together. It identifies the purpose of the meeting and the problems or issues to be addressed. It sets goals, agrees on an operating plan, and spells out what the helper is to do and what the client's role will be. In some settings, the contract is formal, with a written agreement and stated goals. These goals are given measurable outcomes—specific enough that you can determine whether they were met or not.

While we need not be so formal in the one-time astrology consultation, some of these principles can still be helpful. A contract is a negotiation about what the session will cover and what the relationship will be like. You are less likely to meet clients' needs and expectations if you don't know what they are! Sloppy contracts may result in inconclusive sessions, and afterward the clients feel they didn't get what they needed. Or, they might call you back a few times for information they didn't get because you didn't clearly establish the purposes of the meeting.

As Uranian types, we each bring our unique background to astrological practice, as well as a set of personal and often unusual gifts. We all have our own point of view, guiding philosophy, set of heroes, and previous history. Each of us has our own special contributions to make to the evolution and healing of our clients. A retired teacher might do excellent work reading charts of children with school problems. Someone who has been in business might be in a good position to advise clients on business matters. We'll be talking about how you can find your own special niche in chapter Eight. As a result, the form and content of astrology readings vary greatly. Nothing said here is meant to detract from developing your own unique style. What is presented is a method derived from social work principles which works well with the kinds of problems my clients bring.

This is a good time to mention that this book is written through my own personal lens. I am a consulting astrologer with a special interest in understanding the psychology of the individual and in resolving emotional issues. A consultation with a horary or medical astrologer, or even an astrologer who focuses on financial investments, would doubtlessly have some similarities to the process discussed here—as well as some important differences. If your interests are more purely predictive, for example, some sections of the book may not apply to your work. However, other sections, such as how to communicate well with the client or how to keep the session focused, can help you work more effectively regardless of your specialty. And, where the mechanics of pursuing your specialty differ greatly from this method, you would do a service by developing, or asking your teachers to develop, more appropriate curriculum materials.

First Contact—
Handling the Inquiry from the Client

The initial phone call or face-to-face conversation where you discuss the possibility of doing a reading is very important. It initiates the relationship and sets the tone for working together. If the first contact is in a social setting, it is more businesslike to have the person call later. That way you can talk privately and in more depth about the proposed consultation. Let's look at some scenarios that may arise in this first contact and at ways of handling them.

For the purposes of this chapter, we will assume that the caller is already sold on your services and simply wants to arrange an appointment. In reality, however, that assumption is usually not warranted. Thus, part of the first contact often has to do with selling prospective clients on your work. How comfortable are you with sales? (We'll deal with marketing in chapter Eight.)

Let's suppose you have begun by asking what this person needs to get from the session. In the ensuing discussion, you come to understand what the expectations are and whether you can meet them. You know what is bothering the client and what the issues are. When you zero in on the client's concerns, he or she also gets the message that you can put the needs of the client first. These questions help both you and the client to prepare for the appointment. They set a businesslike yet client-centered mood and also make the client think about the meeting. When you know what is needed, you will be able to prepare in an organized way, and will be able to cover the ground the client really wants to cover.

Sometimes callers will say that they are merely curious or that they have no idea what they want. This is more common with astrological virgins—people who have never had a chart done. It's helpful to ask if they've had readings before or studied astrology. If not, you will need to educate them about how you feel an astrological reading can be helpful. Many virgins have no idea what they want because they don't have the foggiest idea what a reading can accomplish. Maybe all they've ever seen is Sun sign columns in the newspapers. They don't know about transits, progressions, composites, electional charts, or solar returns—or any other techniques we use in the field of astrology.

It is up to you to explain these possibilities to first-time clients. It is usually enough to mention the areas covered by the houses and to talk about various applications such as chart comparisons or transits. In simple language, without using jargon, explain what astrology can do. So that you don't bombard them, confine your discussion to the possibilities that meet their current needs.

It often happens in astrological practice that you know the people who call you from another context. Especially when you first begin to practice, personal contact may have been how you met these clients in the first place. Perhaps you know them from work, a social group, through friends, or from some organization. In deciding whether you can read for these individuals, consider carefully what effects the history you share may have on your work. If you decide to see them, continue to be aware that this session is not occurring in pristine Freudian isolation. It is well to acknowledge this history and even ask how these people feel about seeing you in another context.

Many professionals in the "helping" field have fo someone they know becomes a client, it is difficult to co friends because of the ways the relationship changes. That other discussion—quite a valid one—and one where there final answers. You might want to get a tape on the subjec Michael Lutin.[1] For now, it's important to recognize the concer that this shift in the relationship can raise.

Some prospective clients have inappropriate expectations. For example, some people want everything from one session. They want transits and progressions, as well as a look at the charts of several of their loved ones to see what you can tell about that person and about the relationship. That is doubtlessly too much to cover in any useful depth. Explain why depth is preferable to an off-the-top-of-your-head, yes-or-no-answer. With all clients, you will save yourself lots of headaches if you begin defining limits and boundaries even in that first conversation. Before concluding, tell them how long the session will be, what is included, what it costs, and how you prefer to be paid.

Some needy people try to keep you on the phone for a long time. For a variety of reasons, it is best not to listen to their whole life story. For instance, clients who reveal too much on the phone may attribute your accuracy during the reading to the fact that you knew all about them beforehand. Some people calling in crisis are in pain and bubbling over with their problems, and you wouldn't be insensitive to that. However, to let potential clients talk for a long time can be draining and may establish a relationship where they call you as a free therapist. Show concern and warmth, see them as soon as you can, but suggest that you deal with these issues in the session.

Both in the initial contact and during the actual session, it is a good practice to issue disclaimers whenever you operate outside your area of professional competence, and this means when you give advice about decisions your clients are making. The need for a disclaimer holds true whenever you are asked about lawsuits, real es-

[1]Michael Lutin has discussed this issue in various lectures, such as "Counseling with Astrology," or "The Real Live Practice of Astrology." For a complete list of available tapes by a variety of fine astrological speakers, write to the National Council of Geocosmic Research, c/o Nan Milman, 15 Fordham Street, City Island, Bronx, NY 10464.

te, stock options, or any question where a legally-recognized and licensed profession deals with the issue. When health is the major concern, you need to proceed especially carefully, so you can never be accused of practicing medicine without a license. Even if medical astrology happens to be one of your specialties, be very clear with clients that you're not a doctor or a health practitioner. Stress that what you say about health is only based on the astrological chart. Emphatically state that it is not meant to be taken as a medical diagnosis. Suggest that clients follow up with their physician on any medical concerns.

Screening Callers Who Shouldn't Become Clients

Working on our own, we astrologers are very vulnerable to the public. We need to screen our calls carefully, because some callers may not be appropriate clients. Some people are difficult or even disturbed; some people are asking for services you personally cannot deliver; some people want answers astrology isn't constructed to give. By identifying inappropriate clients, you do a service both to callers and to yourself. When you screen out those who want something you can't give, you protect yourself from having clients who are disappointed. At worst, disappointed clients are bad for your reputation; at the very least, they aren't likely to refer anyone to you.

For instance, by asking questions before setting up the appointment, you will identify those people who want something that astrology cannot really do. For example, it may become clear that some callers really want a psychic reading and not a horoscope. They want specific details you can't get from a chart. Tell them so, explaining the difference between what a good psychic does and what information astrology can legitimately provide. Or, looking deeper, they might want to know about their past lives with their current lover. Explain the difference between a past life reading and a relationship chart.

You also educate them, for future reference, about what astrology does. You may need to practice articulating exactly what you do and what astrology is capable of. Many times, when you finish explaining why an astrology reading can't do what they want and what astrology does, they decide they want what you do anyway!

Suppose the caller needs something you aren't good at yet. It is useful to do a periodic stocktaking of what you are and are not ready to deal with. Just as we all have areas where we shine, we also have limitations. There is a kind of relief in not having to pretend that you are good at everything. You may want to limit your work to areas of comfort in the beginning. You can always add new areas of expertise later, when you feel more proficient.

If clients are asking for something you aren't able to provide, it is wiser to refer them to someone who specializes in that area. For instance, financial advising is something I don't have the expertise to do well, and sometimes a great deal of money is at stake. I simply say, "That's not my specialty. Might I suggest some experts in that area?" Callers appreciate this kind of honesty. They remember you, too, and come back.

Some clients harbor magical hopes about what the session will do—whether they express them or not. This is true even in such secular professions as medicine and psychotherapy, but more so with us because of the divine dimension of our work. For instance, you may do a chart for a woman who is well-pleased with the session and especially with the points you make about her marriage. She then pushes her husband into a consultation so you can straighten him out. Or, a caller may ask you to see a friend or family member who is suicidal or heavily involved with drugs.

It is important to address unrealistic expectations directly and to clarify what people can and cannot expect from your services. Even seemingly sophisticated people, underneath it all, may believe you can work miracles. However conscientiously you do this, they can still be disappointed in the result. If expectations like these seem to be operating, you may be better off not doing the reading.

The preliminary conversation serves to screen out people who are very sick. Even if you aren't trained in counseling, you already know by instinct when people are disturbed. The person on the street knows this, and so do children. In the presence of serious disturbance, you may have visceral responses—tingles, goose bumps, or a queasy stomach. You may experience a vague uneasiness and a desire to get away from the person. Respect and cultivate those instincts, rather than overriding them in the understandable desire to help people or to build a practice. For instance, you may hear far too much rage in their discussion of the problem—it passes beyond catharsis to raving. Listening to people like these will doubtlessly set off warning bells you would be unwise to ignore.

Of course, such people deserve help, but even therapists in private practice are cautious about whom they take on. They recognize the need for psychiatric backup when dealing with mentally ill or severely depressed people. Therapists also understand that in complex situations, services other than psychotherapy may be needed, such as inpatient care, legal aid, or financial aid. They are physically and legally vulnerable when seeing people like this in a private office or at home.

We astrologers are even more vulnerable because we have no legal standing and our perceptions aren't taken seriously by other professions. So, if you sense that you are out of your depths, you are safest not making an appointment. You might say that it sounds like an issue that astrology can't resolve. It would take a series of sessions to sort through, more like counseling, and you aren't a counselor. And, no, *don't* give them my number! In fact, if you want to maintain good relationships within your astrological community, don't refer difficult or seemingly disturbed people to other astrologers just because they are more experienced.

Speaking of vulnerability, suppose you are a woman astrologer. A man who is calling about an appointment is inappropriately flirtatious or intense about seeing you, perhaps pressuring you to see him right away. You live alone or will be alone during your hours of practice. Although you generally feel secure with men, you feel threatened at the idea of seeing this particular man. It is always possible that you are wrong, of course, and yet people who ignore their own signals often deeply regret it. Unless you can arrange to have someone around when you do the reading, you might be better off saying that you're booked. The major difficulty with advertising in traditional media like newspapers or the telephone directory, rather than in New Age directories or newsletters, is that you get more of these unwelcome calls. The public still sometimes confuses us with the type of storefront establishment which advertises fortune-telling as a "cover," but which provides sexual favors as well. Legitimate astrologers and legitimate tealeaf or card readers do not deserve to be categorized that way, but nonetheless some segments of the public still believe that of us.

The law still confuses us with storefront fortune-tellers, too. In many cities and states, our work falls under the old statutes against fortune-telling. While such laws are rarely applied, they are still invoked often enough to be a concern for our profession. Therefore, in screening your clients, you could also be saving yourself from legal problems. All it would take would be one sufficiently disturbed, disgruntled, and litigious client, and the astrologer could wind up in court. I testified at one such trial in San Jose, California. It was appalling to see an ephemeris and a natal chart introduced as evidence, the same way a gun or crack pipe would be. The Legal Information Committee of AFAN, headed by Jayj Jacobs, has intervened effectively in communities where those laws were invoked against astrologers or psychics. (If you want more details, write to Jayj c/o AFAN at 216 Reed Street, Mill Valley, CA 94941.)

Ending the Phone Call by Setting the Appointment

Suppose you've gone through this process and determined that the caller's needs are appropriate and that you can meet them. You've identified the issues and explained exactly how the session will address them. For astrologically sophisticated clients, you might have discussed what techniques you will use—e.g., a composite chart for relationship issues. You have reconfirmed the appointment and the birth data, especially when Mercury is retrograde. This procedure also reassures the client that you are painstaking about accuracy. You supply directions to your office, and tell the client what to bring along—for instance, you may want the client to supply a tape so you can record the session.

You might end by suggesting that the client prepares by thinking more about what he or she wants. The client might bring a list of questions. If the client has studied astrology, encourage questions about specific astrological indicators or aspects, etc. Or, let's say it is a relationship reading. Ask the client to do some advance work in defining the areas of conflict that need clarification. If both of you have thought through what the reading should accomplish, the session will be more on target and thus more satisfying.

PRACTICE EXERCISES

Think through the following situations that may come up in phone contacts. You may wish to role-play with a friend or fellow student.

1) Suppose the potential client is concerned about a relationship but knows nothing at all about astrology. Explain what you do with relationship charts, and secure the needed birth data.

2) It's August, the person's therapist is away, and all the potential client knows is that he or she needs some perspective on the emotional issues that are suddenly erupting in the therapist's absence. How would you explain what a chart reading can give this person now? How would you know if it would be inadvisable to see this person?

3) The potential client is in a crisis at work, but the birth time is only an approximation, within half an hour. Explain what rectification could do for the person and what additional information you would need.

Consultation Day—Before the Client Arrives

The day of the consultation is here. You have prepared according to the concerns the client expressed. Of course, this doesn't obviate the need to study the whole chart. For one thing, the list of questions the client brings may include areas you haven't prepared for. For another thing, a holistic approach to a given concern often requires having a grasp of the total person. A question about career choice may mean reviewing the entire horoscope, albeit through the lens of vocation. A chart comparison requires a thorough understanding of the character traits and needs of both parties.

Notice how you feel. Are you nervous about the reading? Thorough preparation cuts down on anxiety, and yet there are some who never feel ready and who suffer from stage fright before each appointment. Meditation and centering exercises can help you get out of concerns about the self and into a form of divine connectedness. Others find that a few drops of Bach's Rescue Remedy concentrate, a flower remedy combination available at many health food stores, immediately calms and centers them. Nervousness is common in the earliest readings, when the new professional understandably lacks confidence. Lessons with a senior astrologer as a mentor can help ease this transition. If stage fright persists and is troublesome, you may need to address it with healers or therapists. Still, a healthy self-doubt can be the Higher Self's attempt to keep us humble and motivated to learn.

Let's say, however, that you are ordinarily calm before consultations and love to give them. You suddenly find yourself filled with dread in the hour or so before today's client arrives. Keep in mind that some feelings you have immediately beforehand may be the person's concerns about the session that you are picking up telepathically. In this instance, it could be that he or she dreads knowing what the chart will say about the future. Becoming aware that such reactions may really belong to the client usually dispels emotions that are not your own. Then, at the beginning, you might ask, "How are you feeling about this reading? Are you nervous?" Discussion of fears and fantasies about what will happen often dissipates clients' anxiety.

Many astrologers have a routine or a ritual they perform before the client arrives. Such routines are part of their mental and emotional readiness, helping them to get centered. Simply setting up the room for the meeting can be part of the process. Some meditate and call upon their guides. Others light candles or clear the energy of the consultation room by burning sage. A process like this is a powerful signal to the superconscious that something out of the ordinary is about to occur, something that invokes the highest part of one's being, rather than the personality self.

When the Client Arrives—First Impressions

The first impression clients get from you is very important. They especially need to know you're not a weirdo, given the reputation the occult sciences have. A pleasant setting and a professional attitude help set the tone of the work. Clients will also be checking to see if you're a caring person who will concentrate on them, or if you're full of yourself and your own importance.

Devote those first few moments to establishing rapport and making clients comfortable. Recognize that most people are ambivalent about seeking help, even from an astrologer. They may be nervous about meeting you and revealing their most private concerns. They may also be worried about what they may be going to hear. You might show concern by asking about their trip or whether they need a moment to catch their breath or to use the conveniences. Don't talk much about yourself. Even when clients ask, it's usually just a polite gesture, because they are there for themselves.

For your part, you will also be sizing clients up to see who you're dealing with. You may get some idea of their intelligence and education, which will give clues about how to communicate. Their age and stage of life can give you a fix on the possible level of maturity and the major life tasks they may be facing. You'd want some sense of their level of sophistication about emotional and spiritual issues. How willing are they to take responsibility for their difficulties versus letting the stars take the blame? Assessments like these can give valuable insights into how to approach the reading.

And Buddy Makes Three . . .

Occasionally clients want to bring someone else along for the reading. Sometimes they will ask permission in the initial phone call. More often, they simply show up with their best buddy in tow, expecting that person will sit in on the reading. You need to find out why the other individual is coming. If it is simply a matter of transportation, the friend can wait in another room, if you have one that is suitable. Otherwise, he or she can come back for the client at the end of the reading.

If, however, the intention is for the friend or relative to sit in on the session, you are better off not allowing it. It is inappropriate and unprofessional. You wouldn't take a friend along to a therapy session—or invite a pal to a pap smear. Whenever a third party sits in, except when the focus of the reading is on that relationship, it greatly distorts the work. You usually get giggles, game playing, and arch in-jokes. The client is generally more focused on the friendship than on the reading. Defenses and facades are high, and the client is unlikely to reach any depth of honesty. I have occasionally made exceptions for very bashful young Latino ladies who arrived chaperoned by their mothers. It may have been wrong to do even that, but you have to allow for cultural differences.

At times, the two buddies regard getting their chart done as a kind of lark, like going to a fortune-teller's tent at a county fair. This misapprehension of astrology as carnival is, unfortunately, still part of our image. We continue to be treated as entertainers by the media and even to be listed as such in some vocational directories. For instance, in its Directory of Occupational Titles, the U.S. government classifies us under amusement and recreation, ranked with entertainers and circus performers. Our image problem is as much our fault as the public's—I have long said that we will get public respect when we deserve it.

However, the time to tackle our poor image is not when you are on the front line. You handle it partly in educating the client about astrology during that initial phone call. You also handle it by presenting yourself in a professional manner during the consultation. By the end of a good consultation, the client should know the difference between a professional astrologer and a fortune-teller. When the Bobbsey twins present themselves at your doorstep, however, just say no.

Sometimes a friend is brought along because your client is inexperienced in the occult arts and is extremely anxious about this first consultation with an oracle. The friend—perhaps a previous client of yours—is more experienced and was brought along for reassurance. In this instance, you will have to work harder to make the client comfortable. Sometimes it is possible to diffuse the tension with humor. Sometimes it is enough to simply acknowledge how nervous he or she might be about this first reading. Then explain that the friend is welcome to bring your client and to pick him or her up afterward, but not to sit in.

When none of the above situations holds true, the presence of the friend, cousin, or whatever, suggests a potentially unhealthy symbiosis between the two. Perhaps your client is a highly dependent individual or prone to codependent relationships—either of which would be a factor to consider as you explore solutions to problems the chart reveals.

Many times, clients object to this ruling. ("Oh, Betty is my best friend in the whole world. We have no secrets from each other.") I stand firm, saying that it is private and that we will be able to go deeper this way. I suggest that if it is important for the friend to hear the discussion, the client should share the tape we make. By the end of the session, most clients seem secretly relieved that the friend wasn't there, as it is indeed a far more private experience than they had realized.

Conducting Joint Readings

It is a different matter when the second person is sitting in because the consultation concerns the relationship. Almost like marital counseling, joint readings require a considerable degree of skill—or many planets in Libra. It is not easy to remain impartial and to keep a balance between the needs and interests of both, especially if one of the two has previously been your client. For this very reason, wise therapists generally will not take a couple on for counseling if one of the parties is already a client.

While the astrologer is not expected to be a marriage counselor, astrology has much to offer in rapid understanding of the relationship. Discussing both charts throws light on what sort of person each is and what each is looking for in a partnership. There is a certain detachment the horoscope brings, in which the nature of the individual is uncovered without blaming or taking conflicting qualities so personally. Skillful chart interpretation, leaving space for each partner to reflect and to talk, can facilitate communication about issues that might not have been clarified otherwise. In addition, the synastry and/or composite will illuminate the strengths and weaknesses of the tie.

Although joint readings are demanding, they can be one of the most rewarding professional experiences. You stretch and grow in your own skills, and you see an immediate impact on the relationship. Still, your own astrological biases and difficulties in relationships may enter into your chart interpretation and approach to the session, perhaps even more strongly than in a reading for one person. Self-awareness in these matters is an important professional responsibility.

Also, whenever you and a client discuss an absent third person's chart, you inevitably only hear one side of the story. The picture is edited and prettified to cast the client in the best possible light. Keep in mind that clients are probably behaving impeccably—at least to the best of their abilities—in order to impress you. In real life, their actions may, in fact, be contributing equally to the relationship difficulties they complain about.

As a naive young social worker, I was often surprised when that terrible husband or wife or parent who was ruining my client's life finally came for a session. Not only were they not inhuman monsters after all, my poor victimized clients were also revealed as less saintly than previously imagined. Experience led me to cast a more jaundiced eye on such one-sided pictures. When you see both parties in a chart reading, it is less likely that one of them will seem the villain. Finally, joint readings are a neat solution to that old ethical pickle of how much a client has a right to know about another person's chart.

What If You Don't Like the Client?

It will doubtlessly be apparent soon whether you and the client are going to like one another. You're going to enjoy some clients more than others, and it's nice to have clients you like. Nonetheless, part of professionalism is dealing with your own preferences and prejudices—*both personal and astrological*—and not imposing them on clients. You will avoid many impossible clients if you do a good job of screening, as discussed earlier. However, some will slip through.

Some obnoxious people who come to me are nonetheless highly satisfactory clients because they are very serious about their use of the tool. On some mysterious metaphysical level, we magnetize the clients who need exactly what we have to teach them—and, conversely, who teach us exactly what we need to know. Clients often mirror the process you, yourself, are going through, albeit in such a grossly exaggerated fashion that it's an object lesson. ("There but for the grace . . . ") For the last several years I seem to be specializing in—excuse me but—tough broads and wild women, so much so that it makes me wonder about myself.

What do you do if clients come and you don't like them much? I PRAY! EARNESTLY! Then, I consciously send the part of myself that doesn't like them away to do something it enjoys. Later, I question it about what was going on, to be able to learn from these negative reactions. (No, no, gentle reader, if you've been a client of mine, this is not about you. Honest!)

When the Client Is More than a Client

We mentioned the concerns that come up when you know the client from elsewhere. Keep in mind that the better you know the person, the more complications the relationship can create in the reading—and the reading can create in the relationship. Acknowledge these concerns with your client/friend both at the beginning and at the end. For instance, with any client, you would want to discuss confidentiality near the beginning of the session. It is even more important that you discuss and respect confidentiality if you know this person from another context.

You would want to set up a boundary around this session in some way that differentiates it from the other settings where you know one another. Sometimes, I do it in a humorous way, for instance, greeting them in a mock serious way as though they were a total stranger. Once, at the end of a week long seminar, my students had requested a sample consultation. They drew lots to see who would get the reading in front of the class. I had the winner go outside and knock on the door. We engaged in the kind of chatter that usually begins a reading, and then she sat with her back to the class. Soon, we were both so engrossed that we were startled when the class laughed at something we said. I can't suggest the correct way to establish the boundary in any particular instance. However, knowing that you need to establish it and acknowledging it with the person is a beginning.

Setting the Scene for the Reading

You next set up a structure for the session itself. Take the client into the consultation room, get comfortably settled, explain the procedure, and put on the tape. Astrologers vary in their routines—e.g., some make tea for clients, while others feel happier with a formal atmosphere. Routines act as an anxiety reducer and also an induction into the special state of consciousness you enter to do this work. If you have a sense of how to proceed for the first few minutes, it is easier than facing a completely unknown situation. It can also give the other person a reassuring sense that you know what you are doing.

Most clients will accept any procedure you are comfortable with, so long as it isn't too outlandish. In social work school, we had to write a verbatim record of each interview. I could barely remember what went on, so I took extensive notes, but worried that this would make clients uncomfortable. Then, I was working with a young girl, and the work consisted of referring her to a well-respected agency specializing in treatment of adolescents. When she came to the clinic again after her first few sessions in that agency, I asked how she liked it. She complained that her new therapist didn't write down anything she said!

It is a good idea to establish what clients know about astrology. Ask how much they've read or studied and with whom, and what other chart readings they've had and how recently. For the astrological virgin, do a short crash course in astrology, pointing out the houses and symbols on their own chart. The unsophisticated attribute too much power to your interpretations unless you show that they come from the diagram, rather than from divine revelation. As we will be finding out how to do in chapter Two, your explanations should be in simple English, not a lot of mystifying jargon about aspects and midpoints and solar arc. Otherwise, what you'll be teaching them is that you don't know how to communicate. Throughout the session, make sure that clients understand what you say and that your interpretations are not cloaked in too much jargon. Near the end, you may want to ask that question specifically.

Taping the Session

Before you begin, ask whether the client wants a tape. Many astrologers, especially those who are just starting out, hesitate to record the session. They fear that they will make a mistake or that someone else will listen to it and judge them. It is important to get over this discomfort, because the tape is a record of the session that many clients listen to over and over. When you are just starting, even when practicing on friends, work with a recorder extensively to get over the shyness. Most people dislike the sound of their own voice on tape, because it is different from how it sounds inside the acoustic chamber of the skull. Listen to your voice on tape enough to get over that—eventually you won't even notice it. (Hearing what you said during the session is also an excellent learning device.)

The tape can be an invaluable tool for clients, a continuing source of help. There is usually too much material for them to absorb in one sitting. Additionally, many first-time clients are so anxious they can't concentrate properly. They often forget much of what you said in the session, and when you record it, they can go over it again as desired. People may need to hear something a few times before they can take it in. For example, when you say positive things about people who have low self-esteem, they might need to listen to it over and over again in order to believe it. Many clients hear only what their current mind-set prepares them to hear, so it is invaluable to be able to go back and discover what you actually said in the session. Finally, your interpretation of upcoming transits or progressions may not make much sense to clients now. When the aspect kicks in, your words may be much more helpful when they listen to them again.

Have the recorder set up and the sound level checked before clients arrive, so there is minimal disruption. You might glue your business card on the flap of the cardboard inside the cassette box so clients have your number handy for future readings. Give the date of the session, both to establish the time frame of any predictions you make and to let them know when an update might be appropriate. It is also a good idea to state the birth information on tape, so you can double check that the data is correct before you get started and so there is a record of the data used, in case of later discrepancies.

Beginning the Session Itself

As the session opens, go over some of the same points as in the phone call. They are important enough to reiterate in order to focus the reading properly. Reviewing the purpose of your meeting helps you and the client focus. There is merit to getting these concerns on tape. When clients relisten to it later, they can hear where they were at the time of the appointment and see what progress they have made since then.

As you did in that initial contact, define what the meeting is to accomplish. Ask once more "What do you need to get from this session?" (Or, "What are the major issues you are working on right now?") This is the time for clients to bring up any additional questions. Assess whether you can handle these additional concerns comfortably in one sitting. The two of you may have to set priorities. Many clients bring along other people's charts and ask if you could, "just take a look." You then have to decide if you are comfortable doing this off the top of your head.

There is still another reason this opening procedure is helpful. Readings that concentrate on clients' own concerns are more likely to motivate them to change dysfunctional patterns. You want the session to make a difference, to be a fulcrum for growth. A consultation is more likely to be effective in motivating clients to change when you direct it toward areas where they are feeling discomfort.

Does this mean you wouldn't discuss a concern you see in the chart if the person hasn't asked about it? In the case of transits or progressions, you have some responsibility to do so. Upcoming aspects may suggest future concerns that the client doesn't have a clue about yet. It will be part of your work to cover these areas, just as a doctor would warn a patient of an unsuspected condition showing up on a test.

However, with the natal chart, rather than overwhelming—and alienating—people by telling them everything you see wrong, confine yourself to what is bothering them now. This way you are more likely to get responsive, actively participating clients rather than resistant and ultimately dissatisfied ones. To proceed any other way is intrusive, acting as judge and jury on their life-style.

Suppose you see a major problem with the mother—as astrologers always seem to do—and this is not what the client wants to work on. You would not dredge up the mother complex and do a complete psychoanalysis unless you could prove its relevance to the question at hand. If a man were complaining of his relationships with women, then his experiences with his mother would clearly be pertinent. Or, let's say you see authority problems based on the relationship with the father. This history would be relevant if there were difficulties with a male boss. When you point out the specific ways that history impinges on the present difficulties, clients are more likely to listen.

Not everyone who asks for a reading has deep-seated problems that they want you to help them grapple with. It is common for astrology students, especially your own, to ask for readings that will help them understand the features of their natal charts. This detailed delineation is part of their learning. Advanced students who are considering going into practice may also request readings from a variety of astrologers in order to learn how readings are done. With your own students, it may also be inappropriate, in your role as teacher, to act as a psychotherapist. It may constitute an invasion of the person's boundaries.

Incidentally, it may not be the best strategy to dive immediately into the heaviest and most painful subjects. Clients need to come to know and trust you gradually before opening up. You might want to cover a couple of easily answered and not terribly threatening questions first, like, "Am I going to travel this year?" or, "When will my raise come through?"

Doing Readings for Clams

One hitch that may come up at the beginning of the session is the client who refuses to say much of anything. You know the sort—the folded arms, the jutting chin. These folks want to be sure that you are genuinely gifted, so they test you. Or, maybe they are secretive and don't want to reveal anything more of themselves than is necessary. This most often seems to happen with Scorpio or Capricorn Ascendants.

It helps to dazzle these types a bit. It's not even that hard to do. These are usually the ones who've never had a chart reading before, so they don't have any idea how revealing astrology can be. You might recap some of the important trends of the past year or pinpoint the most difficult areas of their life through the placements of the outer planets.

Then tell them that they are going to get more out of the session if it is a dialogue. You might tell them that you're not a psychic—I sometimes joke that my crystal ball is out of order. Or, ask them if they'd expect a doctor to guess what was wrong with them without asking questions. Explain that the chart only suggests the general types of situations that will confront them. The two of you can pinpoint the effects much more specifically if they give some details. They're never going to let you see their hole card, but they generally loosen up a little at that point.

Keeping the Focus During the Reading

Once having established a focus, you don't want to stray too far from it, or the reading will lose its effectiveness. Gently nudge clients back to the question at hand. ("Let's stay with the question you raised about ______. If we have time at the end, we'll get back to this.") It's your right as well as your responsibility to keep the session focused. They will be disappointed if the session is over and you haven't addressed the stated concerns.

You may particularly need to redirect Mercury-prominent clients who want to talk about everything under the sun. Try to hook their curiosity: "That's an interesting subject, but there's so much I want to tell you about the issues you brought up." Many clients will rattle on when they are anxious, and then you need to put them at ease. However, others are compulsive talkers who are internally pressured to talk and who can't listen. This is almost a disease. They bombard people with words to keep them at a distance or to avoid being in touch with their feelings. This seems to be especially true when Mercury is within 10° of the Ascendant, even on the 12th house side. True compulsive talkers can be impossible to contain—you may just have to let them rattle on.

When clients want to go too far into what seem to be side issues, you may want to suggest a second appointment. Only with experience, however, can you know what is a diversion and what is important. What about clients who meander and go off on tangents—is it resistance or their *modus operandi*? Their charts will tell—mutables tend to meander, fixed signs to resist. With experience, you learn to set priorities and to know what kinds of questions require the most time to cover thoroughly. (This varies with the astrologer. Each of us has subjects we can shed a great deal of light on and others we have little to say about.)

How Long Should a Reading Be?

How long should a reading last? This is again an individual matter and relates to the format you devise and to the specific issues. Some astrologers do marathon encounter sessions which are a form of healing. Others stick to the psychoanalytic 50-minute hour. Your usual session length may also be modified by the client's special requirements—being from out of town, for instance, or needing several chart comparisons at once. Even if you prefer not to set a definite length, you will still become fatigued at some point and need to finish.

When we have defined the issues so we both are well-prepared, and when we concentrate on those issues, I generally answer all the questions to the client's satisfaction in an hour and fifteen minutes. The hellos and goodbyes take another fifteen minutes or so. When I mix flower remedies related to the discussion, that takes another fifteen or twenty minutes. I leave a half-hour gap between appointments in case we run over, or the subway breaks down, or the client is running late.

It is typical of the earliest stages of practice for readings to last three hours or more. Sometimes the new professional is so glad to have a live body to interview about all the meanings of the chart, that the session becomes a kind of tutorial. Lengthy consultations can be a legitimate learning experience, but ultimately become exhausting for both client and astrologer. Many new astrologers, lacking confidence, feel they have to cover everything in the chart in order to justify charging. It also takes longer in the beginning to identify and articulate what a given chart placement means. As your skill grows, you zero in more quickly on what is important, so your readings are shorter but more effective.

Concluding the Chart Reading—All's Well that Ends Well

It is as important to end well as to begin well. Near the finish, ask clients if you covered everything on their list. Did the discussion answer the questions posed at the beginning, and did it satisfy the expressed needs? In other words, did the two of you meet the contract? Start asking these questions about 15 minutes before the end, so there is still room to deal with any unanswered needs. This kind of closure can make the difference between a satisfied client and one who goes away saying, "We never did get around to what I wanted."

You may wish to make a closing summary about the kind of year they are facing and the major concerns you have discussed. Don't minimize the pain of the transits or progressions. You do want to come to some conclusions about what can be accomplished if clients use these astrological conditions to address major issues rather than to avoid them. You may wish to repeat some of the constructive ideas the two of you discussed about how to meet the challenges they are facing. It is good to end on a positive note—especially with an overwhelmed or discouraged person—but not on a syrupy and false note.

When the allotted time is over, it's up to you to end the session gracefully. Hopefully, you let clients know the approximate length of the session when you made the appointment, so they know what to expect. Remember, however, that clients aren't watching the clock, they're watching you. They probably don't know what time it is, and they would stay forever listening to you talk about their favorite subject—themselves!

Make signals to suggest that the session is winding down. About five or ten minutes before the end, you might ask what last questions they have. For me, the tape is also a timer and boundary setter—my boom box thumps loudly when the tape clicks off. That's an indicator to both of us that we've basically reached the end. When that doesn't work, I close the file folder, put it aside, and then my cat comes over and plunks down on it. If you don't have that kind of rapport with your familiar, or if you don't have one, you may just have to say directly, but kindly that the time is up.

You wouldn't rush clients out if there were still pressing issues you haven't covered—or if they were in a highly emotional state. However, if you two define in advance what you can legitimately accomplish in one session and if you address the expressed needs rather than meandering all over the universe, there shouldn't be many pressing issues left. Organization and focus are the keys. When these elements are present, the reading is more likely to satisfy rather than to overwhelm the client.

Paving the Way for Future Readings

As important as the educational approach is with the potential client, it is even more important and fruitful at the end of a reading. Unless you give clients three-hour sessions covering the rest of their lives and everyone important to them, there's always something more astrology can do. At that moment, hopefully, they are as sold on astrology and on you as they're ever going to be, because you've just given them a demonstration of the worth of this tool. While it is fresh in their minds, and while you still have a picture of their lives and needs, talk to them about other possible services. You do this not necessarily only to sell them something more right now, but to educate them about future applications.

For instance, did a parent tell you about a child who is a worry? Suggest a reading of that child's chart and a comparison with the parent's to understand how to get along better. Is there a lover who's giving them grief? A chart comparison could help clarify what's going on. Did the client ask about relocating? Suggest an Astro*Carto*Graphy. And so on.

Most of all, remember to talk about updates. Many first-time clients leave thinking that a reading is once for a lifetime—"Now that's over! I've had my chart done." If people don't know that there's more you can do for them and don't understand that astrological conditions change, they are much less likely to come back. Those few extra minutes spent on educating the client at the end can make a difference in building a practice.

One Last Thing

One last thing—you should know about the "doorknob statement." That's the provocative statement or the weighty question that sometimes pops out of clients' mouths on the way out the door. The doorknob statement may well be the crux of the whole reading—the true reason they came to you in the first place. Throughout the whole session they've been sitting with this highly threatening question stuck in their throat that they need to ask the sybil, but they just haven't been able to get it out. Now is their last chance—and if they don't like your answer, they can run away without exposing their feelings.

For instance, I did a seemingly ordinary update for the ex-lover of a friend of mine. Everything went just fine. We had some laughs, and the session seemed quite productive. As he went out the door, he gulped, looked down at the floor, and asked how my friend's chart looked. Although not critically ill, the friend had AIDS. What he was really asking was whether I thought our friend would die—and, no doubt, whether he himself was going to die, too.

When confronted with a last minute lulu like this one, ask the client to sit down again, and take time to think before you respond. The doorknob question is generally one that goes so deep and was so hard to ask that your answer will doubtlessly have a powerful impact.

After the Ball Is Over

Now the client is gone. How do you feel? In the beginning, many feel wiped out after a chart reading—so exhausted they have to go to bed. That kind of response is generally a signal that you have been giving healing energy to the client without being aware of it. However, your personal energy can't help the client—only divine energy can help.

Many readers and healers do a closing ritual after a session to reclaim their own energy and release any of the client's energy they absorbed. (Some do this verbally while the client is still present but you need to know if this is a good idea or not.) To release yourself from your client, you might imagine that you and the client are in separate bubbles of white light. Each bubble has a big magnet on the outside. First imagine that your magnet is pulling back your own energy, then that the client's magnet is pulling back the energy you absorbed. If you are reluctant to have the client reabsorb any negativity, imagine the bubble swirling so the energy is simply washed away beneath his or her feet.

Like many practitioners, I clear the energy of the room afterward by burning sagebrush or spraying with a mixture of flower remedies and water. You can get sagebrush (also informally called sage) in many healthfood establishments or New Age bookstores. Light the sage and get the smoke rolling, then waft it through the room. For a flower remedy spray, fill a plant mister with water. Then add four drops each of such remedies as Yarrow, for psychic shielding, Pennyroyal, to protect against negativity, and perhaps Lotus, for spiritual awareness.[2] I also spray between sessions, so that one client is not sitting in another's psychic fallout. I'm not much of a housekeeper by Virgo standards, but I am compulsive about purifying the energy of my workspace.

You may notice a variety of reactions when the person has gone. If you haven't disconnected psychically, keep in mind that some of the feelings that you are picking up on may be the client's. If you begin to suspect that this is so, do a closing ritual such as the bubble exercise. Sometimes it is enough simply to leave the house on an errand or to get engrossed in some mental task.

A successful chart reading is an incredibly intense and intimate exchange, very different from most human encounters. At times, you may feel a sense of loss or loneliness after reaching a particularly deep level of intimacy. A telephone call to a friend or loved one can relieve this sudden sense of isolation.

In those earliest chart readings, you may need to debrief. There can be a need to share what has happened with a mentor or an astrology pal who is also doing consultations. Naturally, you would respect the client's confidentiality, but to discuss your questions about the way the reading went with a more experienced astrologer can be valuable. If there are errors, it is easier to correct them at this stage than once they become entrenched. It is also valuable to identify what you did well, so that you can capitalize on it in future readings.

And, In Closing

So, how are we doing? Did this chapter answer some of your questions about chart consultations? Did you find it easy to understand? Did it give you some insight into how to keep the session focused? Do you feel more prepared now to give effective readings? Were there other issues and questions you would have liked to see covered? Let me know what your questions are, and maybe you can come for an update!

---

[2](For a catalogue, write to the Flower Essence Society, Box 1769, Nevada City, CA 95959.)

CHAPTER TWO

English for Astrologers– No Astrologese Please

Recently I asked a new client if she'd ever had an astrology reading before. She said, "Well, I went to this guy, and he wasn't talking to ME at all! I couldn't understand a word he said. I could tell that he enjoyed it, and that he thought it was a good reading. But he wasn't talking to me at all."

No doubt, the astrologer believed he was communicating especially fluently that day. However, long strings of astrological jargon like quincunx, trine, solar arc, retrograde, and t-square are *not* communication, they are obfuscation. Astrobabble creates unnecessary mystification and anxiety. Inundated with meaningless terms, all clients have to go on is tone of voice and facial expression, which they may well interpret as ominous. If we frown in concentration, they may conclude things look bad for them. Our first responsibility during a reading is to make sure clients understand us. Only through meaningful dialogue can we help them gain a new perspective on their lives.

We easily forget how confusing astrological terms were to us in the beginning. It's hard for us to imagine how bewildering it is for clients when we speak astrobabble. It struck me that it would be fun to substitute unfamiliar and irrelevant terms for our jargon and then to read astrologers' charts using those terms. That way, they can have a fresh experience of how it feels when they bombard clients with jargon.[1]

---

[1]For the many inspirations throughout this chapter, I would like to acknowledge Coyote, without whose help this would never have been written.

I found some delightful words in Webster's and have dubbed them over the astrobabble. They are perfectly good English words, but the meanings assigned to them are arbitrary, for demonstration purposes only. We'll call this Neo-Astrologese. Imagine that you go for a consultation, and the astrologer says:

> You're worried about your job? I'd say you have cause to worry. Saturn is hoovering your Palanquin—wambles it from the sixth. It's holophrastic still, but in December the frenzel is huffish. In January, Saturn goes planetesimal, still wamble the Palanquin, and then it's ratcheting until August. You're not out of the woods until it flenzes and makes that final wamble in about November of next year.

That was difficult to understand, wasn't it? Not difficult enough, however. Words like Saturn, Mars, and Pluto have reams of meaning to us that the layperson can't begin to fathom. When a layperson hears the word Saturn, it means virtually nothing, whereas astrologers have written whole books about Saturn. Therefore, let's switch terms again, so your mind doesn't have those associations to draw on.

Let's call the Sun by its other name, SOL, and the planets by astronomical notations. Mercury is SOL1, and Venus is SOL2. The Moon, strictly speaking, is the satellite of SOL3. Saturn is SOL6. Keep going, up to Neptune, which should be SOL8, and Pluto, which should be SOL9. However, for more than a decade, Pluto has been inside the orbit of Neptune. Therefore, a more accurate designation for Pluto would be SOL8 and for Neptune would be SOL9.

Now, let's try again. To re-create more nearly the client's anguish, first work yourself into a total funk about your future. Then, have someone read the following paragraph aloud, with appropriate head-shaking and frowns, while you sit squirming, with sweaty palms and a dull ache of dread in the pit of your stomach:

> Well, the problem in your relationship stems from that endarch between SOL2 and SOL7 in your seventh house. Of course, the dihedryl from SOL6 doesn't help either. Now, SOL9 is hoovering your Bicuspid, on top of everything else. It's not huffish yet, won't be until this summer. Before

> that it double ratchets and forms another condyl to SOL5, so that should help some.

It sounds awesome and terrible, doesn't it? All these incomprehensible and apparently not very friendly alien forces are messing with your life, and there's nothing you can do about them. No doubt, you wish you'd never come. At least beforehand you didn't know there was all this double-ratcheting and hoovering going on. Like you needed something more to worry about! (If you'd like to amaze and amuse your astrology pals, the Neo-Astrologese glossary appears in Table 1 on pages 30–31. Now they can share the experience of having their charts read this way.)

Astro*Psycho*Babble: Another Error

To switch from astrobabble to psychobabble is not communication either. Many astrologers, myself included, use the insights gained from psychology to enhance our understanding of clients. While a psychological approach to chart interpretation is essential, there is one problem with psychotherapists—they talk funny. For instance, they are always going on about object relations. What do they mean by *object* relations? It is *not* your symbiosis with your computer. No, they mean relationships with people! I submit that any group that confuses relationships with objects and relationships with people has a problem with object relations.

In layering psychobabble on top of astrobabble, the writing of the psychologically-oriented astrologer can become especially dense. Dane Rudhyar set the standard for astropsychological linguistic impenetrability years ago, and the rest of us have struggled to live up to it ever since. As erudite as astro*psycho*babble may sound, clients will not understand it unless they have been through a decade or more of Jungian analysis.

We don't want to imitate psychologists in our quest to serve better, we want to speak the language of those we are trying to help. As a reminder to speak plain English, perhaps we should institute a special award, like the Regulus Awards at U.A.C. We could call it the Dane Rudhyar Award for Excellence in Astro-Obfuscation. (I can

TABLE 1. THE NEO-ASTROLOGESE GLOSSARY*

English	*Astrologese*
Ascendant	Octachord
angular	bosky
aspect	arachnoid
chart comparison	rostellate (v.)
conjunction	endarch
Descendent	Bicuspid
direct, go direct	flenze
exact	huffish
grand cross	double dihedryl
grand trine	triple condyle
harmonic charts	bimorphemic charts
high focus, heavily aspected	meristematic
IC	Mazer
Midheaven	Palanquin
Node(s), n., s.	Phimosis, Phimoses, n., s.
opposition	dihedryl
orb	frenzel
progression	rogation
rectification	zymosis
relocated chart	nummular chart
retrograding (back over)	ratcheting, double ratcheting
square	wamble
stationary	planetesimal
stellium	multiple endarch
synthesize	grizzle
transiting, transited	hoovering, hooverized
trine	condyle
t-square	triple wamble
wide (orb), but valid	holophrastic

(continued)

TABLE 1. THE NEO-ASTROLOGESE GLOSSARY (continued)

Astrologese	*English*
arachnoids	aspects
Bicuspid	Descendant
bosky	angular
bimorphemic	harmonics
condyle	trine
triple condyle	grand trine
dihedryl	opposition
double dihedryl	grand cross
endarch	conjunction
multiple endarch	multiple conjunction or stellium
frenzel	orb
flenze	turn direct
grizzle	synthesize
hoovering, hooverized	transiting, transited
holophrastic	wide, but still operating
huffish	exact
Mazer	IC
meristematic	high focus (many aspects, heavily tenented)
nummular chart	relocation chart
Octachord	Ascendant
Palanquin	Midheaven
Phimosis (pl.Phimoses) n., s.	Nodes, n., s. (true, mean)
planetesimal	stationary
ratcheting	retrograding
double ratcheting	retrograding (back over)
rogation	progression
rostellate	do a chart comparison
wamble (n., v.)	square
triple wamble	t-square
zymosis	chart rectification

**NOTE: All of these words are found in Webster's dictionary, but they have different meanings than are assigned here. The meanings assigned to them in astrologese are arbitrary, for demonstration purposes only.*

think of several astrologers who qualify for lifetime achievement awards in that category!)

Are You Sure They Understand?

You may not think clients have any difficulty with your terminology. Don't assume they understand just because they don't ask what you mean. Many are too intimidated to ask questions. They may have low self-esteem, especially about their intellect or education. They may be convinced they are stupid, especially when faced with waves of unfamiliar terminology coming out of the mouth of someone who sounds like an expert. If they are particularly insecure, they may even nod sagely as you speak so that you don't discover how ignorant they are.

These are the same folks who are afraid to ask the doctor to explain all those medical terms. When I worked in a hospital, one patient was admitted with a diagnosis of borborygmus. What would you think if the doctor told you you had borborygmus? "How long do I have, Doc?" Right? When we looked the word up in the medical dictionary, it turned out that all that it means is that your stomach growls. How they got that one by the admissions committee is puzzling, but they did. The incomprehensible things astrologers tell clients about their charts can be as alarming to them as a diagnosis of borborygmus.

In order to make sure clients understand, reassure them that you're accessible. Encourage them to ask about anything that's not clear. My standard line to clients, especially astrological virgins, is, "Please stop me if I get too technical. I do also speak English." Check back in with them during the reading, if you sense that you are using too much jargon.

While some clients hate it if you use any jargon at all, others feel cheated if you don't fling some mystifying terms around. That way they're sure they went to a knowledgeable expert and got their money's worth. It is entirely possible to do an entire session without any reversion to astrologese. However, sprinkle a few astrological terms into the conversation. If you don't make any reference to the chart, they may think you're getting all this intimate information about them from your crystal ball or your spirit guides. You may also wish to point out on the chart where the information is coming from.

Strangely enough, with astrologically sophisticated clients, you may have to work even harder to communicate. The temptation to relax into strings of jargon is very strong. They can trine, quincunx, and solar arc right along with you, so there is the comforting illusion of two minds running along the same track. If you questioned them, however, they might have very different emotional and intellectual associations to various planets, signs, and aspects than you do. Based on our teachers, the books we read, the conferences we attend, and our personal experiences, each astrophile has different perceptions of and beliefs about various chart factors.

For instance, suppose that you tell the astrologically sophisticated client that transiting Pluto is about to square her natal Sun. You may only be trying to say that a transformation of her self-concept is about to occur. What she hears, however, may not be so different from what the patient with borborygmus hears: "How long have I got?" Maybe you were only trying to say that she might benefit from psychotherapy, but she concludes that chemotherapy is likely to figure heavily in her future. Perhaps that's what happened to her grandmother with that aspect.

Thus, when dealing with someone who has an astrology background, check to be sure that you are communicating. Explain precisely what you mean by any aspect you mention. When the client throws jargon at you, you might say something like, "Let's be sure we understand each other. I have some ideas about what that transit signifies, but I'd also like to hear how you're interpreting it."

How Do You Say It in English?

No doubt you are now thoroughly convinced of the necessity to eschew obfuscation when you talk to a client. Some practitioners of the occult arts deliberately use mystifying jargon in order to enhance their power and influence. I don't believe many astrologers use jargon deliberately as a power ploy—except perhaps on an unconscious level. Many students and new professionals, however, simply don't know HOW to translate this symbolic language they've come to speak so fluently.

How do you change astrobabble into real people's language? You do that the same way you get to Carnegie Hall. Practice, practice, practice! If you're just starting, it's helpful to practice English translations on your beleaguered family and friends. Choose the irreverent ones who will interrupt strings of astrologese with comments like, "That's easy for you to say," or, "whatever that may mean."

Some students have said that they need to give the astrological factors out loud first, in order to begin to understand what is going on. It's a little like learning a foreign language and needing to translate word for word inwardly before venturing a phrase or a sentence. It's fine while you get more fluent in plain English. However, follow it with, "and what that means is . . . "

In those early days, take care of that stage in the chart preparation. Don't do it in front of the client, do it before the client arrives. It's part of the preparation to begin working on the translation. Jot down the striking features of the chart, followed by simple notes about what they might mean. For instance, suppose the client was concerned about a lack of relationships, and the birth chart had Venus square Saturn. You might write down, "Venus square Saturn: obstacles to committed relationships? Ask client."

If you are puzzled about the method of changing a phrase like Venus square Saturn into English, that may be because there's no direct, word-for-word English equivalent. The interpretation of an aspect doesn't come from translating it into English, only from translating it into behaviors, emotions, and history. As you uncover the kinds of feelings and actions this combination produces, you can discover and convey its significance. In other words, translate it into living experience that has meaning for the client.

The English translation by more the traditional, event-oriented astrologer may focus only on the external effects. For instance, Venus square Saturn sometimes manifests as an experience of repeatedly being loved and left. The client may eagerly agree with that explanation—"Yes, yes, they always DO leave me! So, Saturn's causing that, is it?"

We don't want to translate only in terms of external events, leaving clients with the suspicion that Saturn is responsible for their trouble. This approach ignores the inner states which create the pattern—the client's history and the kinds of decisions and choices arising from that history. To get at the true meaning in a way that will help the client understand and change the pattern, look for internal causes and articulate them.

It is useful to ask yourself questions about the client's history, behavior, and choices as you prepare the chart and delineate the salient aspects. Of course, you never know the answers for sure until you ask the client, but you can at least begin to speculate. The questions vary with the aspect, but for Venus square Saturn, here are some that may be productive:

1) What repeated experiences in love might a Venus square Saturn person have?

2) What kinds of relationship choices does the person make that end up this way?

3) What history could have shaped these choices?

4) What kinds of behaviors does he or she engage in that may result in being loved and left?

5) What feelings could shape these behaviors?

While each aspect in the chart plays itself out in multiple ways, one possible scenario for Venus square Saturn is that when a relationship gets close to commitment, one or both parties may become ambivalent or frightened and ultimately break it off. This may come about because the person chooses potential partners who are afraid of commitment and who throw up walls against intimacy. Such choices often historically stem from the relationship with the parent of the opposite sex, who might have been alternately there and not there. For example, one moment the daughter might have been Daddy's little girl, the next moment Daddy might have been withdrawn and silent. One or both parents may have also set up difficult conditions for the child to meet in order to earn love. In adult life, the person is drawn to potential partners who behave similarly to that parent when it comes to love and who are alternately there and not there.

Why does getting close to commitment bring on a crisis of ambivalence in the relationship? For one thing, the person, underneath it all, is just as fearful of commitment as the potential partner, or the person wouldn't choose such ambivalent people to begin with. Secondly, when a formal commitment looms, the Venus/Saturn type may suddenly change the rules in the relationship to a more formalized, traditional, and even rigid set of expectations and behaviors. As this was not what the partner signed on for, he or she may feel trapped and leave. In addition, the possibility of commitment brings on a fear of loss or abandonment as well as evoking painful past losses. Thus, the person might suddenly be fearful, clinging, and even depressed. The partner is often the emotionally unavailable type who does not respond well to demands like these and may well become more distant and closed.

These are some possible answers to the questions posed above. In the preparation, you can speculate on possible causes and effects of a problem, but you cannot know for sure without getting feedback during the reading. You need context and history in order to find the individualized meaning of the aspect. If you see a hundred Venus square Saturn people, they will have a hundred different Venus square Saturn stories. You are never going to be able to pinpoint clients' particular experiences from chart analysis, only from asking them directly. You can give the overview, but only they can supply the context. ("I see that you have Venus square Saturn. Many people with that aspect have had a tough time in love. They seem to choose people who restrict them in some way or who feel restricted by them. Has that happened in your life, and how?")

For simplicity's sake, we have focused on just one part of the translation of Venus square Saturn. In a real chart analysis, you would need to take apart the complete aspect. What house and sign are Venus in, and how does that further clarify the behavior, feelings, and history behind the person's patterns in love? What house and sign are Saturn in, and how does that modify the picture? Venus in Aries square Saturn in Cancer behaves differently and for different reasons than Venus in Scorpio square Saturn in Aquarius. Venus in the 12th square Saturn in the 3rd has a different history and set of concerns than Venus in the 8th square Saturn in the 11th. The total picture is more complex when you include these features and you get more precise information by analyzing them all and, ultimately, by questioning the client.

Chart Particles to Practice on

Pieces of charts are a place to start learning how to articulate astrological aspects and placements. First translate simple phrases, then complete sentences, then whole charts. Of course, in a reading you'd need to take the entire chart into account in answering such questions. Here we just want to make a start in learning to verbalize what we see.

Here are two chart particles to practice on, with examples of the kinds of concerns clients may raise. They aren't pieces of real charts. It's unfair to use clients' charts unnecessarily, and, I don't know about you, but I'm tired of reading long interpretations of the charts of the astrologer's son or ex-boyfriend. The examples we'll use aren't astronomically correct. They are in the Arbitrary House System and in the Speculative Zodiac, but they aren't unlike charts seen in practice.

In Sample Particle 1 a man is grumbling, "I just got fired. AGAIN! Why are my bosses always on my case?"

The relevant features are the Sun/Jupiter/Uranus conjunction on the Midheaven, squared by Neptune on the Ascendant and Mars in Libra in the 12th. About each of these aspects, ask yourself:

1) Why are those mean bosses on his case?

2) Why does he keep getting fired?

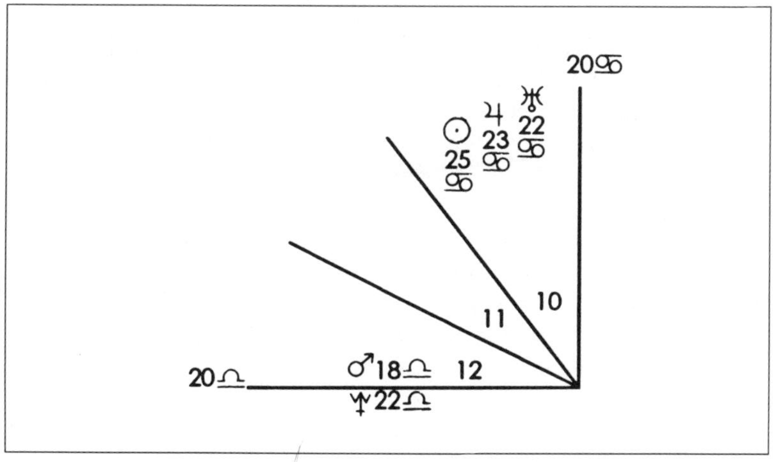

Sample Particle 1. "Why do I keep getting fired?"

3) How does this man see himself vis a vis the world and the world of work in particular?

4) What role models did he have in terms of authority and career?

5) What sort of history is reflected in his behavior?

6) What kinds of job situations might work out better for him?

Let's say that the consultation took place on May 5, 1992, with Saturn at 18° Aquarius, Uranus at 17° Capricorn, Neptune at 18° Capricorn, and Pluto at 21° Scorpio. The transiting Uranus/Neptune conjunction in Capricorn is just beginning to set off all those natal aspects, one by one. Ask yourself:

1) Will his bosses fire him some more?

2) Do you foresee any crises that would impel him to change?

3) What could he do to change the pattern?

4) What long-range career advice could you give him?

Although this is a made-up chart, this man is as real as if he'd come for a consultation. He exists—or someone a lot like him. He's a computer whiz, and he's so brilliant he could program a cow to give chocolate milk if he put his mind to it. He lives out in Silicon Valley with his attractive but domineering wife and his 2.5 kids. He's a good-looking charmer and has stashed away several hopelessly adoring girlfriends acquired in his various jobs.

Where does all that show in the chart? The conjunction of Sun, Jupiter, and Uranus on the Midheaven suggests a computer whiz—even the Neptune squares add to the creative genius. The Libra Rising, with Neptune and that 12th house Mars in Libra conjunct the Ascendant suggest the looks, charm, and compulsive pursuit of romance. However, Libra does tend to marry, and Cancer wants those kids, hence the domineering wife. He has Aries on the 7th, Mars tucked in the 12th, and Neptune in Libra on the Ascendant. These all suggest he'd be the passive partner seeking a mate who would lead/bully.

This is all speculation, and when the client arrives, we could find out we were totally wrong. With the same chart, he could be a radical law professor with an attractive but domineering wife and 2.5 critically acclaimed but out-of-print books, who breaks hearts in gay bars when he's supposedly at political meetings. In real life, we wouldn't be speculating at all. In the initial call, we would have asked what he did for a living, since the expressed concern is his career.

However, let's suppose it is the computer whiz, and let's speculate about the problem with his bosses, since he hasn't arrived yet. (You knew he was going to be late, didn't you? He already canceled once, at the last minute.) One source of difficulty with bosses is that the guy who shows up for the job interview isn't the same guy who shows up for work. With all that Libra on the Ascendant, the initial impression is of someone pleasant, accommodating, and malleable. In Silicon Valley, the C.E.O. has had so many mavericks with big egos to contend with, that it's a relief to find someone both brilliant and workable.

Lo and behold, he settles in at the job and proves to be the maverick with the big ego, after all. The Sun/Jupiter/Uranus on the Midheaven shows not only the brilliance but the rebellion against authority. If he were up front with his defiance, the C.E.O. might be able to contend with it.

However, he's the passive/aggressive type—Mars in Libra in the 12th, conjunct Neptune, squaring the Midheaven and all those Cancer planets. He says he will, no question about it, do what the boss asks, but first he has to . . . Tomorrow at the latest, he'll turn in that report. Can't imagine how those statistics got lost. That brilliant idea he spun out at the job interview? Oh, it's still in development—but it's coming along. Soon. The man could write the book on excuses, but you can't stay mad because he's so personable.

Though the C.E.O. can't quite put his finger on it, he also suspects that this fellow smokes a lot of dope. What would suggest that? The strong Neptune with all the difficult aspects does suggest the possibility of substance abuse. There are no statistics or signatures to substantiate the conclusion that he smokes rather than drinks. However, I've done plenty of them, and the smell of marijuana wafts off the page. Possibly it's the combination of that Mars/Neptune passivity squaring that Sun/Jupiter/Uranus/Midheaven grandiose self-concept. However, in my practice, Uranus has proven to be more implicated with cocaine abuse than Neptune, and Silicon Valley is afloat in the stuff. With Uranus square Neptune, perhaps he does coke on the job to keep pumped up, then smokes after work to chill out.

You begin to get an idea of why he periodically gets fired. What history might be behind this pattern? From the predominance of "male" planets and their relationship to the Midheaven, we'd conclude that his role model was his father. Dad was a maverick also, a law unto himself—maybe even a literal outlaw. Brilliant but flawed, he never lived up to his potential, but he was dazzling. Granted, the old man might not have been around much, but, boy, was his presence felt. To the client, he was a hero, someone to live up to.

How would you approach him? Frankly, it would be very hard to keep from getting drawn into his games. If you become the 7th house counselor, then you get to be the Aries Descendant to his Mars/Neptune in Libra. You nag him to change; he yes-buts you until you're frustrated and give up. Then again, you could be the 10th house authority figure and trigger his arrogance and grandiosity. It would be hard to keep from tripping over either of those roles. No matter how hard you tried to remain detached and objective, the chart is too heavily weighted in those directions.

The first priority, as a counselor, would be to determine if substance abuse is, indeed, a factor. It wouldn't be the first thing you'd discuss—you have to build some rapport. However, if he is using a lot of grass or cocaine, the chances of him being able to change to a healthier career pattern are poor. Marijuana abuse leads to (or, maybe, results from) what people in the addiction business call the "amotivational syndrome." After years of use, it is far easier for those who are dependent on it to dream grand dreams than to do much of anything. Cocaine addiction pumps up the ego and the sense of infallibility, but is a short, precipitous slide into addiction and destructive physical consequences.

If the client does admit drug use, it's going to be hard to make an impact. You need to remain as detached as possible and avoid trying to convert or save him. There is little you can accomplish except to suggest that drugs may be contributing to the career problem. He isn't likely to change until some drug-created career crisis erupts, which would create a bottoming out. Remember, however, that he came in the first place because he'd just been fired. This could be that sort of crisis—or, if he still hasn't hit bottom, you could at least plant some useful seeds. With the Uranus-Neptune transits looming, that bottom could occur any time in the next several years.

If drugs are not implicated (although addicted people rarely tell the truth about that), then you need to stay focused on career goals. He did not ask for—nor is he likely to sit still for—a referral to a psychotherapist. He's an independent Uranian type, after all, and so, of course, he doesn't need help. It's all *their* fault. *They* just don't appreciate his genius. No doubt, the best work situation would be for him to be self-employed or in a consulting group practice. Still, the same problems with passivity and defiance could come up with consultation clients and business partners. Again, you might plant seeds and talk about how the model Dad gave him gets played out in working with authority figures.

Time, transits, and a few more hard knocks will, hopefully, bring him to a place of greater clarity and maybe even a *soupçon* of humility. Am I being hard on the golden-haired boy? Of course, and hopefully if he were actually in front of me, it would be easier to be compassionate. (Wait until you've worked with a few dozen of these, and see if you don't find them frustrating too!)

To give you several more illustrations of this process would be to shift the focus of this chapter to chart interpretation, which is not the intent. However, here's an additional example of the kinds of questions which are productive in translating astrology into behavior and emotions. In Sample Particle 2, a mother is telling you tearfully, "Now that my children are grown, they resent my help and advice. How can we get along better?"

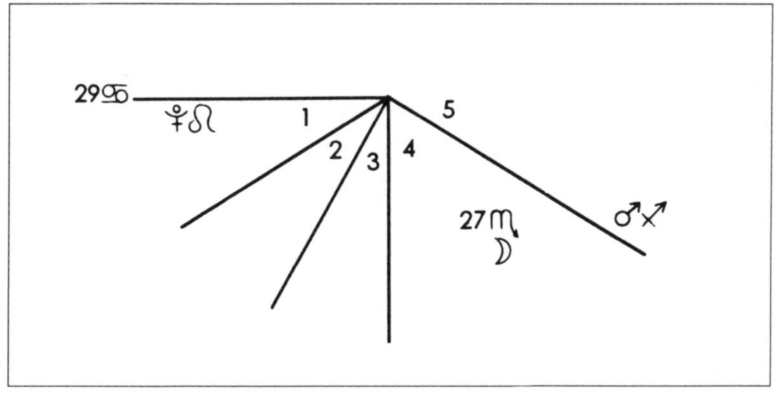

Sample Particle 2. "How can I get along better with my kids?"

The key indicators are the Cancer Ascendant with Pluto in Leo just two degrees off it and the Moon in Scorpio in the 4th house, with Mars in Sagittarius forming an out of sign conjunction to it in the 5th house. Ask yourself the following questions in regard to each of these placements:

1) How has this mother related to her children in the past?

2) What types of behavior might her children be objecting to?

3) What emotions might create or accompany her behavior?

4) Why do you suppose, historically, she developed this parenting style?

Let's say that the consultation took place on November 1, 1992, with Saturn at 12° Aquarius, Uranus at 14° Capricorn, Neptune at 16° Capricorn, and Pluto at 22° Scorpio. The important upcoming transit would be the conjunction of Pluto to the Scorpio Moon.

1) As this transit unfolds, what do you think will happen if she continues in her former style of mothering?

2) What sort of healing work would she need to go through in order to change her relationships with her children?

So that we don't go too far afield into chart interpretation, you're on your own for the answers to these questions and for the English translations. However, this method—asking yourself questions to identify the emotional, behavioral, and historic equivalents of the major chart features—is a useful way to begin translating. Practice making up questions for the next several charts you look at, until this kind of thinking becomes second nature.

Productive Uses of the Client's Verbal Style

To return to our theme of effective communication, one tool is reflecting back clients' language patterns by using some of their own words or matching their conversational style. If you're New England

WASP, it's not going to be terribly convincing if you break into street Brooklynese. "Yo, man! You got Pluto on your case," just won't fly. With less extreme contrasts, however, it's helpful to accommodate your speech patterns to clients' or to use their vocabulary. If a man refers to his girlfriend as his significant other or his lover, you might do likewise. I draw the line at calling her his old lady, but we all have our limits.

Additionally, by listening to the precise words clients use, you find out a great deal about their inner world. What terms do they choose for love, sex, money, or other major life concerns? There are many slang expressions for sex or money, as well as many personal references, but the ones people select are illuminating. Over time, you will become adept at honing in on the precise meaning of clients' words, but no phrase is chosen at random. Each has meaning.

For instance, what underlying differences are suggested if they talk about being financially embarrassed versus having a cash flow problem? The person who talks about being financially embarrassed is primarily concerned about appearances and what others think—a Libra or Leo mode, generally. The one who talks about a cash flow problem is doubtlessly steeped in corporate sector standards and values—Capricorn or Saturn may be implicated.

Picking up on a telling phrase the client has used and showing how that illuminates the problem can be another very effective technique. To return to the example of Venus square Saturn, one client with that aspect asked if she'd ever have a successful love relationship. She was startled when I suggested that thinking of love in terms of success or failure might be part of the difficulty. Looking at what she meant by "successful" when it came to love was one of the most productive pieces of the session. Given an impossible set of predetermined and nonnegotiable criteria that she felt she had to meet, that her dream man had to meet, and that the relationship had to meet, her chances of "success" in love were practically nil. As we talked, she began to see that changing her attitudes and letting go of her perfectionism would enhance her chances of a happy and spontaneous relationship.

You will often be amused to find that people talk their charts. A client with Neptune square the Sun natally had transiting Neptune on her Sun and squaring natal Neptune. She said, "I like to think I'm going with the flow, but really I'm just going unconscious." We had a productive discussion about how to figure out when she was in flow and when she was unconscious. On the whole, she concluded being unconscious was more natural to her. Still, she did, indeed, have moments of going with the flow, and there was value to increasing that quality.

Talking to Various Planetary Types

Over time, as you engage in dialogue with clients, you will also learn how various astrological types think and react. By understanding how they think, you can explain the problem in a way that increases the consultation's potential to catalyze change. You wouldn't talk to a Saturnian the same way you talk to a Neptunian. Uranospeak is a very different English dialect from Plutonese.[2]

You are more persuasive and reach people on a deeper level if you speak their language. That is, use words and arguments that have relevance to their way of life. Then you can be more successful in motivating them to change those things that aren't working for them. (You still won't be successful in motivating them to change things in their life-style that aren't working for *you*, but judging their life-style is not your job.)

You would want to frame what you say in words that will appeal rather than in words that will turn them off. For example, you wouldn't use Taurean turn-ons like money, stability, and security when talking to an Aquarian or Uranian type. Conversely, you wouldn't use Aquarian buzz words like new, trendy, change, and revolutionary with a Taurus. (Even the number of syllables in your words is likely to be different. Uranians can hang in there for four-

---

[2]How would you identify what planetary type clients are? There would be an emphasis on a particular planet or the sign that planet rules or the house connected with that sign. For instance, the Sun, Moon, Ascendant, or Midheaven—or especially more than one—may aspect a particular planet or be in the sign that planet rules. Additional emphasis is created by a stellium in that sign or house, or many aspects to that planet. A planet would also be highlighted if it lies in the Gauquelin sectors: i.e., within ten degrees either side of the angles. Most people can be characterized by at least two planets.

syllable words and throw a few back at you, where Taureans are likely to tune you out after several with three syllables.)

Put yourself in the client's shoes and think of words that have positive value for that sign or planet. Venusians want to hear about loving and mutuality and would be concerned about how any change you discuss would affect their relationships. Aries or Martian people might respond to suggestions couched in terms of taking action, doing something about their difficulties, or winning, even if they're only competing with their own former best performance.

Mercurial people love to hear about variety, new and stimulating experiences, good conversation, and learning. The problem with Mercurial types is not so much how to talk to them as how to get a word in edgewise. Working with Mercury-prominent motormouths, you may need to keep pulling them back from their tangents and going back to the chart. Otherwise, they're likely to still be there when you put the cat out for the night.

Another thing to be aware of is not to confuse *information* with *communication*. They may bombard you with information, anecdotes, witticisms, and questions. You both go away thinking the session was highly satisfactory, when in fact it was merely entertaining. There's nothing intrinsically wrong with that, and maybe all this type of client really wanted was another interesting experience to add to the repertoire of stories. However, if the client has asked you to shed light on serious problems or dysfunctions, then the entertaining barrage may be a defense to avoid dealing with heavy feelings and serious difficulties.

Capricornians or Saturnians like to hear about success and accomplishment, even if you're discussing their spiritual path. Talk to them about recognition, self-discipline, patience, doing quality work, and about things taking time. Characterize their past as coming from hardship or having had a great deal of responsibility as a child. As adults they are late bloomers, ripening into maturity.

Communication with Neptunians is, at best, spotty. So much of what they feel, want, believe, and experience can't be put into words anyway. Like Alice in Wonderland, words may mean whatever they need them to mean at the moment. They can also suffer from lack of clarity and from denial, especially when it comes to their feelings.

Fantasy can feature very prominently in their lives. Still, they like to hear about spirituality, creativity, service, about how they've suffered, and about how karmic it all is.

To go into more detail about one type, how would you speak to a Plutonian? They like to hear about depth, analyzing, overcoming, underlying motives, healing. Begin to speculate about what sort of person you are dealing with. How might you expect them to think? For one thing, typical Plutonians are likely to be wary and not trust you or take what you say at face value. They are cynical. They will look for inconsistencies and dishonesty in what you say. Thus, you need to be honest about your perceptions of their chart.

Additionally, their interpretation of what you say about their horoscope is likely to be negative—seen in the worst possible light, anticipating the most catastrophic consequences. Thus, you need to work at being balanced and positive, though not a Pollyanna. One of their strengths is that they look beneath the surface and analyze themselves and others. They can be trusted not to flinch at talking about the hard stuff. In fact, they won't feel that you did your job unless you go into the heavy situations that have happened to them. (Read my book, *Healing Pluto Problems*,[3] for more helpful hints on how to work with Plutonians.)

It's not my purpose to give you a complete glossary of Plutonese or Uranospeak here—only to alert you that they exist and that you need to talk differently to different planetary types. You pick up the vocabulary by talking to them, and more importantly by LISTENING intently and trying to get inside their heads.

In learning how the various types think, experiential astrology techniques can be more helpful than anything you could read. If an astrodrama workshop isn't available, practice with an astrology friend. Set up a typical life situation, such as a job or career change, an internal debate over a new relationship, or a family problem. Then, try discussing the situation while you are playing the role of Uranus and the other person is Pluto—or play Neptune while your friend is Saturn. If you're an astrological lone wolf in some remote area with no astrology group, try writing a dialogue between the two planets in an aspect. Don't be surprised if they begin to speak out and explain their points of view.

---

[3]*Healing Pluto Problems* (York Beach, ME: Samuel Weiser, 1986).

Communication versus Manipulation

Does this approach to the various planetary types seem like manipulation? I'd like to think of it as persuasion, but, in a sense, all *change agents* are manipulative. Change agents include therapists, healers, astrologers—and salespeople. They all try to influence the client in some particular direction. Whether it is manipulative in a negative sense depends on your motivation. Supposing you have predetermined how the client should behave, think, feel, or be, based on your own values. Then, if you are using your tools of persuasion to control the client, it is manipulation.

It is different when the session is client-driven—that is, if you aim it at the problems clients have identified as the focus of the session. If you are working to help clients change in the direction they desire, then it is probably not manipulation but skilled intervention. At any moment, however, when one of the astrologer's own buttons is pushed, the need to control and, hence, to manipulate can take over. This is one of the reasons we need to be constantly vigilant over ourselves during sessions.

What About the Client's Mercury?

You may be wondering why there hasn't been any reference to Mercury. I started to wonder that, myself, about two-thirds of the way through writing this. Surely, analyzing Mercury's sign, house, and aspects could help you match clients' verbal styles, couldn't it? Yes, it might, but on a superficial level. Suppose a go-getter has Sun, Mars, and Venus in Aries, but Mercury in Pisces. Is speaking in a Neptunian fashion going to work? Or, suppose an unhappy person has Mercury in Sagittarius but the Sun and Moon in Capricorn. Will talking in an upbeat, enthusiastic, frothy mode penetrate to the core of the depression?

Matching Mercuries is like doing imitations—comedians do it all the time. They *sound* like the person they are mimicking, which is why they are funny, but they aren't usually saying anything profound about the person. And, no doubt, the person being imitated feels mocked rather than understood.

We don't want to be comic, we want to be karmic or dharmic. We don't just want to do an imitation, we want to penetrate to the core of the person and communicate at that depth. For profound dialogue to occur, the totality of the chart and of the person has to be taken in, understood, and accepted. Without acceptance, there is no real understanding and no heart-to-heart communication. There may be preaching, there may be rescuing, but there is no meaningful exchange. That is why getting to know the psychology of the planetary type and how that type views life is more important than analyzing the person's Mercury.

Our Goal—Eschew Obfuscation

Hopefully, this chapter has helped you begin to translate astrologese into English—or, better, into experiences and emotions that are meaningful to clients. Communication with the client is an important responsibility for the astrologer. Otherwise, all the astrological knowledge in the world is useless in helping people make sense of their lives. No doubt, I believe that because of my multiple endarch in Gemini, including SOL1. However, many clients have also expressed the distress it created when a previous astrologer used too much mystifying jargon. From now on, let's do our best to eschew obfuscation—at least in astrology readings. Among ourselves, we can throw in as many triple wambles and double dihydrals as we like, but, PLEASE, NOT IN FRONT OF THE CLIENT!

CHAPTER THREE

Counseling Clients in Crisis

Since the *aster* in *disaster* literally refers to the stars, we might infer that emergencies are often provoked by outer planet transits. Thus, professional astrologers, whose stock in trade is outer planet transits, often deal with clients in crisis. An event or condition which poses an imminent threat to the client or a loved one precipitates a crisis. Often a loss or anticipated loss is involved. At times, conditions which may have been difficult but bearable suddenly become intolerable because of some new stress. For instance a dysfunctional marriage may limp along for years, both partners unhappy but too inert to make a move. Then one partner falls ill or loses a job, and the resulting strain on the relationship tips the balance.

Clients in crisis are likely to be anxious, confused, and uncertain what to do. They feel overwhelmed, disorganized, and unable to cope with daily demands. Judgment may be impaired, and many have difficulty in making simple choices, much less the major life decisions that face them. They are likely to ask for advice and to be in a vulnerable state regarding your suggestions. Many are very dependent, although others resist all help and advice.

Crisis also has its positive side. In one of the eastern languages, the pictogram for crisis consists of two characters, one for danger and the other for opportunity. While there is the danger of loss, there is also the opportunity to change undesirable patterns. In emergencies, people question old defenses and become ready to try a new way.

Often, in the earliest stages, they simply do what has worked before. When that fails, they do it harder. Only when old and known coping mechanisms have failed, are they apt to look for a new solution. They are also more open to accepting outside help, so crisis is a prime moment for intervention.

Since many who would be threatened at the idea of a therapist go to astrologers first, we are often in a key position to plant the seeds of change. In this chapter, we will explore how astrologers can respond to clients who come during an emergency. We will talk about specific situations such as the suicidal client, the midlife crisis, and spiritual emergencies like the Near Death Experience. Since we cannot hope to cover all the kinds that will confront you in professional practice, some general principles of crisis counseling will be presented.

Why Are They Coming to an Astrologer?

When you think about it, does it make any sense to run to an astrologer in an emergency? Why not run to a doctor, lawyer, psychiatrist, financial planner, or the police? Many do just that, of course, but the person whose first thought is to call an astrologer is a particular sort of person. Possibly not as well grounded as those who run to financial planners or lawyers, such people think about life in a particular and doubtlessly peculiar way. They think, in short, like we do.

There are two kinds who come at such times. First, there are the spiritually aware who want to understand the karmic and personal growth implications of what is going on. Second, there are the dependent and unsophisticated souls who want to blame their problems on the stars and be told what to do. Type one is more verbal and rewarding, but all too often is merely type two in disguise.

At that moment, you are an archetypal figure—the sybil who can tell the future and placate the gods they may have offended. They hope you will help them control their destiny. With clients in such a frame of mind, it is especially important to avoid giving specific advice. In that vulnerable state where they may regard you as a god-conduit, they are likely to take it. At a certain level, they want to saddle you with the responsibility for their lives. If they follow your advice and the results are disastrous, you may take on part of the blame, at least in their eyes. (There is also a school of thought that says you incur a karmic responsibility for any advice given. For all our sakes, I hope they're wrong!)

People *in extremis* are particularly vulnerable to the implication that the planets are causing this eruption. "It's in the stars," has an odd and seductive comfort. "Ah, it wasn't ME, it was Saturn!" Thus, it is important to avoid talking that way and to get them to see concretely what led up to the event and what part they played. Otherwise, the sense of powerlessness that often accompanies an emergency is compounded by the belief that the stars are in control of their destiny—and not especially friendly at the moment.

Understanding and Monitoring Your Own Reactions

The client's sense of powerlessness can be compounded by the astrologer's reactions. Even though you might feel some of the same panic and upset as the client, it is important to remain calm but compassionate. To panic or get into negativity doesn't help. Most astrologers are psychic to some extent, even those who deny it. You may be picking up clients' feelings and reacting to them as though they were your own. The mere recognition of this possibility may help you disconnect; others need conscious work on psychic shielding with techniques like those given in chapter One.

If you are uncomfortable when clients become upset, be sure you don't stop their tears or anger out of your own needs. If you're having trouble sitting with the emotional storm, breathe deeply and get centered. The feelings we tolerate most readily in clients have to do with our Moon's sign and aspects. Part of being a professional is gaining self-awareness about these emotional tolerances and exercising self-discipline in dealing with uncomfortable emotions. Feelings are apt to be intense during a crisis, so we need self-awareness all the more.

As we'll discuss in detail in chapter Five, a considerable number of astrologers are adult children of dysfunctional families. Many grew up in alcoholic households, where Christmas was often a catastrophe and where payday was not necessarily a day to celebrate. These occasions instead were apt to signal a devastating binge and a family brawl. People from such backgrounds learn to stuff their feelings and to keep everyone cool in order to survive. Free expression of feelings might escalate the crisis, so family members come to consider feelings dangerous.

These defense mechanisms helped adult children of alcoholics (ACAs) and others from dysfunctional backgrounds survive. ACAs in the helping fields need to counteract and heal that programming in order to support clients through times of upheaval. Some may still be too shell-shocked to deal comfortably with clients in crisis. Other common traits of ACAs which are pertinent to crisis counseling are an addiction to excitement, the need to rescue and save, and the need to control, especially when the client's life is out of control.

Blaming the Victim—New Age Style

Clients are particularly sensitive to any underlying attitude of blame. It's human to blame the victim for what happened, and astrologers are not exempt from this tendency. Rape victims are commonly said to have asked for it, battered wives are said to provoke their abuse and to stay with the batterer out of some masochistic need. Crime victims are thought to have been careless to be in that place at that time. Incest victims are told they must have been seductive.

A New Age adage that metaphysical practitioners too often use to bludgeon their clients is that people who are sick in some way caused their illness. This idea leaves clients (or spiritual seekers) who become seriously ill feeling resentful—but also ashamed, guilty, and feeling metaphysically incompetent. The 12th house shows many paths to spiritual growth, and illness is one of them. The time a patient spends in bed is often a time of contemplating the life path and its errors. Since Blue Cross doesn't pay for ashrams, only for hospitals, in modern life, 12th house purposes may more often be achieved through illness than through spiritual retreats.

It is human to feel that the victim was in some way responsible. We do that in order to protect ourselves from anxiety about becoming victims ourselves. Blaming the victim makes us feel more powerful and more in control of our lives. Clearly, we reason, we are smarter, stronger, healthier, luckier, and have our lives more together, so nothing like that could ever happen to us.

Blaming the victim is still another way helping professionals avoid feeling powerless when clients' lives are in crisis. It's a way of dealing with the frustration of not being sure you can help them. However, when clients are running around like Chicken Little screaming that the sky is falling, it doesn't help a whole lot for you to tell them that it's all their own fault.

Although a victim may be angry with the people who blame victims, he or she can also accept the blame, feeling guilty and ashamed. The victim might have been robbed in broad daylight on a crowded street, but decides the mugging was his or her fault. Or, the little boy was 3 years old when his older brother started molesting him, but he concludes that he must have deserved the abuse because he was bad.

Why does a victim accept responsibility? To do so is less threatening than confronting his or her true powerlessness. It is less overwhelming to think that he or she brought about the victimization, and therefore it could have been prevented somehow. It leaves the victim with a strange sense of control. However, accepting the blame makes the victim feel even more guilty and ashamed, as well as feeling alienated from the people who might have given comfort and support.

Blaming the victim takes on an especially obnoxious quality when buttressed by smug New Age platitudes. Here, the reasoning is that because you are wiser, more enlightened, and more pure than the victim, and because you think only in positive terms, this sort of thing will never happen to you.

It's even worse to hear that it's karma. This line of thought concludes that the victim must have been a terrible person back then, or these things wouldn't be happening. Insensitive New Age practitioners have been known to tell a victim that if she was raped in this life, she must have been a rapist in another life. An incest survivor involved in spiritual studies may buy into a similar line of reasoning. It's another way of being told that the victim asked for it and deserved what happened, but the blame is cloaked in pseudo-spiritual pronouncements.

Now, you may believe that such events are karmic. You may even believe you can see the karma in the chart. Your beliefs are your beliefs, but as a practitioner, you should not impose them on your dazed, shocked, and grieving clients. Doing so comes out of the Jupiterian need to have all the answers, to feel superior, and from a less than enlightened need to blame the victim.

Crisis Counseling During the Chart Reading

Unless you have a background in counseling as well as astrology, you are particularly vulnerable in an emergency. When things go wrong, people want to blame someone—witness the high cost of medical malpractice insurance. Thus, you would be wise to issue disclaimers on the tape. ("I'm not a doctor/lawyer/whatever so I can only tell you what I see in the chart.") Suggest that clients see a qualified professional in a relevant field before taking action.

As discussed in chapter One, it is a good idea to do some screening. Ask the caller the reason for wanting a reading. If the emergency is in an area you know little about, it may be best to pass this caller to someone who does. For example, if you would be in over your head when handling a severely disturbed client, send the person elsewhere—like to a mental health facility. This policy protects the client and you as well. Make referrals kindly by explaining that this is not your area of expertise and that you want the caller to get the best help possible. Otherwise, the caller may see it as a rejection of a plea for help and may conclude that you, a messenger of the Gods, see the caller as unworthy and the plight as hopeless.

When a person who is in a crisis comes for a consultation, you may need to give emotional first aid. Rescue Remedy by Bach is a good tool for any practitioner to have on hand. It is a flower essence, and is available in concentrate form in many health food stores. A few drops of the concentrate in a glass of water or a cup of tea help the client calm down. (You can take Rescue Remedy yourself, if you're overwhelmed.) You may also wish to mix four drops of the concentrate in a small bottle of spring water for the client to take home to continue using, a few sips at a time, until the crisis has passed.

It is also calming to wrap the fingers of one hand around the first finger of the other. The first finger corresponds to fear in Jhin Shin Jyutsu, an ancient Oriental form of healing related to acupressure. Hold the finger for a few minutes, until the pulsebeat is strong, then shift to the same finger of the opposite hand for a few minutes. Repeat the process with the thumb, which relates to worry in this system. Toddlers soon find out how soothing this can be, which is why they suck their thumbs.

Clients may talk rapidly, almost incoherently, crying or raging. Ask them to stop and breathe deeply for a few moments before continuing. However, catharsis releases stress and stimulates healing, so be sure you aren't shutting them off just because you are uncomfortable. The chance to express bottled-up feelings and talk things over with a compassionate but uninvolved person is useful. Validation helps—to be told that, yes, what they are going through is hard and sad and that they're not crazy to be feeling the way they do.

Next, evaluate how serious the problem is, and what is at risk. The event which precipitated the crisis may not seem earth-shattering to you, but the client perceives it as such. Gather information by asking questions like these:

1) Is the person or anyone else involved in actual danger?

2) What possible consequences are there? What is the best that could happen? The worst?

3) What are the possible options? (When the client feels there are no options, no way out, the situation is very serious.)

4) What sources of support are there? Who can the client turn to for help? What resources are available?

5) Who else is involved and how might they be expected to react? How could they help? How could they hurt?

6) What is the client thinking about or planning to do?

7) What has the client tried already? What worked and what didn't work?

8) How has the client reacted in similar situations in the past? If, for instance, the person tended to act impulsively, without thinking out the consequences, there is a strong chance of doing so again.

By considering such questions with someone outside the situation, clients can begin to sort out what has happened and how to deal with it. The confusion, the nameless dread becomes less threatening, because they begin to see reality rather than shapeless doom. (In short, the questions move them from Neptune to Saturn.) Sometimes considering possible consequences, options, and sources of support enables them to make a decision.

In listening to their answers, check the chart for expected reaction patterns and for the outcome of various possibilities. The Moon shows instinctive responses and how people deal with emotions. It is important here to limit and focus the discussion, so you help them get focused. You do not want to cover the whole chart, as they couldn't take it in. Confine your comments to relevant parts of the chart and current transits. You will, of course, prepare the whole chart, as in any reading, because you will have to think and react quickly. Put up at least a solar chart of others who are involved, to see where they fit in. It is particularly important to avoid fatalism and to scan the horoscope for strengths and abilities. Even those who generally have a good sense of self may forget certain of their strengths in the face of an upheaval. Your belief that they will make it, when not glibly given, is encouraging.

Finally, as we will discuss in chapter Four, suggest where the person can go for help. A thorough knowledge of local agencies and healers is an important asset in astrological practice. During a crisis, people are more open to seeking outside help, since the usual coping mechanisms are insufficient to handle the new level of stress. Familiarity with resources is reassuring, particularly for those who think there is no way out. Given concrete suggestions, clients can calm down and think about where to go from here.

Whose Crisis Is It?

Folks differ widely in what is vitally important and in what they perceive as catastrophic loss. A crisis for one person may be a way of life for another. People vary in the ability to handle stress. Also, what an individual could cope with easily at one point may cause a breakdown at another point, after a series of blows. It is important not to impose your perceptions about what is or is not a crisis or about the severity of the threat. Instead, judge the severity by clients' reactions and their assessments. The reaction and the aftermath will also be different for different people. So, first, you have to know who your clients are. What does this loss or threat represent? How are they likely to react? What strengths do they have and what vulnerabilities?

The horoscope is an invaluable source of answers to such questions, providing a wealth of information which the usual crisis counselor does not have. For a strongly Uranian or Aquarian type, being fired may be unimportant or part of a pattern that confirms how stupid and power-hungry bosses are. For a strongly Saturnian or Capricornian individual, on the other hand, being fired is a blow, regarded as a failure and a humiliation. It can trigger a major depression. For Saturnians, success can also be a crisis—they are vulnerable to depression after accomplishments, too. Help them to validate and cherish the accomplishment, but also to find another mountain to climb.

For a Cancerian, the death of a parent may be devastating, whether the relationship was good or bad. For a strongly Sagittarian person, it may be an anticipated part of the life cycle, eventually something to wax philosophical over. The Sagittarian, however, may have a strong grief reaction at the loss of a spiritual teacher or the revelation that the teacher has feet of clay. The worst kind of crisis for a Sagittarian or Jupiterian type is a crisis of faith. For a Libra Sun or Moon who has been married and deeply committed for twenty years, the end of a marriage may feel like the end of the world. For an Aries, it may be the opportunity of a lifetime! What kinds of crises can you imagine for other astrological categories? The Mercurial type? The Leonian? The Neptunian? The Plutonian?

How Bad Will It Be?

One reason a person goes to an astrologer in an emergency is to contain the damage. This client wants to find out how bad things might get; this client wants to figure out how to keep the worst from happening. To estimate the outcome of the current predicament, question the person about past patterns to see if the worst has already happened. That is, look at the parts of the birth chart that transits are triggering and that correlate with the current threat. Think about the worst you could expect from that chart pattern, and ask the client tactfully if a similar dilemma has ever come up and how it worked out. Look up the transits at that time to see if they are similar to the current ones.

You need, in short, to take some history, just as a doctor, psychotherapist, or other professional would. We tend to think we should know all, see all, and tell all just from the chart—and our clients often expect that of us, too. We need to let go of such grandiose expectations in order to serve better. There are multiple interpretations of any given chart aspect, and people grow—or deteriorate—in their usage of such aspects during their lives. We should not be expected to zero in on the correct interpretation by some mystical power, any more than a doctor should be expected to make a diagnosis without asking questions.

By not taking a history, you rob yourself of the best possible clues to how the aspect will function. You particularly need this reality check in an emergency. History tends to repeat itself, short of major personal transformation. If the worst has happened once or more before, it may well happen again. If it has never happened and the client is 30 or older, it is unlikely to happen now.

A client had the Moon tightly squared by natal Pluto in the 5th. Transiting Pluto was setting off this aspect, opposing the Moon and squaring natal Pluto. She was in the middle of a bitter divorce from her second husband and had a son by this marriage. I'm not certain what possessed me to say this, as it is definitely not my style, but the words popped unbidden out of my mouth. "Watch out that he doesn't kidnap your son." I was horrified at this prediction, but she wasn't. She revealed that it had already happened once before. Her first son was stolen by her first husband and she had never seen him again. Prepared by my uncharacteristic outburst, she could now take precautions.

Therefore, given a potentially dangerous outcome, as indicated by the current situation, the natal chart, and the triggering transits, you need to ask about the past. Suppose a woman is expressing concern about what will happen if she leaves her current relationship.

Uranus is opposite her 7th house Mars/Uranus conjunction. You would ask if the man she is with has a bad temper. If she says yes, elicit whether he has ever hurt her or other women he has been involved with. You would also want to know whether she has ever been battered by a lover. If the answer to both questions is yes, you have reason to worry and you need to say that there is realistic danger. Hopefully, you will have read something about battering and have resources to refer her to.

If she has never even been threatened by a lover or mate, and the man is not violent but instead is accident prone, you get a different picture. You would still warn of conflict in the relationship that might lead to an explosion, yet might infer a less damaging outcome. Be aware, however, that she may not be telling the truth. Battered women are often ashamed, operate in denial between episodes, and may also have been threatened with harm if they tell anyone what is going on.

Are you concerned that this type of focus is too negative? Would you be scaring the client by asking these kinds of questions? Predicting that a child might be kidnapped or that a woman would be battered would be negative in an ordinary consultation. However, an emergency is by definition threatening and life-altering. People who come in times of upheaval usually want and need to know what could happen. Clients in hard circumstances often express the wish to know the truth. They resent astrologers who give them false reassurances and thus leave them unprepared. To be a Pollyanna just so you and the client can both momentarily feel better doesn't help the client deal with the crisis realistically.

It is upsetting to talk about such difficult situations and be in the presence of the painful emotions they evoke. Yet, they do come up from time to time in astrological practice, so we need to get comfortable. Life periodically dishes up some lulus. We also need to prepare for the fact that the current outer planet lineup can manifest in less than an optimal way. Outer planets create a lot of reality for everyone.

On the other hand, a positive attitude is important. We all know that positive thought can affect outcomes. So, where is the balance? First, acknowledge that astrology cannot predict 100 percent, you can only suggest potential outcomes. A common sense, down-to-earth approach is the most helpful—neither excessively positive nor excessively negative, just realistic and informative. Acknowledge the pain and the difficulty, but let clients know that you believe they will make it. It is also useful for clients to gain perspective on the pain—its meaning, cause, and purpose. Here, again, the knowledge of local resources for dealing with such problems is reassuring.

When Will It Be Over?

Another reason for going to an astrologer in an emergency is to get a sense of the duration and timing of current events. Look at how many times the current transit has hit, since most repeat three times or more with retrograde motion. Count the first station up to two or three degrees before, and the last station two degrees after. The first will bring the onset of the process, and the last will finally tie it together.

If the transit is just beginning, people are at a turning point, which the consultation can help them prepare to handle in a healthy way. They can make use of the knowledge you give as motivation to transform their way of operating. However, the first hit is often overwhelming, an inundation. On repeated passes, they work through the issue. When the transit retrogrades past the aspect to the natal planet, the upheaval may calm down and appear to be over. The second time, they realize that this is *not* going away and they have to do something about it. The third time is a final opportunity to resolve the situation. If the transiting aspect repeats a natal one, usually the issue is a longstanding pattern that gets in the clients' way.

Another feature to look at is outer planet transits over the last several years. A given point in the chart can become sensitized by repeated transits. After people have suffered one blow after another, particularly to planets in a major configuration like a t-square or stellium, the current predicament may feel like the last straw. On the other hand, the series of transits may have evoked a major growth spurt. You would not know this from the chart; you will only learn this by taking a history. Different people react differently to the same transits—and the same person may react differently to a similar transit at different phases of the life cycle.

The Effects of Crisis on Relationships

It is important to note that any personal crisis may well precipitate a partnership crisis. Whenever the individual goes through a major readjustment, it also affects the partner, and so the relationship will have to change to reflect the new condition. This connection between personal and joint readjustment arises because transits or progressions to the Ascendant simultaneously aspect the Descendant. Likewise, transits or progressions to the Midheaven also affect the IC. Uranus transits are notorious for this. The client who comes in saying that he/she just lost a job, fell off a ladder and broke a leg, the roof on the house caved in, and a husband or wife just left—all in the same week—is doubtlessly having a Uranus transit to the angles.

Even when the change is positive, like a career advancement, the new status can be stressful. More difficult adjustments—like parenthood, or taking an elderly parent into the household—can precipitate a major partnership crisis. Where both parties are able to grow and be sensitive to each other, this time can even deepen the tie. Where the bond has already been shaky, it can signal the end. Given the prevalence and acceptability of divorce today, couples are less apt to stand by one another in times of trouble than previously.

Thus, when transits or progressions affect the angles, the astrologer would do well to ask about the status of the love life. Don't focus on the possibility of the relationship ending, as that may not be so, and is one more anxiety the client does not need. You will doubtlessly get reams of information by a simple, non-threatening question like, "How is your partner handling all this?" Counsel the client that attention may be required to keep communication open and that readjustment in the balance of the partnership may be needed.

Many times clients come for a reading because a loved one is in peril—perhaps due to hard drugs, suicidal depression, or a pattern of violence. It is not their problem, yet the status of the loved one is precipitating a personal crisis. Events are out of their control, and they believe their feelings of overwhelming helplessness will be relieved by knowing what is in the stars. They want you to look at the loved one's chart—or to do a reading for the loved one—and magically solve the problem.

In these cases, don't forget who is your primary client—the one who comes to the session needs help, too. The astrologer would do well to know about codependency and the family dynamics of addiction, which we will be discussing in chapter Five. In this way, you will be able to discuss the dynamics knowledgeably and shed some helpful light on your clients' misery. It is also useful to refer clients like these to Alanon, hot line numbers, therapists who work with codependency, and other sources of help. The Bach flower remedy, Red Chestnut, helps those who are deeply or habitually worried about those they love. Red Clover, by the Flower Essence Society, helps people stay centered and calm while others they care for are in upheaval.

What in Heaven's Name Is a Normal Crisis?

Astrologers deal with a variety of crises. Yet, it may surprise you to know that sociologists recognize a category of upheaval called a "normal crisis." That is to say, many crises are not pathological, but predictable parts of life. We may not recognize them as crises because people expect and even welcome them. Yet, they can be very unsettling because they require profound readjustments.[1]

Stressful phases of life include puberty, young adults going out on their own, marriage, the birth of the first child, children leaving home, menopause, the death or dependency of an aging parent, and retirement. For most of us, these events evoke anxiety and require similar kinds of readjustments. Among the flower remedies, Walnut by Bach and the combination by Desert Alchemy called Transitions Formula both help greatly in reducing the confusion and anxiety common during such periods.[2]

It is useful for astrologers to remember such times in their own lives and to read about periods they have not yet experienced. We each have a unique past and thus are uniquely prepared for or sensitized to such changes. We have characteristic reaction patterns—we

---

[1]*Dell Horoscope Magazine* published this section in its 10/92 issue as "What in Heaven's Name is a NORMAL Crisis?"

[2]Desert Alchemy is a flower remedy company that specializes in cacti and other desert plants. For their catalog, write to Desert Alchemy, P.O. Box 44189, Tucson, AZ 85733.

are much the same as children and young adults as in old age. The natal chart and current transits give valuable clues both to past stresses and to the individual's reactions to the change.

As an example of a "normal crisis," women do not automatically and instinctively become motherly just because they have delivered an infant. The birth of the first child requires a major adjustment that takes approximately one year to complete. It is a vast change in status and role, an identity crisis. All the meanings of the Moon come into play—the woman's role, dependency, nurturance, security, and emotions. The new mother is in a vulnerable state, feeling dependent. Yet, she has to relinquish some of her own dependency because she now has a helpless infant who totally depends on her.

Looking at the Moon and its natal aspects, in particular, can suggest what adjusting to motherhood might be like for the woman in question. The woman with a Moon-Uranus conjunction is going to react differently to becoming a mother than the woman with a Moon-Saturn trine. For the Uranian woman, having a baby—even by conscious choice—may represent losing her freedom and individuality. She now must fit the traditional female role she has rebelled against. The Saturnian woman may feel that motherhood finally makes her a true adult and may welcome the change in status and the increase in responsibility. Even with the Moon-Saturn trine, however, there can be some postpartum depression, as the seriousness of this new role hits home.

Menopause is another normal crisis. The difficulties of this phase of life lack reality to those who haven't been there, even women five years younger. It can bring on a considerable upheaval, with an alarming sense of being out of control and inundated with feelings like sorrow, anxiety, or rage. There are also strange physiological processes that can leave one feeling betrayed by the body. Menopausal women who live far from their older female relatives lack experience with "the change" and have little background in this mysterious process. It can begin as young as 40, although it may not finish until the 50s. The modern, liberated woman may be in denial that such an old-fashioned change is happening or that it has such far-reaching effects. We have such a fetish about remaining young that we reject this sign of the march of time.

Major transits or progressions to the Moon often initiate menopause or mark its critical stages. The physiology of the reproductive system is signified by the Moon. So are other aspects of womanhood, and the menopausal woman is often facing changes in role and status as well. If you see an important transit to the Moon in the over-40 female, suggest that she consult her gynecologist about the possible onset of menopause. It also is useful to recommend that she get books about the process, available in the health section of any bookstore. Many of my women clients fitting this picture were relieved that the emotional upheavals they were undergoing had some physiological basis, as they thought they were having a nervous breakdown.

Retirement is another turning point. Many do not survive it, for a considerable number of people die shortly after leaving the work force. (This phenomenon should not be surprising when one considers that retirement often correlates with an outer planet transit to the MC/IC axis.) Those who prepare in advance for this major change in life-style do better. These are the people who have developed significant outside interests, so that they retain a feeling of meaningful activity and purpose.

People who might have a difficult adjustment to retirement include strongly 6th house or Virgoan individuals or those with Saturn, Capricorn, or the 10th house prominent. Where Virgo or the 6th house is prominent, continued health and well-being might require volunteer work, part-time employment, or a fulfilling avocation to replace their vocation. Otherwise, without a feeling of being useful, the 6th house meaning can shift over to illness. If the 10th house is emphasized, the volunteer should ideally enjoy some status, such as a position on the board of directors of a service agency or an officer in an association.

When the Midlife Crisis Hits Home

By now, most of you know the connections between the midlife crisis and the cycles of the outer planets. Briefly, this consists of a series of aspects by these planets to their own natal positions, stretching from age 38 to about 45. They include oppositions from transiting Uranus to natal Uranus, second opposition from transiting Saturn to natal Saturn (the first being at age 14), and squares from transiting Neptune to natal Neptune and Pluto to natal Pluto. If you haven't explored this correlation, read Doris Hebel or John Townley, both of whom have done this era to perfection. We don't have space to cover it in depth here.

These planetary cycles match well the age 40 as described in Gail Sheehy's major book, *Passages: Predictable Crises of Adult Life*. The entire book is worthwhile reading for astrologers, since you will be seeing people who are immersed in the various age-related crises she describes. Here, however, we will focus on the stage that begins around age 40. The cover of *Passages* describes it this way: "THE FORLORN 40S—Dangerous years when the dreams of youth demand reassessment, men and women switch characteristics, sexual panic is common, but the greatest opportunity for self-discovery awaits."[3]

Since the midlife crisis involves outer planet cycles, the individual whose natal horoscope has the outer planets strongly featured would be especially affected. Such people struggle all their lives to integrate the issues connected with those planets into the framework of ordinary reality. The repetition of natal outer planet aspects by the transiting outer planet ushers in a make-it-or-break it phase. This is an important opportunity to clear up dysfunctional ways that a particular planet has been operating. Then, for the rest of this incarnation, these people can get to the higher level of that planet's functions. Being born with a particular planet so strong means they have a special affinity for that vibration and have worked on these issues throughout life.

For instance, suppose natal Neptune aspects the Sun, Moon, Ascendant or Midheaven—especially when more than one of these major points is aspected. The square from transiting Neptune to natal Neptune would set off these points as well. There would be a feeling that, "there's got to be more than this," complete with disillusionments about crucial people or areas of life. At the same time, the individual might bottom out on the less than positive ways Neptune has operated previously. Self-deception is no longer possible, and lifelong illusions that have kept the person living in a dreamworld are shattered. This can be extremely painful for such visionaries, but once they dry their tears or cure the hangover, they are able to function in reality more effectively. Paradoxically, by giving up the dream, they are able to have a piece of it.

---

[3]From the cover copy of Gail Sheehy's *Passages: Predictable Crises of Adult Life*. New York: Bantam, 1976.

For Outer Planet People—those with more than one of the outer planets strongly featured—the midlife crisis is even more crucial. They are visited by a series of intense outer planet cycles and by events, inner and outer, that the ordinary person cannot fathom. But then, we already knew they weren't ordinary people nor do they live ordinary lives! As a rather extreme example of how wild and wooly this stage can get, we'll be looking later on at the chart of UFO abductee Whitley Strieber. Conventional wisdom doesn't help Outer Planet People much. They can be greatly relieved by an astrology reading which explains that they are Outer Planet People and can't be expected to react like their earthling brothers and sisters. The spiritual emergencies discussed later are common to this group at any age, but especially during this cycle.

The Suicidal Client

Let's turn now to crises that are individual, rather than collective. Occasionally, clients will express suicidal thoughts during the session. Sometimes they do it indirectly by saying something like, "I just don't know how much longer I can go on." You then need to question them specifically. "Have you been thinking about suicide?" It is common among beginning counselors to wonder whether a question like this would give clients ideas they didn't already have. Experienced therapists have not found this to be true. People who aren't thinking of killing themselves will probably reply, "Goodness no, I just need a vacation!" Suicidal individuals, however, are likely to be relieved that their inner torment can be discussed openly. If the client answers yes, you have a delicate situation to contend with.

You first need to assess the seriousness of the client's desire to die. Can you tell from the chart? I think not. The National Council for Geocosmic Research, one of the major astrological organizations in the United States, conducted a painstaking and well-designed research project on suicide. They did it over a span of six years, from 1974–1980, coordinated by Nona Press. The researchers acquired death certificates of suicides from the New York City Bureau of Vital Statistics. Out of that group, they were able to secure 310 timed birth certificates. The date, time, and method of the suicide were also known. They paired each chart with a non-suicide, randomly selected.

Then 29 practicing astrologers, including some of the finest in the United States, were given ten such pairs. They attempted to determine which member of the pair was the suicide. We had a fifty-fifty chance of answering correctly, and yet only one of the 29 was able to score significantly above chance. That was Charles Emerson, using the Uranian system. (I was one of the flunkees!) Later, Rory Mercato also devised a rather elaborate formula with some promise, which he is still testing.[4]

This outcome might be regarded as a blow to our credibility. Nonetheless, it is reassuring that we don't know who will or won't kill themselves—that the chart does not show some kind of immutable fate. The study did not vindicate the traditional astrological indicators of suicide. Pluto and the 8th house can represent death and self-destruction, but also transformation and a great healing. In this respect, it is like the Death card in the tarot.

If you can't rely on the chart to tell you, what do you do? Ask your client! There are a series of questions you can use to determine how serious the intention by finding out whether the person has formulated a definite plan. Has the person decided on a method? Are the means to secure that method easily at hand? Does he or she have a definite date or time frame in mind? Have there been previous suicide attempts? Is there a history of family members or loved ones committing suicide? The more yesses you get to these questions and the more definite and detailed the responses, the more cause there is for concern.

One study of successful suicides showed that three-quarters of them had made prior threats. Almost half of them killed themselves *about three months after an emotional crisis from which they seemed to be recovering.*[5] Astrologically, this timing would seem to correspond to direct and retrograde transits over the same part of the chart. Two

---

[4]For a more detailed report on this carefully-designed study, read chapter Six of Nona Press' book, *New Insights into Astrology*. It was published by ACS, San Diego, 1991. Rory Mercato's results were published in the October, 1990 issue of *Urania*. (For information write to Gloria Schwartz, Editor, 498 West End Avenue, #6C, New York, NY 10024.)

[5]As published in Schneidman, E.S. and Faberow, N.I. *Clues to Suicide*. New York: McGraw-Hill, 1957, pp. 204–206.

studies showed that suicidal intent relates to hopelessness about the future, even more strongly than to depression. People who threatened or attempted suicide were unable to look to the future with any hope or enthusiasm. They felt the future was vague and uncertain and that it was foolish to want anything.[6]

There are important implications for astrologers in these studies, namely that those who come to us in such a desperate state need hope for the future. In such cases, I tend not to do long-range forecasting. It isn't helpful to hear that the same astrological conditions accounting for this current emotional black hole are going to repeat themselves over the next two to three years. Instead, look for where help can come from, in terms of chart aspects such as trines and sextiles both natally and by transit. Also look for support in terms of personal or social agency resources.

Support is essential because the astrologer, working alone, does not have the resources to handle suicidal people. Even the therapist in private practice will make sure to have psychiatric backup and to give the client the suicide prevention hot line numbers. Two Bach flower remedies which may be relevant here are Sweet Chestnut, which brightens up the dark night of the soul, and Cherry Plum, for those who fear they will lose control and harm themselves or others. You could also recommend Rescue Remedy to such clients until they are able to find professional help.

The Crisis of Remembering or Confronting Abuse

I wrote extensively about the chart signatures and psychological implications of domestic violence and incest in my book, *Healing Pluto Problems*, and don't want to duplicate that material. What I would like to discuss here is the severe upheaval which erupts when people first confront abuse they suffered in childhood. Perhaps they have always known they were abused but pushed it aside and are now facing

[6]Wetzl, Richard D., Ph.D; Thomas Margulies, MD; Roger Davis, MD; and Elie Karam, MD. "Hopelessness, Depression, and Suicidal Intent," Journal of Clinical Psychiatry, Vol. 41:5, 5/80, pp. 159–160.

it. Others recall the events, but they take on an unreal and dissociated quality, as though they happened to someone else.

An increasing number who come for readings repressed the events for years and are first remembering them. Or, they are struggling to do so and hope to find some answers in their charts. Some suffer from childhood amnesia in which large segments of childhood are a total blank. Except where the person has suffered a brain injury, childhood amnesia is nearly always a sign that extremely traumatic things happened, probably repeatedly, during those early years. Perhaps the abuse was severe and prolonged, or perhaps they were constitutionally highly sensitive to begin with.

For all three categories, opening the door to the abused part of themselves precipitates an explosion similar to opening Pandora's box. Even when the abuse took place thirty or forty years earlier, the reactions emerge as powerfully as if it had just occurred. This is because the child originally closed down in order to avoid devastation.

Unfortunately, the powerful feelings we don't face remain with us, and we deal with them eventually. In the course of confronting abuse, people are inundated with a series of waves of emotions, each lasting a week or longer. The waves generally include terror, rage, guilt, and shame, leading ultimately to grief. The acute phase often lasts about six weeks, though the healing and working through of the abuse may take years.

Those people who blanked out the incidents seem more devastated during the confrontation than those who always remembered. The secret that was too overwhelming to face is revealed, shattering illusions about the abusers. They confront their own powerlessness. They may also feel betrayed by—and terrified of—their own unconscious. For instance, one writer ran into a major writer's block afterward, afraid of what else might surface if she wrote again.

In my practice, it seems that the process of facing, uncovering, remembering, expressing, and healing is often related to Pluto transits. These could be to the MC/IC axis or to the planets involved in the original signature of abuse. Sometimes people uncover and deal with a series of partial memories, each time the Pluto transit recurs, over the two-to-two-and-a-half-years the transit is in orb. Incest survivors began acknowledging and addressing their abuse in a major movement after Pluto entered Scorpio in 1984. By the time Pluto had gone half to two-thirds of the way through that sign, we entered a new stage of awareness, where people uncovered repressed abuse. Men were also beginning to speak out more often and more openly about being sexually abused.

Remembering Abuse

As an example of childhood amnesia, let's look at the chart of comedienne Roseanne Arnold (Chart 1 on page 71). In the fall of 1991, she revealed in the press and on The Oprah Winfrey Show that she had remembered that her mother had sexually abused her during infancy. Following that, her father had sexually abused her for years in early childhood. These repressed memories began to surface in January, 1990, while her fiance, Tom Arnold, was in rehab for cocaine addiction shortly before their marriage. The memories were triggered when Tom suddenly remembered his own childhood sexual abuse, no doubt an underlying cause of his highly destructive addictions. (It is not uncommon for sex abuse survivors to form strong bonds with one another. The surfacing of memories in one often triggers memories or the crisis of confrontation in the other.)

The original signatures of abuse are the square of Pluto in the 7th to her Scorpio Midheaven and the t-square, which has a focal point of Neptune and Saturn in the 8th house in Libra. The t-square also includes Mars in Capricorn in the 12th, and Uranus in Cancer. The 4th house Moon aspects Neptune, Saturn, and Uranus by semisquare and sesquiquadrates, showing the mother's involvement. Roseanne's Scorpio Sun squares the Aquarius Ascendant and increases the Pluto/8th house component of her character. This particular aspect may not have had so much to do with the abuse as with her vengeful and rebellious response to it, in terms of the various scrapes she got into.

With Saturn, Uranus, and Neptune involved in the abuse picture natally, the Capricorn lineup of Saturn, Uranus, and Neptune (by transit) evoked the natal aspects and marked the uncovering of the abuse and the process of recovering from it. The memories began to surface as transiting Saturn crossed her 12th house Mars. The process remained private while Saturn completed the t-square, until 1991, when Saturn began coming out of the 12th house and trined her Moon (the public). Transiting Uranus was quincunx her natal

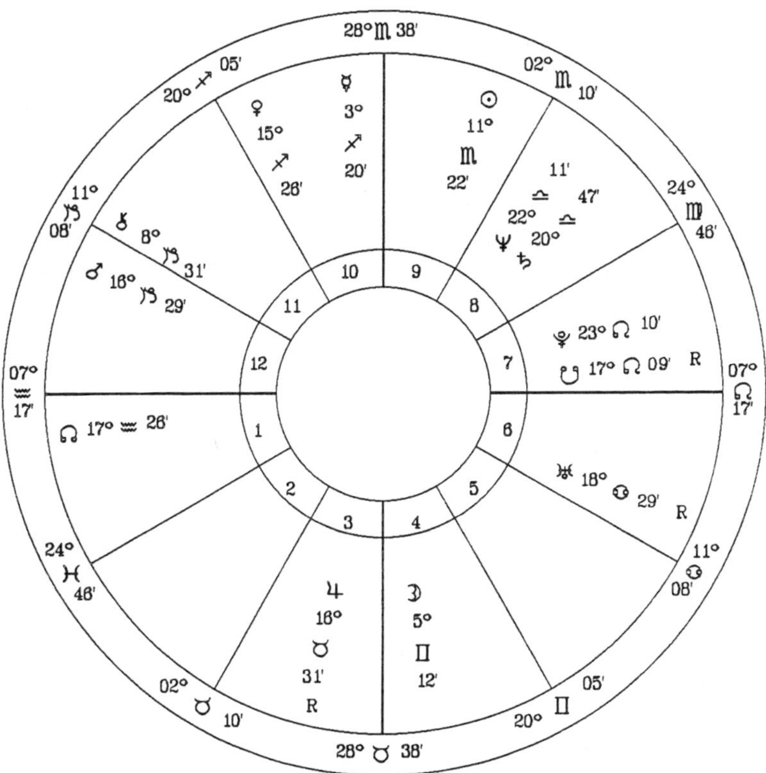

Aspects for Roseanne Arnold – Geo.		
☉ ☍ ♃ 5A09	☿ ⚹ As 3S56	♄ □ ♅ 2S18
☉ □ As 4A05	☿ ☌ Mc 4S43	♄ ☌ ♆ 1A24
☉ ⚹ ⚷ 2S51	♀ ⚺ ♂ 1A03	♄ ⚹ ♇ 2A22
☽ ☍ ☿ 1S52	♀ ⚻ ♃ 1A05	♄ △ ☊ 3S22
☽ ⚼ ♄ 0A35	♀ ⚹ ☊ 2A00	♅ □ ♆ 3S42
☽ ∠ ♅ 1S43	♂ △ ♃ 0A02	♅ ⚻ ☊ 1A04
☽ ⚼ ♆ 1A59	♂ □ ♄ 4A18	♆ ⚹ ♇ 0A59
☽ △ As 2S04	♂ ☍ ♅ 2A00	♆ △ ☊ 4S46
☽ ☍ Mc 6A34	♂ ⚺ ☊ 0A56	♇ □ Mc 5S28
☿ ∠ ♂ 1S51	♃ ⚹ ♅ 1S58	♇ ⚼ ⚷ 0S21
☿ ⚼ ♅ 0A09	♃ □ ☊ 0S55	As ⚺ ⚷ 1A15

Chart 1. This is the natal chart of Roseanne Arnold, born November 3, 1952, at 1:21 P.M. MST, Salt Lake City, UT, 40N45, 111W53. The data comes from Lois Rodden's DATANEWS #29, as given on the birth certificate. Placidus Houses. Tropical Zodiac. North Node is True Node; South Node is Mean Node. Chart calculated by Astrolabe using Nova Printwheels.

Moon, and the first memory she uncovered was that of being abused by her mother.

Transiting Pluto in the 9th (publishing, legal matters) was also sextile the 12th house Mars and trine Uranus during her period of uncovering and intensive healing. Thus, writing and speaking out about the abuse was part of becoming whole again. The happiness and peace that came from confronting, revealing, and dealing with her history was visible in her changed demeanor and appearance. Her public revelations both freed and triggered a great many others with such histories to remember what they had repressed. In her own courageous Sun in Scorpio way, Roseanne was acting as a powerful catalyst and healer for her public.

The Implications for Astrological Practice

There are two important implications for astrologers when dealing with the crisis of confronting abuse. First, when clients come in the midst of such an upheaval, you need to know about the healing process, so you can help them deal with it. For instance, you need to be comfortable with listening to their stories and allowing them to express their feelings. Many clients who confront the abuse fear they are having a nervous breakdown. They worry that they can't face or cope with the emotional eruptions marking the earliest phase. It helps to know that the eruptions themselves are normal, that this is part of the healing process, and that it is time-limited. It helps to be listened to and cared about.

You also need to know books and resources to recommend. Directing clients to the multitude of books now existing for survivors is helpful. One of the most empowering is the very compassionate self-help manual by Ellen Bass and Laura Davis, *The Courage to Heal*.[7] Reading these books yourself would help you to be more knowledgeable and authentic in your responses. It would also increase your level of comfort in listening to their stories.

Developing a knowledge of local resources for incest and abuse survivors is an important contribution. You should be able to tell

---

[7]Published by HarperCollins, New York, 1988.

people about support and therapy groups for survivors, so they don't go through this alone. There is something incredibly healing about sharing the process with others who have been through the same wounding. It cannot be gotten from loved ones or healers who have not had the experience. It is not the astrologer's job to be a support group of one either!

The second important implication is that it is important not to precipitate this crisis in clients who aren't ready for it. You may know the chart signatures of abuse—they are given in my book, *Healing Pluto Problems*, for instance, and others have taught them. Once you know the signatures, there may be an urge to get clients to acknowledge the abuse and its aftereffects, but this may be a costly mistake.

An alarmingly irresponsible use of the knowledge of abuse signatures came to my attention recently. I received an agitated letter from a woman who was told by a stranger over lunch at an astrology conference that her chart showed she was sexually abused. When she said that wasn't true, the man told her that she was indeed abused, but she had repressed it. Whether she was or was not abused is uncertain, but how could anyone prove they hadn't repressed something of this nature? His action was itself a form of abuse—an abuse of astrological knowledge and power! I'd have to call this a hit and run chart interpretation style, with no concern for the effects upon the receiver.

While few professional astrologers would behave this way over lunch, it becomes less clear when such a pattern shows up in a chart consultation. You may feel strongly that dysfunctions in various areas of the client's life are due to the effects of abuse. Survivors display a wide range of such severe symptoms as recurrent involvement in abusive relationships, phobias, gynecological ailments, extreme isolation, sexual compulsiveness or frigidity, addictions, and even multiple personalities. When focusing on such difficulties, you may be tempted to push the client to confront the abuse which both the chart and the life so strongly suggest.

However, we do not have the right to break down defenses and create the emergency we are talking about. People erect psychological defense mechanisms for good reasons. The wisdom and integrity of the psyche construct them to do just what the term implies—defend the individual from harm. In cases of childhood amnesia, it would be especially important to respect the wisdom of the psyche in blocking out the devastating events. I've known people who had done years of quality recovery work who suffered devastating—and dangerous—relapses of their addictions when repressed memories of sexual abuse surfaced.

Therefore, any probing in that area needs to be incredibly gentle. You might ask, for instance, if the client suffered from cruelty as a child. You may have a sense of who the offender was, based on the chart. If so, you might point to difficulties in the relationship with that person as a possible cause of current difficulties. If the client vehemently denies any difficulty there, claiming that it was a wonderful relationship, it is wise to back off.

Even when there is some acknowledgment that, yes, father was a problem, that does not give us a green light to draw out all the details. Unless the client is brimming over with a need to talk about what happened, a chart reading is not the appropriate place to elicit specifics. Be alert to any resistance to your questions, testing to see if clients are ready to deal with the abuse. The timing for confronting these issues must come from within, not from the astrologer. A friend's mother was 70 and dying of cancer when she finally revealed that she had been sexually abused for several years by an older brother, the family hero, when she was a girl. Only the pressure of imminent death had pushed this very proper woman to face and speak about the abuse.

Unless you are also a counselor and seeing the person regularly for therapy, you are not going to be around to pick up the pieces if you breach the denial. Even in ongoing counseling, therapists hesitate to batter down a client's defenses and force a confrontation with the abuse history. Far more damage can be done in a one-time consultation with a hit-and-run interpretation, especially given the quasi-supernatural power clients can project onto the astrologer. With abuse signatures, a little knowledge can indeed be a dangerous thing.

When Clients Ask If They Were Abused

When clients who suffer from childhood amnesia ask outright whether you believe they were abused, based on the chart, you should still be cautious in what you say. It is one thing for the rational part of them to think they want to know, and still another thing for the wounded inner child to face what happened. If chart indications seem clear cut, you might say that there does seem to be a strong possibility of abuse, but that no one can be 100 percent certain.

This is not altogether a hedge. I have seen what looked like abuse signatures and, upon discussion, found that the actual history involved other difficult occurrences. Several clients with prominent Mars-Pluto or Mars-Saturn configurations had recurrent, painful surgery in childhood due to some physical malformation. They had positive relationships with their parents, but the experience of having so much pain inflicted on them by doctors, although necessary, gave them many characteristics of abused children. Or, I have seen charts with a badly-aspected Pluto in the 3rd where the trauma was not abuse by a sibling but the sibling's death. You can't know for certain what some of these chart patterns mean without interviewing the client.

There are also people whose chart signatures are hazy—maybe yes, maybe no. Some seem not to have been actually abused. Instead they seem to have soaked up sexual energy psychically from parents with a strong sex drive who were still not so uncontrolled as to molest their children. This can result, for instance, from sleeping in the parental bed for some time when the parents are passionately involved. (Neptune is more often implicated here than Pluto.) I have also had clients who were as traumatized by watching their parents physically abuse their siblings as if it happened to them personally. The threat of violence was still present, even though they were "good" and avoided it.

Many who ask such questions are considering hypnotic regression. Counsel them not to force memories to the surface. Instead, urge them to respect their defenses and allow memories to emerge at a pace they can handle emotionally. Suggest they seek out healers who will provide a safe space in which to do this work, as safety often allows memories to come up. *Gentle* body work—like massage—is especially helpful in evoking memories. The body remembers everything that has ever happened to it, even when the mind does not. (Body work that *hurts*, like Rolfing or shiatsu, is very stressful for abuse victims.)

The Spiritual Emergency

There is another type of crisis that the psychiatric establishment is likely to regard as a serious mental disturbance or even psychosis. This category includes such paranormal experiences as sudden psychic opening, kundalini awakening, UFO contacts, the Near-Death Experience (NDE), and possession by discarnate spirits. Although the secular world is likely to label this type of upheaval as a breakdown, it is actually a breakthrough to another level of reality or another plane.

These events are, in effect, spiritual emergencies. A growing number of transpersonal therapists and healers recognize them as valid forms of spiritual passage or initiation in which the person may require outside help. Not easy in any era, our uneducated, secular culture's lack of acceptance or understanding makes dealing with such events very difficult.

The astrologer can help by being knowledgeable about such experiences and validating them. We are on the front lines, virtually an "emergency room" for spiritual upheaval. People need to be reassured that they're not going crazy when weird and supernatural events begin happening. They may also need help in coping with supernatural events, so astrologers need to know resources. Forming connections with knowledgeable and well-balanced spiritual practitioners is especially important here. We need to keep the knowledge current, also. The Neptunian nature of such work means that the person who is an excellent psychic, trance channel, or past life reader this year could be a burnout case next year.

Recommending appropriate books is also an important service, since these upheavals often strike in the middle of the night, when there is no one to turn to. It is calming to see your seemingly bizarre experience in print and to discover that there is a long and well-documented history of such events. A very important book is *Spiritual Emergency*, edited by Stanislav and Christina Grof. This is a collection of essays on many of these phenomena written by transpersonal psychologists and other well-versed practitioners.[8] Since we won't be able to cover all possible types here, I highly recommend this anthology.

---

[8]Stanislav Grof, MD, and Christina Grof, editors. *Spiritual Emergency*. Los Angeles, CA: Tarcher, 1989.

The transits of the outer planets through the universal signs are likely to stimulate many more such experiences than in ordinary times. Masses of people will be touched by phenomena like these. All those whose charts contain major placements—Sun, Moon, Mercury, or Ascendant—in the range that Uranus, Neptune, and Pluto are transiting are candidates. The combination is so unusual, I wouldn't be at all surprised if a UFO touched down at a Superbowl game!

The Near-Death Experience and Its Aftermaths

Raymond Moody popularized the Near-Death Experience (NDE) in his book, *Life After Life.*[9] The prototype is of leaving the body, perhaps floating above it and observing what is going on. Next, people who have this experience commonly pass rapidly through a dark tunnel, emerging into a brilliant white light. They are greeted by loved ones who are deceased or by beings of light. An awesome spiritual presence conducts them through a review of the life just ended. At some point, they are told that they have not completed their earthly work and must go back. Typically, there is a reluctance to return to Earth, followed by re-entry into the body and a sense of disappointment at being revived. In any given NDE, some of these ingredients may be missing, as this is a composite picture.

There has been considerable publicity about the NDE in recent years. Medical advances have saved many lives that once would have been lost, so the experience itself is no longer rare. As long ago as 1981, a Gallup Poll showed that over 8 million Americans had already had NDEs. Since then, a great many more have had them. The Grof anthology has an excellent chapter on counseling people who have had NDEs. In it, Bruce Greyson and Barbara Harris conclude, "Thanks to modern technology, the NDE may become our most common doorway to spiritual development."[10]

P.M.H. Atwater, a major writer on NDEs, similarly commented in a letter to me that, "The aftereffects of a Near-Death Experience are the *same* as those from a spiritual transformation. This broadens con-

[9]Raymond Moody, *Life After Life*. New York: Bantam, 1988.
[10]*Spiritual Emergency*, p. 201.

siderably the amount of people involved, and gives us a neutral model whereby the transformation process can be more objectively studied."[11]

Ms. Atwater has written an excellent and readable paperback on the life-transforming, long-range effects of this phenomenon called *Coming Back to Life: The After-Effects of the Near-Death Experience.*[12] After having died and been revived three times in 1977, she has talked, worked, corresponded with, and lectured to thousands of people with NDEs and finds common threads. It takes about seven years of intense work to assimilate the NDE, but the first four years are the hardest. It is as though they have to learn how to be in the physical world all over again. Family and friends often have great difficulty comprehending what has happened and how deeply these people have changed. They may seem mentally disturbed to others, especially to people with no spiritual background. Many are sent to psychiatrists and committed or sedated to take away their reactions and their struggles to readjust.

Here are Ms. Atwater's observations on the pattern of aftereffects and changes in personality from the NDE:

1) The inability to personalize emotions, especially those of love and belonging to anyone. They experience a feeling of overwhelming and unconditional love and acceptance for the whole world, but love which is not personalized. Their loved ones may experience this impersonal love as rejection and abandonment.

2) The inability to recognize and comprehend boundaries, rules, and limits.

3) Difficulty in understanding time or references to the past, present, and future—a sense of timelessness. They often experienced the future, but see the past, present, and future as all one.

4) Expanded or enhanced sensitivity, becoming more intuitive and psychic. Many reject or try to suppress this overwhelming psychic bombardment.

[11]From a private communication with the author on 10/4/1991. The emphasis is hers.

[12]P.M.H. Atwater, *Coming Back to Life: The After-Effects of the Near-Death Experience.* New York: Ballantine Books, 1988.

5) A shifted or changed view of physical reality, becoming more detached, objective, and seeing through events and problems with a noticeable reduction of fears and worries. They refuse to worry about things that have most of us going and may also no longer care about material things.

6) A different feeling of physical self, a certain detachment from the body and any identification of it as self.

7) Difficulty with communication and relationships, finding it hard to say what is meant or to understand language phrasing by others.[13]

In trying to find chart examples, it was interesting that I have never knowingly had a client with a NDE. Clients have revealed every kind of secret and traumatic experience imaginable—especially since my Pluto book came out. Furthermore, when asked for data in 1991, the massive ISAR-Rodden Data Bank contained only five, including several who are astrologers. I hypothesized that few of them come to astrologers because they no longer need us. Atwater's list of characteristics says they may develop paranormal abilities, including seeing beyond time and experiencing the future. We might be more likely to get their distressed family members.

However, when I wrote to Ms. Atwater about that, she replied, "Counselors, be they astrologers or not, *are* often needed by near-death survivors and others so transformed. This helps them to understand who they once were and where they might be headed in their development."[14] Since astrology seems an excellent tool for precisely this kind of exploration, it's still puzzling why so few seem drawn to us.

The ISAR-Rodden data bank provided the chart of a woman who had a Near-Death Experience, shown here as Chart 2 (pages 80–81). This woman's life was filled with tragedies. She had lost a child, a son attempted suicide on April 26, 1950, her house burned down on August 23, 1965, and her first husband hung himself on February 4, 1983. She certainly qualifies as a Plutonian! The birth chart has a strong Pluto. It is only degrees away from the Descendant as the focus of an Eye of God, the 10th house Scorpio Sun in the

[13]*Coming Back to Life*, pp. 67–68. Used by kind permission.
[14]From a letter dated 10/4/1991.

Aspects for Woman with NDE – Geo.		
☉ □ ☽ 4A20	☽ △ ⚷ 3S05	♄ △ Mc 4S01
☉ ☌ ☿ 1A51	☿ ✶ ♂ 3A08	♅ ∠ ⚷ 0A05
☉ ✶ ♂ 5A00	☿ △ ♇ 2S26	♆ ✶ Mc 1S05
☉ ⚺ ♃ 1S33	♀ □ ♂ 1S47	♆ □ ⚷ 3A05
☉ △ ♇ 0S34	♀ △ ♅ 0A43	♇ ☍ As 3A29
☉ ✶ As 4A04	♀ ∠ Mc 1A11	☊ ⚺ As 0S39
☽ ✶ ♃ 2A47	♂ ∠ Mc 0S35	☊ ☍ ⚷ 2S42
☽ ✶ ☊ 0S23	♃ ⚻ ♇ 0A58	Mc ⚻ ⚷ 2A00
☽ ⚺ As 0S16	♃ ☌ ☊ 3A10	
☽ □ Mc 5A05	♄ ☍ ♆ 2S56	

Aspects for Her NDE – Geo.		
☉ ∠ ☽ 1S33	☿ ⚻ ♄ 0A53	♅ ☌ ☊ 1A16
☉ ☌ ☿ 1A10	☿ ☌ ♅ 2A10	♆ ✶ ♇ 1A24
☉ ☌ ♅ 3A19	☿ ☌ ☊ 3A25	♆ ☌ As 6S32
☉ ☌ ☊ 4A35	♀ ∠ ☊ 1S37	♆ □ Mc 0S03
☽ ∠ ☿ 0S24	♂ △ ♃ 0A28	♆ △ ⚷ 3S54
☽ □ ♀ 4A38	♂ △ ♄ 4S31	♇ ⚺ Mc 1A27
☽ ∠ ♅ 1A46	♂ ⚺ ☊ 1S59	♇ ☍ ⚷ 2S30
☽ ⚺ ♆ 0S26	♃ ☌ ♄ 4A59	☊ ✶ As 5S00
☽ ⚺ ♇ 1S50	♃ □ As 2S33	As △ ⚷ 2A39
☽ ✶ Mc 0A23	♄ ⚻ ♅ 1S17	

Synastry Aspects for Woman with NDE, Geo. and Her NDE, Geo.		
☉ ⚼ ♀ 0A25	♂ ⚻ ⚷ 0A37	☊ △ ☉ 1A54
☉ ✶ ♂ 0S03	♃ □ ♂ 1S30	☊ △ ☿ 0A44
☉ ✶ ♃ 0A25	♃ ⚺ ♃ 1A57	☊ ⚺ ♄ 0A08
☉ □ ☊ 2S02	♃ △ ♅ 1S45	☊ △ ♅ 1S25
☽ ☍ ☉ 2S17	♃ △ ☊ 0S29	☊ ∠ ♆ 0A47
☽ ⚼ ☽ 0S44	♄ △ ♀ 1A59	☊ ⚼ Mc 0A44
☽ ☍ ☿ 1S07	♄ ∠ ♃ 1S09	As ⚻ ☿ 1S24
☽ ⚺ ♄ 0S15	♄ ⚼ As 1S24	As ☌ ♄ 0A31
☽ ☍ ♅ 1A02	♅ ☍ ♆ 2S01	As ⚻ ♅ 0A46
☽ ☍ ☊ 2A18	♅ △ ♇ 0S37	Mc □ ☉ 2A48
☿ ✶ ♂ 1S54	♅ □ Mc 2S04	⚷ ✶ ☉ 0S48
☿ ✶ ♃ 1S27	♅ ✶ ⚷ 1S53	⚷ ✶ ☿ 1S58
☿ ⚺ As 1A06	♆ ∠ As 1A32	⚷ ⚼ ♆ 1S55
♀ ⚼ ☉ 1A37	♇ ✶ ♂ 0S31	⚷ ∠ Mc 1S59
♀ △ ♇ 1A20	♇ ☍ ♃ 0A59	
♀ ✶ ⚷ 1S10	♇ ⚺ ☊ 1A28	

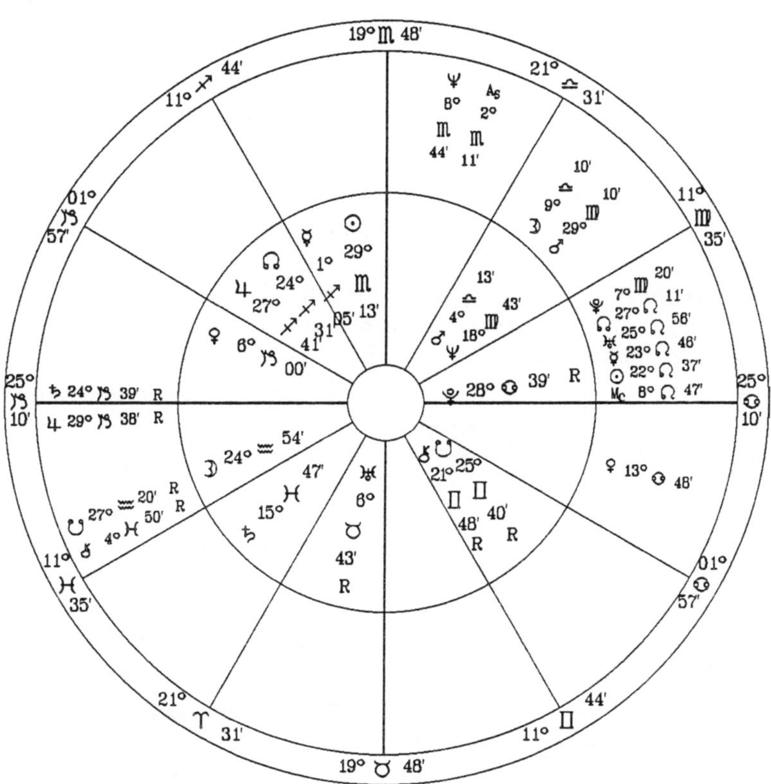

Chart 2. Inner wheel is natal chart for a woman born November 21, 1936 at 10:58 A.M. CST in Chicago, IL, 41N52; 87W39. Data is from the ISAR-Rodden data bank, given to Lois Rodden. This woman had a NDE in August, 1961. As an approximation of the transits, the planetary positions for August 15, 1961 are printed in the outer ring. Placidus Houses. Tropical Zodiac. North Node is True Node; South Node is Mean Node. Chart calculated by Astrolabe using Nova Printwheels.

Gauquelin sector 10 degrees off the Midheaven, and two planets in the 8th house. Though the exact date and time are not known, she had a NDE in August, 1961. The transits for mid-August are printed in the outer ring so you can get an idea of what was happening. The triggering factor appears to be a conjunction of Jupiter and Saturn crossing her Capricorn Ascendant and opposing natal Pluto.

Emotional Reactions of UFO Contactees

In considering UFO contactees, a delicate situation arises. Even stalwart Alice in Wonderland types who routinely believe ten impossible things before breakfast have trouble with this one. Those who accept the possibility of life on other planets and even of UFOs still tend to question the sanity of people who claim to have been contacted or abducted. Fortunately, we do not have to decide those questions here, only to consider the crisis endured by those who believe they have been contacted. It erupts either after consciously experiencing contact or, as the experience is more often repressed, after remembering the event. Many of the things said earlier about the crisis of remembering abuse hold true here as well.

Once more the Grof anthology contains a sound and sane approach to counseling such people. I highly recommend Keith Thompson's chapter, "The UFO Encounter Experience as a Crisis of Transformation."[15]

Mr. Thompson observes that contactees' most perplexing question is, "Why me?" They experience a sense of being selected for some unknown reason to carry out some unknown purpose or mission. As in the mythical hero's journey, there is the unwilling summons. Contactees often pretend the experience wasn't real or repress it, in order to preserve their sanity. At some point, memories begin to surface, precipitating a crisis. They are overwhelmed with terror, disbelief, and self-doubt, feeling they must be going crazy. They try to talk to others, and when met with disbelief and ridicule, they re-

[15]Thompson, Keith. "The UFO Encounter Experience as a Crisis of Transformation," in Stanislav Grof, MD, and Christina Grof, editors. *Spiritual Emergency*. Los Angeles, CA: Tarcher, 1989. pp. 122–134.

treat to secrecy, feeling isolated. The positive effect is often a changed view of life as vastly bigger and more complex than previously known. The experience is reality-shattering and yet can lead to a feeling of being very special, with compensatory ego-inflation.

Chart 3 (pages 84–85) is that of Whitley Strieber, the noted author of *Communion* and other books about UFO abductions. Although difficult to sit through, *Communion* is worth reading for its evocation of the emotional upheavals an abduction experience brings about. Strieber describes a period for several years afterwards of terror, paranoia, fleeing from place to place, and not being able to get his life together and function.

His book, *Communion,* particularly deals with a series of events in 1984–1986. The first in the series of contacts, which involved his whole family, took place in upstate New York through the evening until the middle of the night on October 4, 1985. The next remembered experience, again in upstate New York, was on the evening of December 26, 1985. A third major occurrence happened on February 7, 1986, in New York City, from near midnight until 4:00 A.M. of the next day. (Mr. Strieber eventually also retrieved memories of being missing for 24 hours in late August, 1967, at the age of 12.)

Mr. Strieber qualifies as an Outer Planet Person (OPP). His natal Sun-Mercury-Uranus conjunction, square Jupiter, suggests an extremely unusual or eccentric person, prone to exceptional experiences. UFOs and contacts with alien beings seem related to Uranus. His Pluto is also strong, on the IC, conjunct the Moon and squaring a 12th house Mars-Venus conjunction, suggesting powerlessness to prevent things done to him against his will. Naturally, many people have one or more of these aspects and are not visited by aliens—at least, not that they can recall. The same Pluto aspects can also be seen in abuse survivors, and the same feelings of fear, rage, victimization, and shame are experienced.

Transits for the first abduction are also shown in Chart 3. During the three abductions, Strieber was having the series of transits described earlier as evoking midlife crisis. Uranus opposed natal Uranus, Neptune squared natal Neptune, and Pluto squared natal Pluto. At some points in the process, one of the three aspects was closer to exact, at other points still another was more exact. (If you are going through midlife crisis, read *Communion*, and your midlife crisis will feel like a picnic compared to his!)

Aspects for Whitley Strieber – Geo.		
☉ ☌ ☿ 3A12	☽ □ ♂ 2S07	♂ □ Mc 5S16
☉ ∠ ♀ 0S09	☽ ∠ ♃ 0A16	♃ △ As 3S28
☉ □ ♃ 3S11	☽ ⚹ ♆ 0A06	♄ ☌ ☊ 2A10
☉ ∠ ♇ 1A32	☽ ☌ ♇ 4S59	♆ △ Mc 3S03
☉ ⚺ As 0A17	☽ ☍ Mc 3S09	♇ ⚺ ☊ 0A41
☉ ⚼ Mc 0A18	☿ □ ♃ 0A00	♇ ☍ Mc 1A50
☉ □ ⚷ 5A18	♀ □ ♇ 1A41	☊ ∠ As 1A56
☽ ∠ ☿ 0A15	♀ ⚹ ☊ 2A22	As △ ⚷ 5A01
☽ □ ♀ 3A18	♀ □ Mc 0A09	

Aspects for W.S. Abduction – Geo.		
☉ ☍ ☽ 1A24	☽ ⚻ ♄ 0A42	♂ ☌ ♇ 0A50
☉ ☌ ♀ 5A36	☽ ☍ ♆ 0S32	♂ ☍ ☊ 0A00
☉ ⚹ ♂ 2A16	☽ △ ♇ 2A51	♃ ⚹ ♅ 1A58
☉ ⚺ ♄ 0S42	☽ ⚹ ☊ 3A41	♃ ∠ ♆ 1A10
☉ ☌ ♆ 1A57	☽ □ As 4A37	♄ ⚺ ♆ 1S14
☉ ⚹ ♇ 1A26	☽ ☌ Mc 4S44	♆ ⚹ ♇ 3A23
☉ △ ☊ 2A17	☿ ⚹ ♃ 1A08	♆ △ ☊ 4A13
☉ ☍ Mc 6A08	☿ ☌ ♅ 3A06	♆ □ As 4A05
☽ ☍ ♀ 4S12	♀ ☌ ♆ 3A39	♆ ☍ Mc 4A11
☽ △ ♂ 3A41	♀ □ As 0A26	♇ ☍ ☊ 0A50
☽ ⚼ ♃ 1S42	♀ ☍ Mc 0A32	As □ Mc 0A06

Synastry Aspects for Whitley Strieber, Geo. and W.S. Abduction, Geo.		
☉ ⚼ ♂ 0A38	♀ ☍ ♇ 0S03	♇ □ ♂ 0A54
☉ ☍ ♅ 2S47	♀ ☌ ☊ 0S48	♇ □ ♇ 1A44
☉ ⚼ ♇ 0S12	♂ ⚼ ☿ 0A19	♇ □ ☊ 0S54
☉ ∠ ☊ 0A38	♂ △ ♀ 1A40	☊ △ ♂ 1A35
☽ ⚻ ☉ 1A49	♂ △ ♆ 1A59	☊ ⚹ ☊ 1A34
☽ ⚺ ☽ 0A24	♃ ⚻ ♃ 1A34	☊ ⚺ ⚷ 1A27
☽ △ ♄ 1A06	♃ □ ♅ 0A25	As ⚼ ☉ 1S55
☽ ⚼ ♅ 0A40	♄ ⚺ ⚷ 0S43	Mc ⚺ ☉ 1S20
☽ ⚻ ♆ 0S08	♆ □ ☉ 1S42	Mc □ ♂ 0A56
☿ △ ♃ 1S33	♆ □ ☽ 0S18	Mc □ ♇ 0A06
☿ ☍ ♅ 0A25	♆ ⚼ ♃ 1A24	Mc □ ☊ 0A56
♀ △ ☉ 1A29	♆ ⚹ ♄ 1S00	⚷ ☌ As 2A02
♀ ☍ ♂ 0A47	♆ □ ♆ 0A14	⚷ □ Mc 1S56

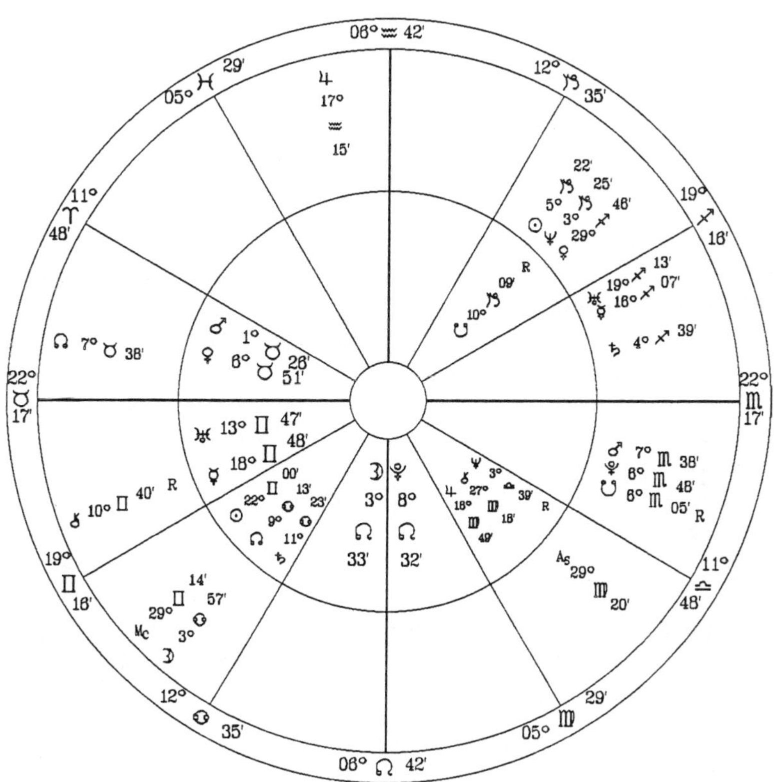

Chart 3. Whitley Strieber, born on June 13, 1945, 4:45 A.M. CWT in San Antonio, TX, 29N25, 98W30. The birth data comes from Lois Rodden's DATA NEWS, #17, 6/89, p.1, as given on the birth certificate. Outer ring: transits for his abduction on October 4, 1985. Placidus Houses. Tropical Zodiac. North Node is True Node; South Node is Mean Node. Chart calculated by Astrolabe using Nova Printwheels.

As Pluto squared natal Pluto, it repeated the natal Pluto aspects to his Moon, Midheaven, Mars, and Venus. The theme of things being done to him which were out of his control was thus activated. Jupiter in Aquarius had just crossed his Midheaven and set off all the same aspects, and publishing books about these events did ultimately enhance his fame. The Uranus opposition to natal Uranus also set off the natal Uranus conjunction to Sun and Mercury. As mentioned earlier, any time natal aspects are repeated by transit or progression is an especially significant period. The person is likely to experience events suggested by the natal chart.

And This Is Just a Sample!

Even if we devoted a whole book to the subject, we wouldn't be able to cover all the kinds of crises, spiritual or mundane, that confront the practicing astrologer. We have progressed from common or "normal" crises like menopause to more arcane ones like being taken for a ride on a spaceship.

You will doubtlessly find it informative to read books about these and other common turning points in people's lives such as divorce or the unexpected death of a loved one. The more you know about the stresses people encounter in the course of living, the more helpful you are able to be. Therefore, this chapter has just been a starting point in an ongoing process of self-education. What we hopefully have accomplished is to provide a few examples and some principles of crisis counseling that will help you support clients in emergency situations.

CHAPTER FOUR

Finding Resources for Your Clients

The personal problems uncovered in the process of doing an astrology reading can be complex. The tools astrologers use are brilliant for clarifying dysfunctional patterns of behavior and thought, and for highlighting current issues. Having reached this level of clarity during the session, however, clients are likely to ask, "Now what?"

When the astrologer has no answer, clients are apt to go home with a sense of frustration. Self-hate may even increase because they now have insight and still can't do anything to change unwanted patterns. The practitioner may also feel frustrated. Many who could be talented astrologers simply do not practice, as they feel powerless to do anything about the difficulties people bring up.

Having identified the problem, no doubt you, too, are asking, "Now what?" Part of the answer is for astrologers to learn about local resources. Then clients can be referred to places where they'll get help. Learning to develop a resource network and to make effective referrals are the goals of this chapter.

When we work in the helping fields, we have the responsibility of acknowledging our limitations, so that we don't harm either the client or ourselves by overestimating the extent of our skills. One of the major limitations of astrology itself is that it is a superb diagnostic tool, but not a cure. The horoscope has been likened to an x-ray of the soul. If you broke a leg, and all the doctor did was take an x-ray and diagnose a broken leg, you'd rightfully say, "I knew that." This is one reason astrology isn't more popular. We ought to be more than x-ray technicians, albeit divinely-inspired ones. We should be able to suggest some solutions for our clients' concerns.

Many professional astrologers, myself included, have dealt with this limitation in part by learning some healing tools and including them in their practice. Quite a number have gone back to school to study counseling. However, we cannot all be therapists, and, even where we have the training to do some counseling, we still could not meet the entire spectrum of concerns. Identifying a variety of resources makes you more useful to clients who must follow up on the concerns you've discussed. Many who come to us, especially with abuse backgrounds, could profit from body work. Many want groups. Many clients have health concerns. Some need crisis care or even a place to stay in an emergency. Their children may require special services. Their loved ones may have to undergo drug or alcohol detoxification.

Astrologers are in a special position to make referrals. Many who wouldn't ordinarily dream of going for therapy find it less threatening to go for a chart reading. Saying that you're "just curious" about your future is less humbling than saying that you need help. We are on the front lines and often see those whose lives are at major turning points or in crisis.

At such vulnerable times, people are more open to changing self-defeating patterns because it is clear that they are no longer working. Often, clients are simply unaware of services or healing methods that could make it possible to establish healthier behaviors. The astrologer who has a working knowledge of good sources of healing can have a profound impact.

Types of Referrals Indicated by Various Transits

Transits to natal planets or personal points by Saturn, Uranus, Neptune, or Pluto pinpoint times when people can do essential work to clear out old patterns. Pluto is most often implicated in psychotherapy or other healing efforts, but people can also make useful progress during other major transits. You may even be able to make recommendations about the gender of therapist and the type of therapy from the transits.

For instance, difficult transits to the Moon indicate effective intervals for psychotherapy. Here, clients often find it productive to delve into emotions—in fact, they'd be hard pressed to avoid it! They may also review their childhood, particularly any issues related to the mother, security, and dependency. Since the Moon is involved, a nurturing female therapist would be the best choice, thereby providing a corrective mothering experience. If the client is more comfortable with a male therapist, perhaps having had an abusive mother, then a lunar male would be best. However, you would want to explain that issues related to the mother are likely to be pressing and that it would be an excellent time to address them.

During other transits, a male helper might be the more appropriate choice. Challenging aspects to the Sun, such as from Saturn or Pluto, are likely to bring up issues related to the father and his effect on self-esteem and the self concept. Thus, a benign paternal figure, possibly older, would be healing for that part of the personality which is still seeking Father's approval. Techniques related to self-esteem would be productive here. Helpful tools during these aspects are self-esteem affirmations, inner child work, clearing of the solar plexus chakra through Reiki or meditation, and flower remedies for self-worth.

Male role models could also be useful for both male and female clients during outer planet transits to natal Mars. These are key times for learning assertiveness, releasing past accumulations of anger, developing new techniques for dealing with conflict, and giving the self permission to experience healthy competition. The indicated methods might be assertiveness training, bio-energetic therapy, or the martial arts, with tai chi being more likely when Neptune aspects Mars.

Transits through the 1st, 6th, or 12th houses or aspecting planets in those houses often suggest the need for health care or for body work, like shiatsu, acupuncture, or therapeutic massage. Aspects to the Ascendant are other indicators. Even trines and sextiles to these placements can indicate a physical approach. People often spontaneously use these softer aspects to institute new health and fitness regimens like yoga, jogging, or improved nutrition.

Although all three of these houses are related to health, transits through them are not necessarily marked by illness. They do show when progress can be made through releasing the bodily residue of past difficulties. For instance, one woman chose to undergo Rolfing while Saturn was squaring her 1st house Pluto. A great deal of crystallized fear and tension came to the surface during this rather painful form of body work that involves stripping knots out of the muscles. However, she was completely free of a chronic back problem for a full seven years afterward.

Transits through the 11th house or to 11th house planets show times when working with groups can be productive. Uranus transits, in general, carry the suggestion of group process, not just when they involve the 11th house. Neptune transits to the 11th house or to planets in the 11th suggest times when meditation groups and other spiritual fellowships or Twelve Step programs are a saving grace. Still, people would be wise not to surrender their individuality, as disillusionment might well follow. Pluto transits to these same placements may indicate great healing coming from groups. However, such clients should be cautioned not to become involved in group politics or to become codependent on fellow members, to avoid the less enlightened ways of using Pluto's energy

The 11th house Saturn transits or aspects are periods when membership in professional associations or networking can support a solid sense of vocation and can result in career advancement. When Saturn transits the 11th, this joining with one's colleagues is a natural impulse. It is an unfolding of the previous transit of Saturn through the 10th, wherein a new foundation was built for the career. Jupiter's one-year journey through the 11th is a time when groups can bring growth, supporting a more general expansiveness. (The following year, as Jupiter transits the 12th, people may pull back from so much social contact, but continue this growth through inner work and contemplation.)

I don't mean to make outer planet transits sound fabulous, since they often bring pain. They may also bring memorable confrontations with reality and with other people. However, it is precisely because of difficulties like these that we become willing to change. In addition, by foreseeing times when critical issues come to a head, people can begin work on detoxifying and healing those areas of life where the transits are occurring.

Used in this way, astrology can also be a powerful preventive tool, and astrologers who can suggest resources for healing can be of great service. With advance work and preparation, the worst ramifications of a transit need not manifest and the higher uses of those planetary energies can be experienced. For instance, suppose a client is having a Pluto transit to a much-suppressed natal Mars. There is a history of attracting violence, and you are rightfully concerned that history might repeat itself, with devastating results. You could do some prevention by referring the client for assertiveness training or for bio-energetic therapy to clear out blocked anger that was turned inward.

Motivating the Client to Seek Treatment

Later, you will learn about developing a resource network. Let's begin, however, by discussing how to make an effective referral. Unless clients are approached with skill and sensitivity, they may never make use of your recommendations. Suppose that during the reading, you have touched on some painful issues. You have discussed areas of the client's life that aren't working or are self-destructive. You believe these areas could improve with proper treatment. Now your task is to motivate the client to seek help.

This is all the more reason not to spend hours pointing out everything wrong with the chart, but instead to concentrate on clients' current concerns. Chapter One discussed the wisdom of beginning by setting a contract about the issues the reading will cover. When you focus on areas of expressed discomfort, you are more likely to get active participation rather than resistance. A session that deals with issues the client has identified is more likely to motivate him or her. Conversely, a session in which the astrologer hammers home every problem, flaw, and shortcoming in the entire horoscope is likely to make the client give up in despair.

Outer planet transits and the associated upheavals inherently provide motivation. Timing is everything. People often live with a bad situation for years—miserable, but not ready to address the problem. Many people change only when the discomfort of not changing is greater than the discomfort of changing. Periods of crisis are often associated with outer planet transits and provide a powerful impetus to transformation. Threat of loss particularly spurs growth.

Even when no emergency is present, the pain outer planet transits may bring is often a turning point, a window of opportunity for modifying long-standing difficulties. These aspects often bring old dysfunctions to a critical point. Former psychological defenses no longer work, so effective intervention can promote a healthier new approach. Saturn-Neptune transits come to mind, as do Pluto transits to personal points. No doubt, you have your own nominees.

For example, suppose a client with a Venus-Neptune conjunction in the 5th house has a long-standing pattern of painful relationships with alcoholics. Now Pluto is transiting the conjunction, and he or she is embroiled in the Love Affair from Hell. This would be an opportune time for you to suggest Alanon. If you've been to an Alanon public meeting yourself, you can speak more convincingly about how it works. Try one.

Outer planet transits are particularly crucial when transiting aspects repeat tough natal ones. For instance, suppose the birth chart has a Sun-Pluto square and now transiting Pluto is opposing that Sun. When natal aspects are repeated in this way, the individual may finally get tired of some self-defeating behavior or become ready to let go of some toxic person or situation. It is common to experience a painful bottoming out on a repetitive pattern and to decide to turn it around. The inner re-evaluation such aspects bring are a spur to growth. In the midst of the soul searching, people are more open to suggestions about healing.

Assess, from their reactions, how ready they are to accept a referral. If the response is cool, maybe it's too early in the transit, which usually repeats three times. On the first pass of the aspect, it's easy to pretend that the upheaval will blow over and life will return to normal. If clients *yes* you about going somewhere, but are lukewarm to your suggestions, they may still be in a state of denial. They may not accept that something has to be done until the second or third pass. This is another reason the tape is vital. By listening to it, clients can hear your recommendations again later—when they can actually *hear* them.

Another source of motivation is knowledge of various therapies. Many people stay in undesirable behavioral loops because they do not know that other choices are possible. Or, perhaps they do know that there are other ways to react, but have no idea how to get from where they are stuck to a healthier place. By telling them about helpers who can work with them to transform uncomfortable patterns, you give hope of a better future.

Finally, support and encouragement also strengthen the will to change. You support clients by showing the more evolved uses of chart placements and by aligning yourself with their better qualities. Never underestimate how significant a reading can be in clients' lives. It can restore their vision and put them back in touch with their abilities and life purpose. Many people are discouraged by the obstacles they have encountered and also suffer from low self-esteem. Some lack a support network, or—worse—significant others belittle them. They will sense it if you are being falsely encouraging, but your sincere belief that they can do better is a source of hope. Sometimes the role of astrologer as cheerleader has to come first, before the role of astrologer as resource person can be effective.

Understanding Clients' Feelings about Going for Help

Just handing clients a card with a name on it does not ensure that they are going to make that call for additional help. You have to work with their concerns about seeking treatment. Resistance to such suggestions is normal and even, to some degree, a sign of healthy independence. Only the very dependent are thrilled at the suggestion that they find someone to take care of them. For most people, going outside their circle of family and friends about their problems is an alien concept. Admitting to a stranger that you aren't capable of helping yourself is painful. We defend ourselves and our fragile self-love strongly against a world that is often unkind.

In New York, this reluctance is not so universal. Educated people go to therapy at the drop of a hat. When you go out to eat, people all around you are talking about what they said to their therapist and recounting their therapist's brilliant interpretations. In August, when all good therapists are on vacation, you should hear the bitching and moaning! While I lived there, I ran a very successful ad each summer with the lead, "What to Do While Your Therapist is Away." Outside New York, and outside this elevated circle, you have to work harder at making referrals.

Men, in particular, have difficulty admitting they need help. (This is even true in astrological practice. You may well find that you have about four female clients to every male.) Due to a combination of cultural conditioning and biology, most men believe they are failures if they can't handle their problems alone. They may find the emotions addressed in therapy—like sadness, dependency, or lack of confidence—especially threatening.

Adult offspring of alcoholic and dysfunctional families are another group that has difficulty asking for assistance. For reasons we will discuss in chapter Five, a disproportionate number of astrological clients come from such families—more than their percentage in the population. It behooves us to know the far-reaching effects of backgrounds like these and to be able to discuss the relevancy to the issues brought out in the reading. We also should be able to suggest books, groups, and other resources that can heal the syndrome, such as those discussed in that chapter.

There are several reasons this often-troubled group has difficulty accepting referrals. For one, they were strongly conditioned not to talk about the family to outsiders. They experience great embarrassment about their backgrounds, and a deep sense of personal shame, which makes it difficult to open up to others. They are often in denial about the effects of their childhood and present a determined facade of: "I've got it all under control." In that troubled environment, nurturing may well have been sparse or emotionally costly. In order to survive, the child may have learned a fierce self-sufficiency which carries over into adulthood.

Finally, many of these children became caretakers at an early age, not only of their siblings but often of the parents themselves. As adults, these caretakers feel far safer being the helper than seeking help for themselves. Their self-esteem and wish to remain in control is at stake. Focusing on the needs of other people is also an escape from their own pain.

A disproportionate number of astrologers also come from such families. They may have many of these same defenses—and many of the same difficulties in their personal lives. Thus, they, too, may feel safer being the helper. It can be more comfortable focusing on clients' problems while living in denial of the effects of their history on their own lives. There is a problem with insisting that a client needs help while denying one's own hang-ups. Astute clients tend to notice the discrepancy and to reject the referral along with the source. (Watch out for those eagle-eyed Plutonians, especially. Nothing gets past them!)

Various planetary types have their own difficulties in accepting referrals. The reason Plutonians scrutinize you so intently is that their trust has been badly betrayed in the past, probably repeatedly. Such experiences make it hard for them to trust you or anyone you suggest. Plutonians also have more horror stories about their therapists and healers than any other group. It may well be that they play games and wind up creating abusive reactions from their helpers.

Saturnians like to feel they have it all together and can take care of themselves. They perceive admitting that they need help as an admission of failure. Uranians zealously defend their independence, with contempt and defiance being among their primary defenses. So what if they don't fit in? It's society's problem, so society has to change. (Who knows, maybe they're right!) Aries, too, are fiercely independent. When it comes to solving their problems, the proper term for all three groups is counter-dependent. That is, it's not so much that they think they can do everything themselves—it's relying on others that feels dangerous. Thus, they fight dependency—and you—off with all their might. Neptunians may not go for help because they don't feel worthy. Although we've been talking about clear-cut planetary types, at some level we all have some of these resistances related to Saturn, Uranus, Neptune, and Pluto.

Given the aversion so many people have to going for treatment, how would you broach the subject? First, be sure that you make the suggestion with great sensitivity. Put yourself in the client's shoes and imagine how you would feel hearing those words. Talk about going for healing in a way that leaves the self-esteem intact. Do it gently, tactfully, as you yourself would like to be handled in the same position.

To get some sense of how clients feel, imagine that you, yourself, are going for therapy and are arriving for the first interview. How would you feel about meeting a stranger and discussing your problems? How would you like to admit your failures and shortcomings to someone you've never met before? What would it be like to tell your life story and the intimate details of your current situation? How would it sit with you to know that these private facts were being written down in a case record?

It would be particularly important to think these questions through if you have never gone for any form of therapy. This would give you a sense of what your clients might be feeling. If you have gone for help in the past, remember how the application process and initial sessions felt.

An Exercise in Empathy

Let's make the experience of going for help more real for you. Either within your astrology group or class, or with one other practitioner, pair off and take turns being the astrologer and the client. If possible, it would be important not to choose a friend as your partner. The whole point is to find out how it feels to talk to someone you don't know well.

In order for this exercise to succeed, it is essential that participants' right to confidentiality be assured—even for the astrologer member of the pair to acknowledge out loud. (Possibly the primary discipline for any helping person to learn is never to repeat what is told to them in confidence.)

Now the client member of the pair admits to the astrologer an area of life he or she would like to improve and where there is some discomfort. Once the client's concern is identified, the astrologer will suggest that the client seek help in this area. If the client is hesitant, the astrologer explores what the hesitations are.

When the discussion feels concluded, switch and let the member of the pair who has been the astrologer now become the client. Repeat the process. Afterward, the group will discuss how it felt to be in the position of client.

If any member has no area needing improvement, then the entire group should stop the exercise, genuflect, and call *Ripley's Believe It or Not*. Such total perfection is almost unheard of on the planet. The individual should not waste time on astrology. There is a very good position available as the next world avatar.

When the Client Resists the Referral

Often, during the reading, clients resist acknowledging that they need treatment, so you may feel you haven't made an impact. Know that you've planted the seed for later self-questioning and have given hope for change. I've worked with some real mules who didn't seem to appreciate my brilliant insights and inspired solutions at all! When some of them were seen again later, it was gratifying to discover that not only had they taken hold of the suggestions, but they'd gone further than I could ever imagine.

Many seemingly resistant clients call back six months later, when the anticipated transit is hot and heavy, and ask, "Now, who was that person you said I should see? I lost the phone number." This usually is more than a simple request for a piece of information. It is generally a plea for reassurance that they are doing the right thing in going for help. You might open up the discussion of their readiness at that point by asking, "Where are you now with the difficulty we discussed?"

When confronted with a seemingly resistant client, plant the seed and let it go. Don't keep pushing out of a misguided wish to rescue, or the Jupiterian need to be right. Rest in the knowledge that those seeds can sprout as the transit continues and the process intensifies. Many clients will find it easier to hear what you said when they review the tape. In the privacy of their own home, without having to face you and admit their need for change, they can be less defensive.

You may find, however, that you meet less resistance as you become more knowledgeable about what's available and more confident about making referrals. You'll either be more convincing or attract clients who are ready for the kinds of resources you're familiar with. Like most forms of human interaction, astrological practice is governed by the laws of magnetic attraction. In operation, this means that the people who need what you have will be attracted to you, even when they don't consciously know why. Therefore, as soon as you get to know about a particular source of healing, clients who need it are likely to show up. The very process of seeking out resources is likely to magnetize many new clients who need what you now have to give them. (Conversely, when an astrology practice dries up or goes stagnant, it usually means the astrologer has gone stagnant and needs to find something new to offer.)

Understanding the Concept of Secondary Gain

To the frustration of the well-meaning astrologer, there are clients who seem to need to hang onto their problems. They do not grow through their difficult transits, nor do they particularly want to. Many of them have what I call "The Beloved Affliction." Watch their faces when they talk about their problem. You will observe a kind of self-satisfaction, almost a pride in the affliction. It has defeated the best efforts of family, friends, and helping people.

When you suggest a solution, a smirk crosses their faces as they tell you they already tried it and it didn't work or as they offer the perfect excuse. Now, clients may legitimately offer objections to a particular method and tell you that it didn't work for them. That's not resistance, it's information. The difference is that the game player persists in countering every suggestion, often not even hearing you out before offering the excuse. Furthermore, they are thoroughly enjoying showing you up!

Why would anyone get more gratification out of remaining in the pain than in getting free of it? Therapists call this phenomenon *secondary gain*. No, astrologers, secondary gains are not the goodies you get when progressed Venus or Jupiter does something nice to your chart. These gains are the side-benefits of having a symptom that outweighs, in certain clients' minds, the benefits of getting well. The drama and suffering may be all that makes them important. It has become part of their self-concept, a quality that makes them special. It may also seem to be their only legitimate way of seeking attention and caretaking.

Different planetary types find different secondary gains in their symptoms. In my experience, Neptunians are particularly prone to this phenomenon. They are accustomed to suffering, even a mite attached to it, as though it will give them Brownie points in heaven. After all, look where it got Jesus! The suffering may also serve as a punishment that they believe they deserve, for whatever nebulous reason. With Uranians, the problem may make them individuals, and having it may prove society—not to mention their parents—wrong.

Plutonians cling to difficulties for the sake of revenge. (I call the house where Pluto is located the fail-for-spite house.) Plutonians may also use their illness or symptom as a way of manipulating and controlling those around them. For Virgos, their various illnesses authorize them to take much-needed time off. What would be the payoff for Libras? For Cancers? For Capricorns?

When you encounter clients who receive rich secondary gains from their symptoms, the prognosis is questionable. Trained therapists and healthcare workers have a hard time getting anywhere with them, too. Rather than becoming caught up in the game, detach—compassionately if possible. In such lives, the symptom fills a great spiritual void and lack of meaning. The underlying question for these people is, what will they get if they give up the problem? What will fill the void left behind? It had better be good!

Respecting Clients' Choices

Consider, also, whether clients who refuse referrals are being resistant or whether they are instead acting upon an unconscious or super-conscious choice. The concept of freedom of choice is in itself liberating. However, what I call "Wonderbread Metaphysicians" often turn the idea that we create our own reality into a hostile form of one-upmanship. They feel vastly superior to others whose reality isn't as successful in worldly terms as their own. I can hear them out there now saying, "Why do you CHOOSE to get into one betrayal after another in relationships? Where does it get you to choose that?" [1]

Clients then feel guilty for having a problem, because it obviously means they're incapable of choosing properly, even though you've now informed them that they have a choice. A smug metaphysical sophomore even told me that she doesn't feel bad when a gay man dies with AIDS because, after all, it was his choice. That's not spiritual wisdom, folks, that's sugarcoated, New Age homophobia. (It wouldn't have been so bad, but she owned the New Age bookstore in the community and was setting herself up as the local guru.)

What defense do clients have when told they chose this self-destructive experience or that their negative thinking must have created it? The thing is, there are choices and choices. People make some extremely difficult life decisions at levels that aren't accessible to the conscious mind. One level is in the unconscious. Motivation and past programming are often repressed and thus operate without the individual's awareness. When that is so, you can point out all the

[1]This section is excerpted from my foreword to Gail Fairfield's excellent book, *Choice-Centered Astrology*, 1990 (Ramp Creek Publishing Company, Box 8, Smithville, IN 47458).

options you like, but the individual may still be powerless to take the positive ones.

For instance, some people make crucial decisions in childhood and then forget having made them. ("I'll never get married," or, "I'll fix them—I'll fail at everything I try.") For such people, insight alone is not enough. Therapy, healing work, and perhaps the support of a self-help group may be needed to work the insight through to release past programming.

Uncovering such decisions and canceling them may well be necessary before these people have the freedom to choose anything else. Metaphysical writer Sondra Ray developed one tool that my clients have found powerful in revoking such decisions. She recommends that you write the same statement seventy times a day for seven days, seventy times seven being a magical number of completion.[2] Students of metaphysics are often frustrated when their repeated positive thoughts and visualizations do not work. Sugary affirmations like, "Love and abundance flow into my life," are often ineffective. This is because negative decisions or beliefs countermand them. Here are some examples of effective statements for this technique: "I release my parents' opinions about my talents," "I let go of my attachment to my family's poverty," or "I am willing to release the pain of my divorce." Frequently, we have to deprogram before we can reprogram.

Beyond that, we make some extremely important choices like those that relate to addiction at the soul level, during the period before birth when we select life tasks, associates, and even parents. Those who resist therapy or who don't seem to benefit from it may have made decisions on that level. It may not empower people who are addicted to alcohol, drugs, food, or to being in debt to be told that they have a choice about how to use Neptune—to continue in the addiction, or to seek the spiritual path. The heavy drinker or drug user may still have some degree of choice. However, those who are truly addicted have lost the power to decide whether to use the substance or not.

Adults are generally not conscious of prebirth choices, and yet those choices can override conscious decisions. They can even appear

---

[2]In particular, see Sondra Ray's use of this technique in her two excellent books published by Celestial Arts: *The Only Diet There Is* (1981) and *I Deserve Love* (1987).

contrary to the best interests of the individual. Such experiences are not necessarily punishment for past life misdeeds, but may be selected for soul growth. In order to be complete, each soul seeks out each possible major experience in the course of hundreds of incarnations. It's important to know, however, that even tough selections like addiction or having an abusive mate need not be a lifelong sentence. If you become conscious of the reasons behind the choice and heal yourself of the residual effects, that particular lesson need not last a lifetime.

Finally, there are collective choices to be taken into account. It is a mistake of the Pluto in Leo generation to think they are the center of the universe and have unlimited freedom. Humanity as a whole makes certain decisions at various times in history. People born within that era must then live within the matrix created by that decision and to some extent have individual destiny delimited by the consequences. The strength and position of the outer planets in the horoscope show the extent to which we participate in the collective unfolding.

In our era, we are experiencing great difficulty with relationships. Taken individually, this may feel like failure or neurosis. The key here, I feel, is a collective desire to reshape the nature of relating itself—a major contribution of the Neptune in Libra generation. We are trying to move away from a traditional model of dependency and rigidity of roles. The new model will be that of two independent, equal human beings together by choice rather than bio-determined necessity. As individuals, this period of the evolution of commitment may at times be painful; as a collective, it is a period of hope. And, yes, individuals still apparently choose to be born in a given era and thus to be part of that collective experience.

Part of motivating clients to seek treatment can involve showing that there are options other than remaining in the painful pattern. However, it is important that the practitioner be gentle when discussing these principles. Be sure judgment is not lurking under the surface. Have some compassion and respect for the person who has made a tough choice in order to strengthen the soul, to learn a particular lesson, or to pay off karmic debts to others. In order to complete our soul development, we all eventually have to make hard choices like these. Maybe such people aren't less intelligent than you are—maybe they're just more brave!

Monitoring Your Own Judgments of Clients' Problems

This leads to an important principle—practitioners' attitudes and actions may well be the cause of resistance. The way clients respond to your suggestions has much to do with your reactions to their problems. Even when unspoken, negative reactions register with clients, who then conclude, "She thinks I'm sick—really, really sick." If their self-esteem is very low, your judgment can be a final, crushing blow. The passive type may withdraw from you and shut down. If they are less passive, they may become angry and confrontational.

Clients are also sensitive to judgments underlying your referrals. This is particularly true when recommendations stem from your personal values and beliefs, as opposed to what is really paining them. Judgments include opinions about how you think their lives ought to be and what you think is wrong with them.

Your values might lead you to think a gay person should become straight. Or, you might feel that a 40-year-old career woman who has fallen for a 23-year-old surfer is a fool. Clients' life choices and life-styles are none of your business. You don't know the karma—maybe that young surfer is the treasured soul mate who has been with her through many lifetimes. You also don't know what important qualities people are developing through a life-style that our materialistic, production-oriented culture labels dysfunctional.

For example, you may feel a chronically unemployed artist has a problem and should become a civil servant. Codependency treatment is one of the fastest-growing sectors of the therapy industry. However, I shudder to think what would have become of Vincent van Gogh if his brother, Theo, had spoken to someone who was knowledgeable about codependency. Van Gogh, whose paintings are now worth millions, never earned a dime at painting in his lifetime. Theo believed in his talents and supported him financially. I can hear the discussion now: "Theo, you simply have to stop enabling Vincent. He's never going to make it as a painter. He had a perfectly good job as a mailman. Tell him to go back to work."

Speaking of codependency, the tendency to want to rescue the client is another response to monitor. Many children who grow up in dysfunctional families become caretaking adults. They are often led to a calling in the helping professions, astrology being no exception.

Their self worth may depend on finding people in dire circumstances to save. When they encounter someone with a serious problem, the rescuer within them may kick in.

Unfortunately, emotional residues of childhood caretaking are also often evoked—such as panic, grief, and resentment. Underlying these responses is terror that they won't survive if they don't help Daddy or Mommy feel better. For astrologers from such families, these feelings can be activated during readings and when making referrals. For instance, they may feel frantic when people don't want help, evoking their need to control.

Finally, be sure your suggestions aren't coming from a judgmental, smug, or know-it-all place. (All too often, one's Jupiter is doing the reading.) Smugness, fortunately, is more common to the New Age sophomore or new convert. Time gives a deeper perspective and shows that life's questions are more complex and difficult than we thought. After a few outer planet transits to natal Jupiter, we recognize that we don't have all the answers—not for other people, often not even for ourselves.

Does it sound like I'm contradicting myself? On one hand, I am saying that it is important to let go of the attitude that you have all the answers. On the other hand, the purpose of this chapter is to help astrologers find some solutions to their clients' problems. It is one thing to present clients with possible solutions that they can investigate. It is quite another thing to assert that you have *the* answers to their problems. Especially, it is important to avoid the *S* word—should. You really don't know what is right for other people—you can only make suggestions.

Toxic Shame as a Barrier to Change

Another *S* word is shame. Many clients suffer from severely damaged self-esteem. Particularly if they come from dysfunctional backgrounds, their level of shame may be so high, that the idea of exposing their inadequacies to a therapist or other helper is daunting. They may also feel they don't deserve a better life.

If you, the astrologer, also come from an alcoholic or dysfunctional family, your own level of shame may be so toxic but so unconscious that you are unaware when it is operating. We also carry a certain level of shame at practicing a profession that is held up to public ridicule. Unaware, we may get relief from our own shame by feeling superior to clients, especially morally or metaphysically. ("I'm okay because I can tell you all the ways you're not okay.") Shame often creates a need to judge others and to feel more evolved, more metaphysically correct, or more together—whether or not such judgments are voiced.

Some clients project such omniscience onto astrologers that you may end up being a devastating judge, even if you don't mean to be. So, on the one hand, you may be trying to build the clients' self-esteem by listing the positive qualities you see in the horoscope. On the other hand, the way you discuss difficulties and urge clients to seek help may reinforce the shame. Many of the self-esteem problems that many clients complain of are shame-based. Adult children of alcoholic or dysfunctional families—and sex abuse survivors—are especially prone to shame.

As a caring person, no doubt you are watchful of what you say to clients, so that you'd never knowingly shame them. However, it may not be what you say out loud, but what you are thinking and feeling that clients pick up on. Your tone of voice, body language, or even telepathic messages affect clients. Neptunians and Plutonians, in particular, are keenly sensitive to messages like these and also struggle with feeling like outcasts.

Naturally, it is difficult to control judgmental reactions to clients, some of which can come from the astrologer's own unhealed shame. Ask yourself if this could be true of you. Remember that shame is particularly likely if you come from an alcoholic, dysfunctional, or abusive family background yourself. If so, it would be important to work on healing your own shame so that it does not intrude on your work with clients. (We will learn more about how such backgrounds can affect your astrological practice in chapter Five.)

For shame issues, I would particularly recommend John Bradshaw's book, *Healing the Shame That Binds You*.[3] At any rate, it would be a good reference for most astrologers to read, since so many of our clients suffer from low self-esteem. The bottom line is, unless ad-

---

[3]John Bradshaw, *Healing the Shame That Binds You* (Deerfield Beach, FL: Health Communications, 1988).

dressed, either clients' shame or your own may get in the way of your making effective referrals and their accepting help, since they may not feel worthy of a better life. By understanding shame yourself, being able to articulate its causes, and having a good resource book to suggest, you can help clients make a breakthrough.

Getting the History of Past Change Efforts

One theme in various chapters is the importance of getting a client history. In order to counsel effectively, you do not need to find all your information in the chart. History-taking is useful. You'll find out what your clients have already tried. When the discomfort is severe, people may have tried a variety of solutions before coming to you. Not all those solutions would be formal ones—going to a therapist or social service agency is generally the last resort. By learning about clients' past efforts to help themselves, you acknowledge and simultaneously evoke the health-seeking part of their nature. You also determine what inner resources they have to call upon.

As in gathering any history, ask open-ended, non-leading questions. That way, clients don't limit what they tell you and don't feel they have to please you by giving a particular answer. You might ask the following:

1) What sorts of things have you done about this problem in the past?

2) What happened when you went there (or did that)?

3) What was helpful about that work? What was not?

4) Tell me about the person you worked with there.

5) How did your family or mate react to your efforts?

6) Why did you stop going (or doing that)?

7) Would you go back there or somewhere similar again?

In asking questions like these, you find out what worked and what hasn't worked and why. You learn what kinds of situations are productive and valid and what kinds are not. (For one thing, you don't lavish praise on some method that the client has already tried and found seriously wanting!) You learn a great deal about how clients might operate in a future healing context. You discover how they respond, generally, to helping professionals and what types of helpers might be best. You also discern how able they are to persevere in the painful process of confronting the past, present difficulties, and the associated emotions.

Another side benefit of this line of inquiry is that the client gets a chance to work through any past negative experiences with helpers. Unfortunately, many people have had their problems compounded by the institutions or systems which are supposedly designed to help. For instance, rape victims often find silence preferable to their treatment by the police and courts. Too many battered wives have died as a result of the system's inadequacies to protect them. Clients will tell you harrowing experiences with disturbed priests, doctors, and therapists who wound up hurting more than they helped.

When clients have bad experiences in seeking assistance, they are doubly hesitant to allow themselves to be vulnerable again. Once more, the astrologer is in a unique position, because clients who tell you such stories may not regard coming for a reading as seeking help. Given the opportunity to discuss healing efforts that left painful residues and to be heard compassionately rather than blamed, they are often freed to seek a new solution. Thus, talking with you about what happened can open the way.

Kinds of Therapies Indicated for Various Astrological Types

Traditional therapies may not be much help to Outer Planet People. Students of metaphysics and other spiritual teachings may ultimately find traditional therapy frustrating. Working with concepts like karma and trying to get a traditional therapist to validate them is like talking French to someone who only speaks a few words. Astrology students also can find the language barrier frustrating. Fortunately, within the transpersonal psychology community, there are a growing number of therapists who have studied spiritual teachings or astrology. When you look for resources, it will be especially important to seek out therapists like these, as many who come to astrologers are on a spiritual quest.

A case in point would be Neptunians in need of therapy. (Is that a redundancy, perhaps?) I believe they cannot become truly healthy unless they spend part of their therapeutic work considering how spirituality fits into the picture. On the other hand, traditional social work, with its concrete, practical focus on current functioning and problem-solving may be the approach some spaced-out Neptunians need. Another useful resource might be a vocational counselor.

The determining factor in the choice would be whether you need to uncover your archetypes or pay your rent. Spending years dancing with archetypes or gestalting dreams can sometimes be just another way of avoiding change and responsibility while still being able to insist to your mate or family that you're working on the problem. "Maybe I'm still smoking pot and maybe I still don't have a job, but, hey, I'm going to therapy, aren't I?" Therapy does take time, of course, but I'm talking about career patients who use analysis or other forms of therapy to cop out on adult responsibilities.

Uranians respond better to groups, especially leaderless or peer groups. The self-help movement may appeal to these independent souls—unless, as is too often the case, they consider themselves too intellectual and evolved for their fellow members. Social action groups formed to address problems they share in common with many others could be good therapy.

Be aware, however, that one major Uranian trait is hard to address in a peer group—the problem with authority. This can best be ameliorated in individual therapy with a benign authority figure. Only therapists who are secure in their own authority can be helpful here. Someone who spent the last seven years working with delinquent adolescents would have just about the right qualifications for dealing with the diehard Uranian.

Plutonians, on the other hand, HATE groups. It is much more difficult to control a group and harder to avoid exposing those deep, dark secrets and not-so-pure motives. One-on-one therapy is much easier to control, and you get into such neat codependency rackets. However, a group led by a well-qualified therapist may be just the thing that is most healing to the Plutonian. To be stuck with people you haven't chosen and can't control week after week is a great learning experience. You learn that others share those ugly feelings you keep secret and that you're not such an alien, after all. You also learn that people can get mad at you and they don't disappear—and that you can get mad at them and nobody dies from it. One Plutonian said that she detested group therapy each and every week for the entire year she attended. However, she made more real progress than she had in years of individual therapy. It was not so much the insight she gained—she already had *too* much insight—it was the experience of belonging despite herself.

Finding the Resources

There are many ways to find resources. You may be surprised to notice that once you turn your attention to this need, possibilities suddenly pop out at you from everywhere. The local library's reference section will have directories of community agencies and national associations. In the New York area, there is one gigantic directory—*The Source Book: Social and Health Services in the Greater New York Area.*[4] The same company produces directories for many other metropolitan areas.

You may find listings in the yellow pages under social services and psychotherapy. Newspapers, magazines, or media carry features from time to time about agencies or groups which are meeting a need. Classified ads may include a section on counseling. There are hot lines for a large variety of problems. Self-help groups often have phone numbers where you can find out about meetings.

Almost every major spiritual community has New Age newspapers and annual directories where body workers, therapists, and other healers advertise. Ministers may know about community groups. Clients or friends may be able tell you where they've found help and their personal experiences with such places. Keep in mind, however, that troubled clients may present a distorted view—exaggeratedly positive or negative.

---

[4]Phyllis Andrews, Editor. Onyx Press, Phoenix, AZ, 1989 edition. Library Catalog # Ref 361.9741 S.

One way to get to know some healers well is to propose an exchange of services. You do a reading for the healer and the healer gives you a body work session, past life regression, or whatever his or her specialty may be. Not only does each of you get to know the other's work for potential referrals and collaboration, but you also get an additional opportunity for personal growth. In addition, you experience firsthand the vulnerable position of being the client, rather than always being in the safe, seemingly superior role of helper. This experience can increase your empathy with how the client feels about seeking help.

You might keep a file box or roladex which includes cards of practitioners you often refer people to, hot lines, and other resources. You can write for meeting lists of various self-help groups. Keep good self-help books on hand to show clients. Books can start the recovery process when the person is not ready to seek more formal treatment. I also provide preprinted lists of traits of adult children of alcoholics, codependents, and incest survivors. The client who is unsure or in denial about such a pattern can take a copy home and think about it.

It's best to provide the client with more than one name or referral. Not every healer is right for every client. I tell clients that although I have a good impression of the various practitioners that I know, there is no way to know whether the two of them would fit well together. It is important that clients respect their own instincts. They have the right to keep looking until they find someone they can work with comfortably.

Once you develop a referral network, it's important to keep it current. Healers move, they burn out, they shift the focus of their work. Nothing detracts from a client's motivation more than calling up and learning that a service is no longer available. Call your practitioners from time to time to learn if they are still taking referrals, what new services they may be offering, and what the current rates may be.

It is also useful to get feedback about clients you have sent to various "helpers." You will learn more precisely the right types of referrals to make and how to prepare clients for this particular service. Be sure, however, to respect clients' rights to confidentiality in such discussions. They may well have revealed secrets to you that they have not yet been able to tell the practitioner. Whenever possible, it would also be sound practice to get feedback from clients themselves about the treatment they received. You might ask them to call and tell you how the work went. (Don't call them yourself, as they may not have gone for the services you discussed and may experience the call as pressure.)

If you come from a dysfunctional family, you may harbor magical expectations about what various forms of healing can accomplish, or you may think individual helpers in your referral network can work miracles. These expectations are not unlike the ones you have of yourself that you are forever failing to meet. You may expect that others can stop an unmotivated alcoholic from drinking, or cure a deep-seated emotional problem or serious illness in a few sessions. Since it would be hard for helpers to live up to such demands, you may find yourself periodically disillusioned by the healers in your network. Clients from dysfunctional families may buy into these fantasies and be disappointed, too. Learning to be realistic about results is part of the seasoning that comes with professional experience. On the other hand, when you are able to be realistic, making a good referral to someone you trust can calm down the part of you that needs to rescue others.

Why Personal Knowledge of Resources Is Important

Personal knowledge is important in determining where to refer clients. If a social service agency specializes in the kinds of clients who frequently come to you, they may allow you to visit. (Ask for the social work or public relations department.) Likewise, it would be useful to attend some meetings of Alcoholics Anonymous or other self-help groups that are open to the public. You can say from first-hand experience what it was like, and you hear the stories of the members. Their stories will doubtlessly convince you of two things: first, that alcohol is more powerful than you ever imagined, and, second, that there is hope, no matter how far down the person has gone. Your conviction will be more persuasive to the addicted person or concerned family member who has lost faith.

Part of making an effective referral is being able to answer questions about what happens when the client goes for an appointment. Clients may be too intimidated to raise these questions, but it is important to address them. ("You seem hesitant. What are your concerns about going?") Otherwise, fears and fantasies about what will happen can make clients too frightened to follow up on the referral. Particularly with nontraditional forms of healing, lack of knowledge can cause clients to imagine all sorts of strange practices. When you are able to say what happens, especially from firsthand experience, you dispel clients' fear of the unknown. More even than the words, your unspoken conviction of the safety and effectiveness of such services comes across.

How do you get this kind of information? We couldn't hope to describe all the possible kinds of therapies and healing modalities in less than a separate book, and new methods are continually developing. However, you need to familiarize yourself with major ones like Reiki, rebirthing, acupuncture, shiatsu, gestalt work, Feldenkreis, bioenergetics, Rolfing, and the Alexander technique. The health and science section of the library—or your local bookstore—may carry books describing various therapies. New Age newspapers and magazines feature articles about the healing arts. In talking to practitioners or agencies in your search for resources, ask for details about how they work.

A side benefit to interacting with other therapeutic disciplines is that they in turn become more familiar with astrology. They see that we are also professionals rather than weirdos or storefront readers. In the long run, ending our isolation by reaching out in this way will help astrology's image. Although you will meet skeptical responses from some, remember the statistic that says that 65 percent of the public has some belief in astrology—which includes 65 percent of helping professionals as well!

Suppose you locate therapists or body workers for such common concerns as adult children of alcoholic families, incest survivors, or recovery from addictions. It would be important to call or even meet with them, so you get a clear picture of who they are. Your reputation is on the line when you make a referral. When a client has a bad experience with someone you recommended, you, yourself, can lose credibility. Anyone can advertise, and you don't want to send clients to unbalanced or incompetent healers! Keep in mind also that just because practitioners are "nice" and know the buzz words doesn't mean they're capable.

Adding a New Piece to Your Job Description

Astrologers fulfill many roles, but the role of resource person is an important one. Knowledge of local services can be considered a professional responsibility. It's time-consuming to become informed, but it's time well invested. If you make a good referral that enables someone to break free of a painful pattern, you're doing a finer form of service. If that is not enough reward, consider that *clients you assist in this way are more likely to come back—and send other people to you.*

CHAPTER FIVE

Relationships in Jeopardy–Codependency, the Adult Child Syndrome, and Their Implications for Astrologers

Far and away the two major issues that clients bring to the practicing astrologer are love and career. This chapter and the next present my insights into those issues. I find that the most troubled relationship histories—and, all too often, the most snarled-up career patterns—have a common root of growing up in a dysfunctional family. Dysfunctional families, including those with alcoholic or abusive parents, incline their offspring to form codependent relationships with mates, bosses, and friends.

Codependency is a major self-help buzz word, and groups for codependents and adult children of alcoholics (ACAs) have spread throughout the United States. People are also talking a great deal about defining boundaries. Since you'll be hearing these terms from clients, you need to be familiar with them. We'll discuss how these concepts apply to astrological clients, including the chart patterns to look for, and case examples based on the charts of some famous people. We'll find out about the types of services your clients might benefit from and we'll look at the ways codependency (or being an ACA yourself) can influence your astrological practice.[1]

---

[1]This chapter was originally my contribution to the anthology, *Astrological Counseling*, edited by Joan McEvers for the Llewellyn New World Astrology Series, 1990. It is reprinted by permission. I highly recommend the book for its fine chapters by a variety of astrological counselors.

What Is Codependency?

Codependency is an addiction to an addict or to some other person. The obsession with trying to help or change that individual grows in strength until it takes over your life, giving you no peace. It doesn't change just because that person leaves, but instead can become a pattern carried over to new relationships. Melody Beattie, in her best-seller, *Codependent No More*, defined it in this way: "A codependent is one who has let another person's behavior affect him or her, and who is obsessed with controlling that person's behavior."[2]

The term codependency originally derived from the field of chemical dependency and applied to families and significant others of alcoholics and addicts. Because of the way they grow up, the majority of untreated adult children of alcoholics form codependent relationships with mates, lovers, family members, friends, and even bosses. In particular, they tend to get involved with one alcoholic or addictive personality after another. Alternately, they may stay away from codependency by staying away from committed relationships.

Rather than lavish all that energy on fixing one person, many ACAs work long, poorly-paid hours in service fields like astrology, where they may play the role of rescuer. There's nothing wrong with service, but when it's compulsive and driven by codependent needs, it can ultimately be damaging to both practitioner and client.

ACAs aren't the only people who develop codependency. It can develop at any stage of life when you love someone who has a severe physical or emotional problem. Parents aren't the only source—it could happen if a beloved brother started using drugs or a mate began drinking alcoholically. Grandchildren of alcoholics can also have the full-blown ACA syndrome, even when the parents are teetotalers. The grandparent passes it on to the parent who passes it on to the child.

Many traits common to ACAs apply to members of severely dysfunctional families as well. It's been estimated (Lord knows by whom) that 95 percent of all families are dysfunctional to some degree. But here I'm not talking about your average unfulfilling, emotionally illiterate, uncommunicative parents who don't validate your creativity or worth. I'm referring to families where there was physi-

---

[2]Melody Beattie, *Codependent No More*, New York: Harper/Hazelden, 1987, p. 31.

cal or sexual abuse, or where a parent was chronically and severely physically or mentally ill. It can happen where a parent died early or committed suicide, where a parent was a gambler or promiscuous, or where there were other severe or bizarre eruptions and disruptions. It could happen if your bedridden grandmother lived with you and her illness controlled the entire family, or if your sister was a child schizophrenic.

Since books on the topic have topped best-seller lists and sold millions of copies, it is fair to say that codependency is a widespread problem. Popular awareness of codependency grew throughout Neptune's stay in Capricorn, but first gained widespread professional and popular recognition during the Neptune-Saturn conjunction of 1989–1990. Saturn represents boundaries and limits, and Neptune represents the dissolving of them, so defining boundaries and learning to set limits became issues in the world at large. In particular, it seems to be an issue for the Neptune in Libra generation, for whom that perfect relationship has been the Santa Claus that never came.

As recognition of codependency grew, so did knowledge of how to get free. There are many helpful books on recovery from codependency and the adult child syndrome. Both regular and New Age bookstores commonly have special sections dedicated to these needs. Self-help groups, workshops, trained counselors, therapy groups, and even inpatient treatment programs have grown rapidly. In addition, approaches developed elsewhere—like assertiveness training and work with the inner child—can also be useful, keeping in mind the part dysfunctional backgrounds and codependency play in the problem.

The Hidden ACAs in Your Client Population

Statistics show that one person in four has been deeply affected by a relationship with an alcoholic. Therefore, at least 25 percent of the people who come to you for readings are family members, lovers, or close friends of alcoholics. However, I suspect it is more than that, for reasons we will presently discover. If you aren't finding this to be true of your own clients, it may be that they're not telling you this family secret out of shame. It's not the kind of information people readily volunteer, and they don't necessarily view you as having a need to know. After all, they're not coming to you about the firmly-buried past, but about the future and about when their relationships are going to get better. Until I came to know the chart patterns and began asking the crucial questions, very few of my clients told me about the alcoholics in their lives.

It isn't always simply a case of being secretive, either. One of the major traits of families of alcoholics or addicts is that everyone, beginning with the alcoholic, tends to deny the addiction. This protects the addict from having to give up the habit and protects the family from the pain and shame of seeing how destructive a problem it is. A Neptunian defense mechanism, denial means that they either don't recognize that an addiction exists or don't recognize that they're addicted to the addict. Many see the addiction and yet deny the extent of the damage. ACAs say things like, "Yes, my Dad drank, but he stopped when I was 16, and it was so many years ago, it doesn't have any impact on my life today." As we'll see later, the residuals are considerable, especially in the ways these people relate and work.

So, in the consultation, if clients deny the addiction or its impact, and we don't recognize it, it's not addressed. Then there's no answer as to why their relationships are so crazy and addictive, why they're so isolated, why they just can't get along with their bosses, and why they're in so much pain. All they get is the momentary comfort of hearing, "It's just your Neptune." And yet this momentary comfort carries a long-term sense of helplessness. You can't do anything about where Neptune is in your chart, except to die and be reborn.

Why ACAs Are Drawn to Astrology

Many adult children of alcoholics or other addicts come to astrologers, psychics, and other readers looking for an answer to their inexplicable confusion, turmoil, and pain. A major reason they come to us is that when you grow up in a chaotic, unpredictable household, predictability has its appeal! Another reason they're drawn to us is that astrology and other such disciplines help ACAs solve that puzzling question of who they really are, as opposed to roles their families conditioned them to play. Alice Miller, an important writer about treatment for ACAs, speaks of the path to health as finding the TRUE SELF, as opposed to who parents and others needed and expected one to be. In *The Drama of the Gifted Child*, Miller says that the alcoholic parent is narcissistic and may love the child, but only as an extension of the self. Love is given only on the condition that the child's true self be buried to meet the parent's need for attention, admiration, and approval.[3] Astrology, numerology, and other related tools can be major arenas for exploring the true self.

Our clientele may also have a higher proportion of ACAs than the general population because, I suspect, more ACAs believe in us than do other kinds of people. When you're a little kid and you have a grandiose parent whose brain is befuddled with alcohol, you get programmed with some remarkable ideas. (A kinder interpretation is that alcoholics are visionaries who stimulate offspring to look beyond everyday reality.) Like Alice in Wonderland, you may be required to believe six impossible things before breakfast. So, it's not that much of a stretch to believe in astrology, past lives, absent healing, holes in your invisible aura, parallel realities, or, for that matter, snake oil.

Finally, ACAs and people from dysfunctional backgrounds may have a special yearning for spirituality, unless they've been so wounded they wind up hating God. Those who had disturbed or addicted parents may have a strong need to find closeness with a Father/Mother/God who is loving, understanding, wise, and all-powerful and who cares deeply about them personally. And, yes, it's profoundly comforting to know that this life, this crazy set of parents, this troubled history is not the only chance.

Since we inevitably confuse the relationship with the divine with the relationship with our parents, rarely is the spiritual path without potholes, detours, and false turns for ACAs. Often, the problem is not so much with the Divine, but with the messengers, to whom they transfer that need for an all-knowing, all-loving parent. They look for godlike qualities in astrologers and others who seem to be in touch with the Divine. When the messengers, themselves, are

---

[3]Alice Miller. *The Drama of the Gifted Child: The Search for the True Self.* (New York: Basic Books, 1981), p. 14.

ACAs, the potential for distortion is compounded. For example, one such messenger—the fundamentalist evangelist, Jerry Falwell—is an ACA. His father was a wealthy bootlegger who murdered his own brother and then became alcoholic out of guilt.[4]

Why Astrologers Should Know about Codependency

Astrologers need to learn about codependency for several reasons. First, it will help explain why so many of our clients repeatedly become involved in painful, crazy, abusive, addictive relationships. Second, we're on the front line for referrals to treatment resources. Many come to us who would not go elsewhere, even if they only come to ask when the alcoholic is going to straighten up. The codependent is used to being the helper and has difficulty asking for help. When you go to an astrologer, you aren't asking for help, oh, no, you're just curious as to what the future holds. Because there are resources for codependents, astrologers need to be able to recognize the syndrome, educate clients about what's wrong, and suggest where they can go for help.

Most importantly, we need to educate ourselves about the ACA syndrome and codependency because many of us are ourselves codependent without knowing it, and, as we are going to see, it has an effect on the way we practice. Talking to astrologers around the country and the world, I find that, like myself, a very high percentage—including many of the top speakers and writers—are ACAs or come from severely dysfunctional families. The reasons given earlier as to why ACA clients are attracted to these disciplines are also reasons we're attracted to study them. They become our path for understanding ourselves and other people. Even more, they're an outlet for the common ACA need to rescue and fix people, as we were never able to do for our parents.

---

[4]Lois Rodden's DATA NEWS #5 (8/87) p. 2, gives the birth information from his twin brother as about noon, EST, August 11, 1933, Lynchburg, VA, 37N25, 79W09. Family history is discussed in Falwell's autobiography, *Strength for the Journey*, (New York: Simon & Schuster, 1987). The chart is not included here because this time doesn't seem to be exact.

Common Characteristics of Codependents and ACAs

In his important and readable book, *A Primer for Adult Children of Alcoholics*, psychiatrist, Timmen Cermak discusses the major characteristics of codependents:

1) Codependent people will hide or even change their identity and feelings in order to please and be close to others.

2) A sense of responsibility for meeting other people's needs comes first for codependents, even at the expense of their own needs.

3) Low self-esteem and very little sense of self to begin with is common to most codependents.

4) Compulsions and addictions drive codependents and keep them from having to confront their deeper feelings.

5) Just like alcoholics and other addictive personalities, codependents hide behind denial and have a distorted relationship to will power.[5]

Cermak, who was the first president of the National Association for Children of Alcoholics, lists traits many ACAs share. Although not every ACA has all of them, these are common. They are fearful and especially fear their feelings, losing control, conflict, authority figures, and angry people. Although they're fiercely self-critical and suffer from low self-esteem, they're frightened of criticism from others, so they constantly seek approval. ACAs take on too much responsibility and feel guilty standing up for themselves. Intimate relationships are a special area of difficulty. Because they're afraid of being abandoned, they'll do almost anything to hold on to their relationships, which are often with addictive personalities or other unavailable people. They confuse love and pity, often attaching themselves to people who are victims or whom they can rescue. They can also place themselves repeatedly in the victim role.[6]

---

[5]Timmen L. Cermak, MD, *A Primer for Adult Children of Alcoholics*, (Deerfield Beach, FL: Health Publications, 1989), pp. 19–23. Reprinted by permission.
[6]Cermak, pp. 34–37.

One statement in a list of traits circulated at ACA Twelve-Step meetings is that, "even if we never picked up a drink, we took on all the characteristics of the disease of alcoholism." That is, ACAs who never drink can still act like alcoholics at times because, like all children, they pattern much of their behavior on parental models. Specifically, grandiosity and defiance are two main characteristics of alcoholics, and a great many New Age people are massively grandiose and defiant. (It sounds like Neptune and Uranus!)

In their cosmic dimensions, studies like astrology encourage grandiosity. We may see ourselves as very, very special because of what we know and may subtly or even unconsciously encourage clients to see us in the same way. We may even come to see ourselves as having a direct pipeline to the Divine. This arises from ACAs' need for a close tie to an all-loving Heavenly Father or Mother without the problems we experienced with our earthly parents.

The defiant, rebel ACA often masks these traits by rigidly acting just the opposite. This doesn't mean they've overcome the conditioning from their alcoholic families, but rather that they're controlled by having to act out the opposite pole. As Cermak and others in the field have remarked, ACAs are reactors, rather than actors. For instance, rather than showing their fear of authority figures, they may glory in defying authority. Rather than seeking approval from society, they may go out of their way to dress and act in ways that get negative attention. (In astrological terms, these are the Uranian types.)

Astrological Indicators of the ACA Syndrome

Let's take a look at chart signatures that go along with the ACA syndrome. No single aspect can be taken as a certainty, so you'd be looking for several confirmations. Neptune, naturally, is prominent, often in the 1st, 4th, or 10th, or in aspect to the Sun or Moon, or with Pisces in any of those spots, or many Neptune aspects or Pisces planets. The 12th house may also figure strongly, with the Sun or Moon often appearing there. An individual who has many of these signatures would be classified as Neptunian. It is often possible to distinguish which parent was alcoholic, as when the Moon is aspected by Neptune, the mother is either an addictive personality or rendered severely dysfunctional by the situation. Sun-Neptune or Mars-Neptune aspects hint at the males of the family. Saturn-Neptune aspects often show that the authority figures were unable to provide consistent structure, security, or discipline, with alcoholism only one of the possible reasons.

Neptune aspects also indicate psychic abilities, in which we obliterate our boundaries and blend with others. *Psychic abilities* and *boundary problems* may just be two ways of defining the same phenomenon. As discussed in *The Medium, the Mystic, and the Physicist*, Lawrence LeShan found that healers were able to heal when they could let go of self and become one with the person in need.[7] The problem for many with psychic abilities is shielding—i.e., establishing boundaries so that people's thoughts, feelings, and needs do not bombard them.

Psychic merging is common in addictive and dysfunctional homes, as the child or spouse uses psychic radar to monitor how the troubled person is doing in order to prevent an eruption. Thus, psychic gifts are common in ACAs as a survival skill. Many intuitive astrologers are ACAs who use this gift in their work. We who are psychic need to examine ways in which we may be codependent or have difficulty with boundaries in our practice. Many who study but don't practice wisely hesitate. They may sense that they haven't established firm boundaries and don't know how to set limits or to shield themselves psychically.

Chart Examples of ACAs

Just in case your client files aren't full to overflowing with examples of Adult Children of Alcoholics, Table 2 (page 124) shows data for some famous ACAs whose charts you may want to work with. As an example of the Neptunian type of ACA, Drew Barrymore's chart is shown here as Chart 4 (page 122). Part of the famous Barrymore theatrical family, Drew began her career in the movies at age 6 in *E.T.*

[7]Lawrence LeShan, *The Medium, the Mystic, and the Physicist* (New York: Ballantine, 1982).

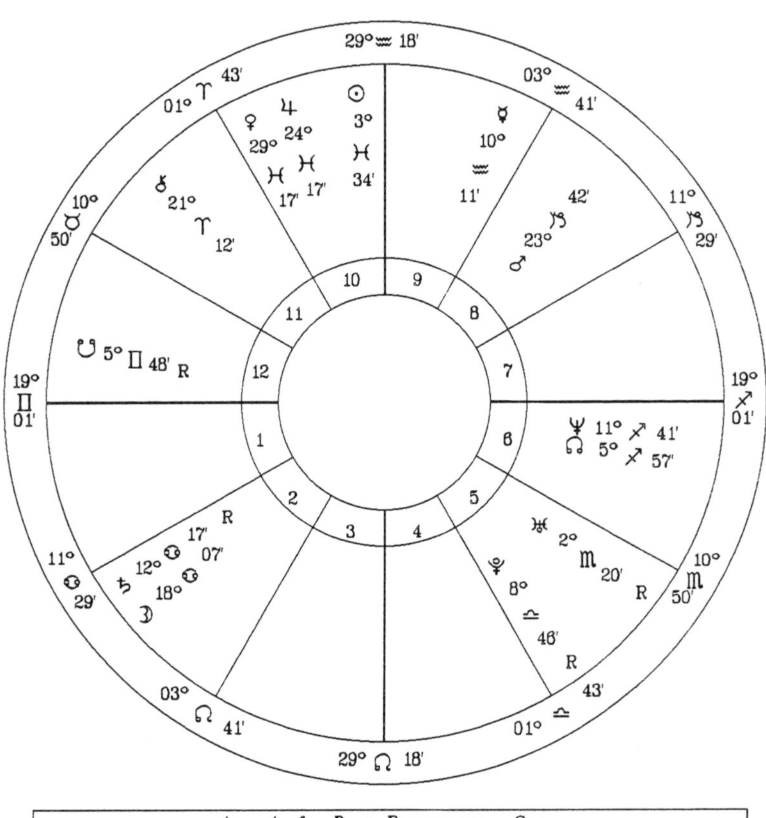

Aspects for Drew Barrymore – Geo.		
☉ ⚼ ☽ 0A27	☿ ⚹ ♆ 1A30	♅ ⚼ As 1S41
☉ △ ♅ 1S14	☿ △ ♇ 1S25	♅ △ Mc 3A02
☉ □ ☊ 2A23	♀ ☌ ♃ 5A00	♆ ⚹ ♇ 2S55
☉ ☌ Mc 4S16	♀ ⚺ Mc 0S01	♆ ☍ As 7S20
☽ ☍ ♂ 5A35	♂ ⚹ ♃ 0A35	♇ ⚹ ☊ 2A49
☽ ☌ ♄ 5A50	♂ □ ⚷ 2S30	☊ ⚼ ⚷ 0S15
☽ ⚺ As 0S54	♃ □ As 5A16	As ⚹ ⚷ 2A11
☽ □ ⚷ 3A05	♄ ⚻ ♆ 0A36	
☿ ∠ ♃ 0A54	♄ □ ♇ 3A31	

Chart 4. Drew Barrymore. Data from birth certificate in Lois Rodden's specialized quarterly newsletter, DATA NEWS #15 (1/89), p. 4. She was born February 22, 1975, 11:51 A.M. PST, Culver City, CA, 34N01, 118W25. Placidus Houses. Tropical Zodiac. North Node is True Node; South Node is Mean Node. Chart calculated by Astrolabe using Nova Printwheels.

and has appeared in many movies since. The Barrymores have been noted for alcohol problems, including Drew's father, John Drew Barrymore, and her grandfather, John Barrymore. In fact, Drew has called herself a fifth-generation alcoholic. Drew began drinking at 9, smoking pot at 10, and using cocaine at 12. By 1989, her drug problem was serious enough that, at age 14, she went to rehab centers twice and tried to commit suicide.[8]

Neptune is angular in her chart, in the 6th house of work. This suggests that the pressures and terrors of fame at an early age may have contributed to the addiction. The father's side of the family and their addictions are shown by the Sun, Venus, and Jupiter in Pisces in the 10th house. Although the relationship is a difficult one, the mother does not drink and is the main stabilizing force, as seen by the Moon-Saturn conjunction in Cancer.

Strangely enough, Pluto is often co-prominent with Neptune and is also often found in the positions noted above. Thus many ACAs would also be classified as Plutonians. Here Pluto signifies the sober or less addicted parent who struggles mightily to keep the addiction and the addict under control. It also signifies the child's efforts to control his or her environment and keep it safe, efforts that continue into adulthood, long after the original threats have passed. These same signatures, undiluted, often appear in the charts of grandchildren of alcoholics whose parents are not alcoholic. The ACA patterns of behavior and relating get passed on through the parents. Although a great many ACAs themselves have addictions, the strongly Plutonian may at least resist the parent's drug of choice in an effort to maintain control.

Chart 5 (page 126) for Suzanne Somers, is an example of the Plutonian type of ACA. In her autobiography, *Keeping Secrets*, she is open about her alcoholic family background.[9] Pluto squares Suzanne's ascendant, a potent aspect which is easy to miss in these charts. It is in the 4th house, conjunct Saturn, the ruler of the 10th, a combination in itself suggesting a difficult childhood and possibly abusive parents. (Drew Barrymore had a square. I've seen Pluto-Saturn aspects in the charts of several child stars.) The conjunction

---

[8]Family and recent history discussed in, "Falling Down and Getting Back Up Again," by Jeannie Park and Robin Micheli, *People Magazine*, 1/29/90, pp. 57–61.
[9]Suzanne Somers, *Keeping Secrets* (New York: Warner, 1988).

TABLE 2: A WHO'S WHO OF FAMOUS ACAs.

CAROL BURNETT: It is well known that both Carol's parents were alcoholics, and she was raised by a grandmother. Lois Rodden's *Profiles of Women* (p. 53) says that the birth data is from the birth certificate, and she was born April 26, 1933, 4:00 A.M. CST, San Antonio, TX, 29N25, 98W30. (She, herself, gives the time as 4:15 A.M.)

JAMES CAGNEY: The alcoholics in his family were his father (who died when Cagney was a child) and his maternal grandfather. *Astro-Data II* (p. 276) gives July 17, 1900, 9:00 A.M. EST, New York, NY, 40N45, 73W57 as his birth data. Listed as DD. Although the year has been questioned, this chart has a t-square with Neptune in the 10th, Saturn in Capricorn in the 4th, and Moon in Aries. His mother was a quick-tempered red-head who didn't hesitate to take a bull whip to people according to family history mentioned in *Cagney by Cagney*, Pocket Books, New York, 1976, pp. 16–17.

LYNDON B. JOHNSON: The alcoholics were his father and brother. Lois Rodden's *Astro-Data III* (p. 233) gives the data from his mother's diary as August 27, 1908, at sunrise, 4:18:20 A.M. LMT in Gillespie County, TX, 30N04, 98W40. Family history from Doris Kearns, *Lyndon Johnson and the American Dream*, Signet, New York, 1976, pp. 24–26.

JOAN KENNEDY: The alcoholic was her mother, as discussed by Joan in a speech at the Houston Council on Drug Abuse and Alcoholism in April, 1987. Joan's birth certificate information comes from *Profiles of Women* (p. 184) as September 5, 1935, 6:10 A.M. EDT, New York, NY, 40N45, 73W57.

JACQUELINE KENNEDY ONASSIS: The alcoholic was her father, Black Jack Bouvier. Her data, from *Profiles of Women* (p. 159) is July 28, 1929, 2:30 P.M., Southampton, NY, 40N53, 72W23. Time variously given as EDT or EST, but EDT puts Neptune closely conjunct the MC, trine her Aries Moon. Family history from Bill Adler, *All in the First Family*, G.P. Putnam's Sons, New York, 1982, pp. 112–113.

ELEANOR ROOSEVELT: Her father was an alcoholic, and away most of the time, and at age 9, her mother died of diphtheria. Birth

(continued)

TABLE 2: A WHO'S WHO OF FAMOUS ACAs (continued).

information from Lois Rodden's *Profiles of Women* (p. 214) based on a family birth record submitted by Joan Negus as October 11, 1884, 11:00 A.M. EST, New York, NY, 40N45, 73W57. Family history discussed in her book, written with Helen Ferris, *Your Teens and Mine*, Doubleday, Garden City, NY, 1961, pp. 21–22.

RED SKELTON: His father was a circus clown who died of drink two months before Red was born. Family history is discussed in Arthur Marx, *Red Skelton: An Unauthorized Biography*, E.P. Dutton, New York, 1979. Birth information given on p. 5 of Marx's book as July 18, 1913, 1:15 P.M. CST, Vincennes, IN, 38N41, 87W32. Marx says that the year is given on birth certificate, discharge papers, marriage license, and passport as 1913, but Skelton has also been known to say he was born in 1906. The 1906 chart makes little sense either astrologically or in light of family history, while the 1913 map appears very valid.

LILY TOMLIN: *Profiles of Women* (p. 169) gives birth certificate information as September 1, 1939, 1:45 A.M. EST Detroit, MI, 42N20, 83W03. This puts Neptune on the IC in a grand trine with Uranus and Mars.

squares angular Jupiter, Mercury, and Mars in Scorpio, additional Plutonian energy. The Moon again is in Cancer, which does not in itself suggest an alcoholic background, but may show that the issue of nurturing is a critical one for the individual. Neptune is quincunx the Ascendant, but otherwise unaspected except for a mild sextile to Saturn. Richard Idemon used to say that an unaspected planet was like a loose wire, often more important in the native's life than would be expected.

Chart Signatures of Codependency

Astrologically, who are the codependents? Obviously many of the same patterns will be seen as in ACA charts, but there are additional indicators and interpretations. People with Neptune aspects to the

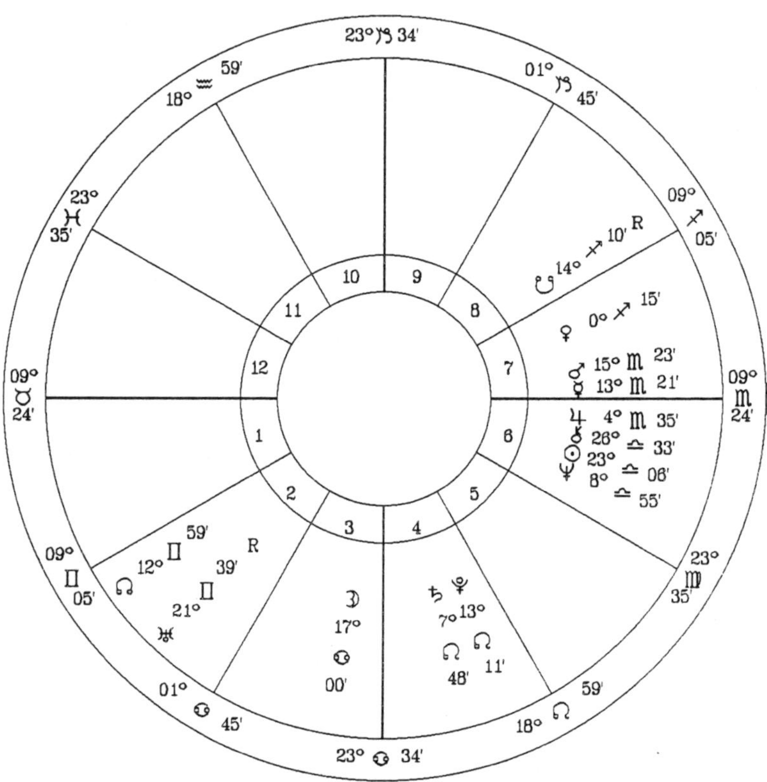

Aspects for Suzanne Somers – Geo.		
☉ △ ♅ 1S27	☿ ⊼ ☊ 0S22	♅ ⊼ Mc 1S55
☉ □ Mc 0S27	☿ ☍ As 3A57	♅ △ ⚷ 4S54
☉ ☌ ⚷ 3A27	♂ □ ♇ 2S11	♆ △ ☊ 4A04
☽ △ ☿ 3S39	♂ ☍ As 5A59	♆ ⊼ As 0S29
☽ ⚼ ♀ 1S44	♃ □ ♄ 3A14	♇ ✶ ☊ 0S12
☽ △ ♂ 1S37	♃ ☍ As 4S49	♇ □ As 3A47
☽ ☍ Mc 6S34	♄ ∠ ♅ 1S10	☊ ⚼ ⚷ 1A26
☿ ☌ ♂ 2A01	♄ ✶ ♆ 1A07	Mc □ ⚷ 3A00
☿ □ ♇ 0S10	♄ □ As 1S36	

Chart 5. Suzanne Somers from data in Lois Rodden's ASTRO-DATA II. *According to her birth certificate, she was born October 16, 1946, 6:11* P.M. *PST, San Mateo, CA, 37N34, 122W19. Placidus Houses. Tropical Zodiac. North Node is True Node; South Node is Mean Node. Chart calculated by Astrolabe using Nova Printwheels.*

Moon are often addicted to giving the nurturing they themselves never got. Those with Neptune aspects to the Sun may have self-esteem and identity bound up in rescuing. People with Neptune near the Ascendant keenly feel the needs of everyone they meet. When Neptune is near the Midheaven, rescuing can be a career choice. People with Neptune in the 7th or aspecting Venus are especially prone to committed but agonizing relationships with addicted people. People with Pisces planets in any of these places can have similar tendencies. Note that many of these placements can also signify the addict or dysfunctional person. Such people can become vulnerable to addiction, even as they rescue. It can be a way of coping with the depletion and sorrow of rescuing.

While not all of us are codependent, we all have Neptune somewhere. We could become vulnerable to the syndrome, given the right predisposition, the proper transits, and a painful set of circumstances. (The child you adore starts using drugs, your beloved mother has a massive stroke, your spouse develops cancer.) Neptune's house and aspects in your chart show areas of confusion about where you leave off and other people begin—where your boundaries are blurred. In those areas, you may have trouble setting limits and can be taken advantage of or even victimized. Thus, Neptune in the natal chart is often where we feel powerless—a victim or martyr. It is also the area where you would be most likely to get involved in codependency if the right set of circumstances triggered it. With Neptune in the 3rd, one could be a life-long sucker for siblings, some of whom may be alcoholic or addicted; in the 5th, with your love affairs or children; in the 8th, with sexual partners; in the 11th with friends.

The Liza and Judy Show—A Case Study

As a case study in codependency, let's look at the charts for Judy Garland and her possibly equally talented daughter, Liza Minnelli. Their charts, based on birth certificate information from *Profiles of Women*, are printed here as charts 6 (page 128) and 7 (page 129). Judy's long struggles with alcohol, pills, and suicidal depression are a Hollywood legend. Liza herself was at the Betty Ford Clinic in 1984 to kick her cross-addictions to diet pills, tranquilizers, sleeping pills and booze.

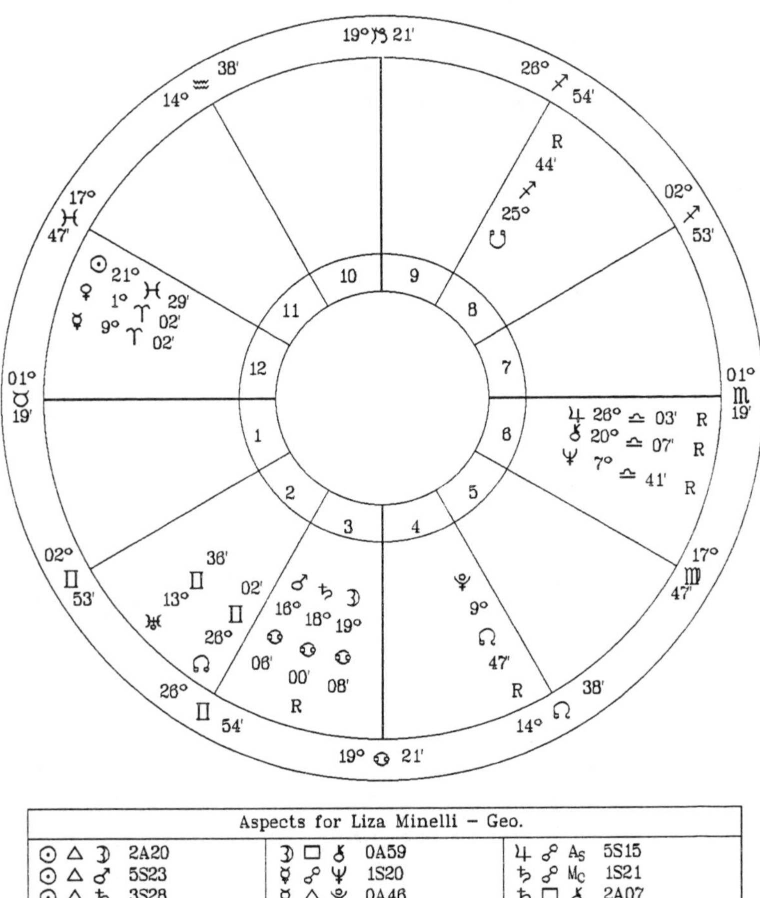

Aspects for Liza Minelli – Geo.		
☉ △ ☽ 2A20	☽ □ ⚷ 0A59	♃ ☍ As 5S15
☉ △ ♂ 5S23	☿ ☍ ♆ 1S20	♄ ☍ Mc 1S21
☉ △ ♄ 3S28	☿ △ ♇ 0A46	♄ □ ⚷ 2A07
☉ □ ☊ 4A33	♀ □ ☊ 5S00	♅ ⚹ ♇ 3S49
☉ ⚹ Mc 2A08	♀ ⚺ As 0S17	♆ ⚹ ♇ 2S06
☉ ⚻ ⚷ 1S22	♂ ☌ ♄ 1A54	♇ ∠ ☊ 1S15
☽ ☌ ♂ 3A02	♂ ☍ Mc 3S15	Mc □ ⚷ 0A46
☽ ☌ ♄ 1A08	♂ □ ⚷ 4A01	
☽ ☍ Mc 0S13	♃ △ ☊ 0A01	

Chart 6. Liza Minnelli. Birth certificate data from Lois Rodden's Profiles of Women *(p. 353) as March 12, 1946, 7:58 A.M. PST, Los Angeles, CA, 34N04, 118W15. Placidus Houses. Tropical Zodiac. North Node = True Node; South Node = Mean Node. Chart calculated by Astrolabe using Nova Printwheels.*

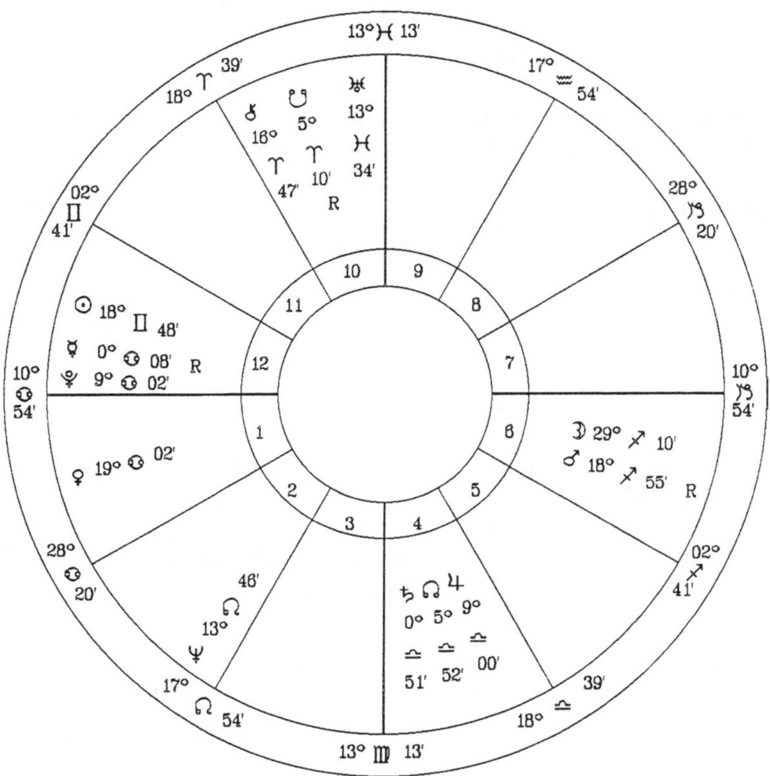

Aspects for Judy Garland - Geo.		
☉ ⚺ ♀ 0S13	♀ ⚻ ♂ 0S06	♅ △ As 2A40
☉ ☍ ♂ 0A07	♀ △ Mc 5A48	♅ ☌ Mc 0S21
☉ □ ♅ 5S14	♀ □ ⚷ 2S14	♆ ⚻ Mc 0A32
☉ □ Mc 5A35	♂ □ Mc 5A42	♆ △ ⚷ 3S02
☉ ⚹ ⚷ 2S01	♂ △ ⚷ 2A08	♇ □ ☊ 3S10
☽ ☍ ☿ 0A58	♃ □ ♇ 0S03	♇ ☌ As 1A52
☽ □ ♄ 1A41	♃ ☌ ☊ 3A08	♇ △ Mc 4S11
☽ ⚼ ♆ 0S25	♃ □ As 1S54	☊ □ As 5S02
☿ □ ♄ 0S43	♅ ⚻ ♆ 0S11	As △ Mc 2A19
☿ ∠ ♆ 1A23	♅ △ ♇ 4A32	As □ ⚷ 5A53

Chart 7. Judy Garland. Birth information from the birth certificate in Lois Rodden's Profiles of Women *(p. 84) as June 10, 1922, 6:00 A.M. CST, Grand Rapids, MN, 47N14, 93W31. Placidus Houses. Tropical Zodiac. North Node = True Node; South Node = Mean Node. Chart calculated by Astrolabe using Nova Printwheels.*

Although Liza remains intensely loyal to her mother's memory, her childhood sounds like an ACA's nightmare. By age 10, Liza was begging for food for herself and Judy and sneaking out of hotels and apartments to avoid paying bills and back rent. She was her mother's confidant, comforting Judy after her many suicide attempts.[10] In her teen years, the relationship between them became more explosive, and Judy would periodically kick Liza out. In 1962, Liza left home for good at age 16, going to New York with $100 to pursue her show business career.

Liza's chart is a prime ACA profile. Her Sun in Pisces is in the 12th house. The trine from the Sun to her angular Moon-Mars-Saturn-IC conjunction in Cancer shows her closeness to her mother, but also the mutual dependency. As a 12th house Cancer Sun, I seem to have had a personal blind spot to the role of Cancer planets in ACA charts until writing this! Liza's Venus and Mercury are also in the 12th, opposite Neptune. Pluto in the 4th makes a wide square to Liza's Ascendant—8°, but wouldn't you say it works—plus a 3° sesquiquadrate to that 12th house Sun. Thus Liza qualifies strongly as a Neptunian and less obviously as a Plutonian.

Judy's Neptune does not immediately register as a strong one, and yet she was both a sublime musician and actress and an addictive personality—all Neptunian pursuits. Then we note that her Neptune forms an eye of God with her Pisces Uranus-MC conjunction and her Descendant. The strain of being constantly in the public eye and being a sensation from her teens onward must have contributed to her addiction. We also discover that Neptune forms an odd-shaped triangle of semisquares and sesquiquadrates with Mercury and her Sagittarius Moon (definitely somewhere over the rainbow!). Like Liza, she has a strong 12th house containing Sun, Mercury and Pluto, although Pluto is closely conjunct the Ascendant. Both had a waif-like, lost quality, which can be attributed at times to the 12th house. Once more we see the prominence of Cancer, with the Ascendant, Mercury, Pluto, and Venus. Pluto isn't exactly pallid, being on the Ascendant, widely conjunct both Venus and Mercury (a midpoint), trining the Uranus-MC conjunction, and squaring the Nodes and Jupiter. (Once more, there's that

---

[10]Family history discussed in Alan W. Petrucelli, *Liza! Liza! An Unauthorized Biography of Liza Minnelli*, (Walled Lake, MI: Karz-Cohl Publishing, 1983).

child-star signature of a Pluto aspect to Saturn, although it is a wide square.)

When you look at the connections between their charts, you will note that Judy's Venus at 19° Cancer is exactly conjunct Liza's Moon and IC, and closely conjunct Liza's Mars and Saturn as well. Liza's Neptune falls in Judy's 4th, conjunct Judy's Jupiter-North Node-Saturn conjunction, suggesting confusion about which one of them was the parent. Liza's South Node on Judy's Moon suggests that nurturing her mother was an automatic reaction, possibly due to past-life connections. Judy's Neptune is widely conjunct Liza's Pluto. Even though those are generational placements, they do suggest a truth about the relationship, which was that Liza perennially had to keep the situation under control when Judy was falling apart. There are wide Sun-Uranus contacts on both sides. They not only show the stormy nature of the relationship and the wildness shared by both women that the relationship may have sparked, but also that each supported the genius, charisma, and uniqueness of the other. The contacts also form a restless but lively t-square in mutable signs involving Pisces, Gemini, and Sagittarius. The outlet is on Judy's Virgo IC, and the two traveled constantly during Liza's childhood, never successfully establishing a home.

Since both Judy and Liza have strong 12th house placements, then, as a mathematical and behavioral inevitability, so does the composite, shown here as chart 8 (page 132). Self-destructive pursuits (such as addiction), the need for privacy, and the lost child qualities are present in both. The strong 12th house in this chart suggests that the very fact of being together may have increased the tendency for each to be addictive. The Mercury-Venus conjunction suggests a good and loving communication between the two, an understanding of each other that could not easily be verbalized to the world. Neptune in the 4th squares the Ascendant, further increasing the Neptunian qualities, but also suggesting that there must have been a strong psychic tie and mutual blending of boundaries. Pluto makes a 3° semisquare to the Ascendant as well. The difficult 4th house, with Neptune and Saturn, show a painful struggle to find a place to feel at home. The Moon, Mars, and Jupiter in Libra further testify to a loving, albeit often angry connection. The fact that the trio is in the 5th house shows mutual support for their performing abilities.

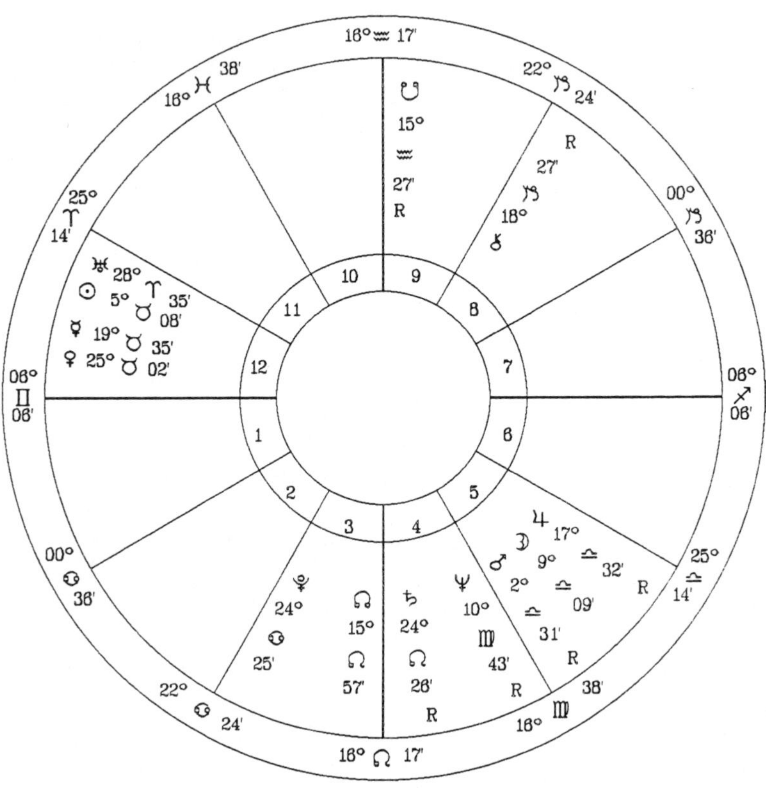

Aspects for Judy Garland – Liza Minelli		
☉ ☌ ♅ 6A33	☿ □ ☊ 3S38	♃ △ Mc 1A14
☉ △ ♆ 5A35	☿ □ Mc 3A18	♃ □ ⚷ 0S56
☉ ⚺ As 0S58	☿ △ ⚷ 1S08	♄ △ ♅ 4S09
☽ ⚼ ♀ 0A52	♀ □ ♄ 0S36	♄ ⚺ ♇ 0A01
☽ ☌ ♂ 6A39	♀ ⚹ ♇ 0S37	♅ □ ♇ 4S10
☽ ∠ ♄ 0A16	♂ ∠ ☊ 1A34	♆ ∠ ♇ 1A19
☽ ⚺ ♆ 1A34	♂ △ As 3S36	♆ □ As 4A37
☽ △ As 3A03	♂ ⚼ Mc 1A13	☊ ☍ Mc 0S20
☿ □ ♄ 4A51	♃ ⚹ ☊ 1A34	

Chart 8. Composite chart for Judy Garland and Liza Minnelli, for Los Angeles, CA. Placidus Houses. Tropical Zodiac. North Node = True Node; South Node = Mean Node. Chart calculated by Astrolabe using Nova Printwheels.

How an ACA Background Can Affect Your Practice

As we got to know the astrological profiles of the ACA and codependency syndromes, did you find some of your chart in it? You're not alone—as mentioned earlier, a great many of us in the field of astrology, myself included, are ACAs. It is up to us as individuals, of course, to recognize and work on how the dysfunctional background affects our personal life. My immediate concern here is to explore how it can affect your astrological practice.

Many of us have worked very hard to transform ourselves through a variety of healing tools. Thus, we are generally able to give good service. By now, many of us have already done some work on our ACA issues. And yet, unless we remain conscious and vigilant, we may still be triggered into ACA and codependent patterns when clients' problems are similar to those of family members or others we love—or to our own problems. I myself attended ACA groups and later Al-Anon for several years and thought I had some good quality recovery. Yet, when reading the material on codependency, I was dismayed to see my blind spots.

The issue to think about now is your practice. Many ACA astrologers and most of their ACA clients are still in ignorance and/or denial about the effects of growing up in an alcoholic or dysfunctional background. When we don't deal with this information consciously, the personality traits identified with the adult child syndrome can profoundly affect the ways we relate to clients. The following exploration of traits of untreated ACA therapists was developed by Cermak in *A Primer for Adult Children of Alcoholics*.[11] My comments about how these traits may manifest in readings or healing work are interspersed in brackets.

Cermak says that untreated ACA professionals can be recognized by the way they encourage you to be angry for their own purposes. They often push you to take action before you're ready. [Although clients may come to you about a life concern like marital separation, they aren't necessarily ready to make a move.] They intellectualize, rather than encourage you to express your feelings. [For instance, if you suddenly find yourself inundating clients with jargon

---

[11]Cermak, *A Primer for Adult Children of Alcoholics*, pp. 69–70. Used by permission.

and technical material, ask yourself if the emotional content of the session is making you uncomfortable.] They are uncomfortable with silence. [When the client pauses for reflection, do you rush in with a metaphysical lecture or information about their fixed stars, asteroids, and so on?] Untreated ACAs resist exploring Twelve-Step programs and are certain that they've already dealt with all their codependency issues.

Reading other writers on the subject like Claudia Black, Melody Beattie, Alice Miller, and Janet Woititz led me to consider additional ways the ACA syndrome and untreated codependency can cause difficulty in chart readings. For instance, in *The Drama of the Gifted Child*, Alice Miller says narcissistic practitioners, as many ACAs can be, have a great need for approval, understanding, and validation from clients. There is a pressure for the client to meet one's expectations and to present material to fit one's concepts and belief systems.[12]

The codependent practitioner easily becomes defensive and needs validation and stroking from clients. Do you get upset if a client questions your interpretation or doesn't tell you how right on target the reading is? Many of us are overly-attached to the client's approval and admiration. We feel we have to know it all and have the right answers. We do tap dances to dazzle and amaze. We may also be overly-attached to being right in our predictions and interpretations, at the cost of having a true dialogue with the client. We can get depressed after the reading if we don't get enough positive feedback. Then we question ourselves, our work, and our worth.

Boundary problems show up in readings as over-identification in its various forms. The client's problem becomes your problem, or conversely, your own difficulties get confused with the client's. You may feel pain or anxiety about giving clients other than what they want to hear, even though the transits or progressions are anything but positive. There may be problems in setting limits—e.g., taking too many phone calls from a client who becomes excessively dependent or allowing your readings to go on for hours. Fuzzy boundaries can also result in being drained after a reading. (This may also mean you're doing healing without conscious awareness and need to channel divine energy rather than your own energy.)

[12]*The Drama of the Gifted Child* (New York: Basic Books, 1981), p. 24.

The common ACA need to fix people may have motivated us to do readings in the first place. That need may lead us to want to rescue clients who are addicted or in difficulty. We may try very, very hard to solve every problem in the client's life through three-hour sessions. Where we are overly responsible, we may take on too much of our clients' problems or spend too many hours preparing. For instance, astrologers may think they have to do several years' worth of transits, progressions, harmonic charts, midpoints, and fixed stars. The pervasive trait of low self-esteem may result in not charging or charging too little.

Untreated ACAs and codependents also tend to be extremely controlling, although they can be subtle and gifted at manipulation. (Keeping things under control was a survival skill at home. Are we talking Pluto?) When clients don't respond by doing what ACA astrologers recommend or don't believe that this is THE ANSWER, ACAs can sometimes become agitated, enraged, or vindictive. They may respond by invoking their divine connection, scaring clients about their Pluto transits, or threatening clients with cancer if they don't straighten out their way of thinking. Similarly, there can be agitation and even rage when clients don't change in the way the ACA thinks they should.

There are two main issues clients come to us about—career and relationships. Unfortunately, two primary characteristics of untreated ACAs are that they have authority problems and distorted relationships. If we haven't addressed these issues in our own lives and are in denial, it's a matter of the blind leading the blind. If we have difficulty around intimacy or anger, can we teach clients how to have healthy relationships or be positive role models for them? Let's suppose you're still living out the victim role and have a history of being betrayed in relationships. You bring your ACA mind-set to the chart reading, so when clients ask about difficult relationships, you counsel them to watch out for betrayal.

Similarly, out of unresolved anger toward our own parents, we may encourage clients in anger against their parents or bosses. If we're grandiose, we may encourage clients in grandiose career plans, rather than taking a grounded and realistic approach to vocational astrology. Many ACAs live on the edge financially, due to improper grounding in their unstable families, and the financial path in career astrology is anything but sure. Many of us have serious difficulty working for anyone else, and that's part of the attraction of being self-employed. With difficult 8th or 2nd house transits, we may ignore the fact that a client has gone deeply into debt with credit cards, second mortgages, and bill-payer loans.[13]

Traits like low self-esteem explain why some ACAs study astrology for many years and never feel they're good enough to do readings. Many don't practice, or practice infrequently, because they don't feel they CAN fix people and yet expect themselves to. Or they don't practice because they feel it's too much of a responsibility. Given the grandness of our tools, they may expect themselves to be all-knowing and feel self-hate if they're not as grand as their sources of knowledge.

Finally, ACAs are especially susceptible to addictions and compulsive behaviors. In our field, more of us than we like to recognize are alcoholic or suffer from some form of addiction. We practice individual and collective denial about it, but it's an occupational hazard. It's a way of dealing with the sometimes overwhelming responsibility, sense of isolation, endless giving out of energy, and psychic bombardment that readings entail. We also may want to stuff feelings that get stirred up in a session when we deal with major life issues in such a concentrated form. If your role models used substances or compulsions to deal with stress and keep feelings at bay, you tend to live what you learned.

The Adult Child Syndrome and the Politics of Groups

The combination of grandiosity and defiance, as you can imagine, plays holy heck with the politics of astrological organizations and other New Age groups. Many of the traits Cermak mentions also play into group dynamics. They include the leader's need to be in

[13]An astrological aside: Pluto rather than Neptune appears to be the predominant theme for people who are addicted to their credit cards and to ruinous debt. It may show up in the 2nd or 8th or forming important aspects to planets in those houses, or with Scorpio placements in those houses. Here, the issue seems to be spite and revenge. Many incest survivors have debt compulsions.

control, the members' fear of conflict, fear of angry people, inability to take criticism, the tendency to see things in a black and white perspective, the need for agreement and approval, and the tendency to feel like a victim. Put a large number of defiant, grandiose, unrecovered and in denial ACAs together, and you're likely to see some bizarre group behavior. You may find feuds, splintering, casting out those who dare to question, and crowds who are oohing and aahing over the emperor's non-existent new clothes.

When such groups predominantly consist of ACAs, it's not unusual for top positions to be filled by the equivalent of alcoholic parents. That is, even if they never pick up a drink, leaders have been known to behave alcoholically. Strong denial and a high tolerance for bizarre behavior are ACA characteristics that can be carried over into group life. Thus, members may indulge and overlook even the most astonishingly dysfunctional behavior from leaders. The members' need to create a happy, close family-type experience is a powerful one. The painful isolation they've suffered, and the lifelong sense of being different and not belonging, makes the group so precious to its ACA members that they tend to deny dysfunctionality in order not to threaten the sense of finally belonging. With these blinders on, everyone and everything is WOOOOOONNNNDERFUL.

If you should be so unwise as to point out that the emperor is not, in fact, wearing any clothes, this group may turn on you as though you'd done something indecent. "Oh," they say, "but he's sooooo spiritual!" The group may ostracize you, and they certainly won't ask you back to speak. Truth is an unwelcome commodity in places where denial is king.

Further characteristics of alcoholic families that may be replicated in groups made up largely of ACAs are codependency and fuzzy boundaries. Many ACAs (myself included) elect to stay out of even healthy groups and out of group politics because of family histories that wildly violated personal boundaries.

Some astrological groups have been guilty of boundary violations, but we are models of mental health when compared to what goes on in cult-type organizations. Unfortunately, ACAs, especially young ones, are quite vulnerable to questionable spiritual teachers and groups. A close-knit spiritual group can be a priceless gift, but a group that insists you give up your individuality to belong is destructive. A group mind intent on invading boundaries can do great damage to an individual whose boundaries are shaky in the first place. Cults that profess to be spiritual are notorious for this, but even a more loosely organized group can at times lose respect for individual members' rights, beliefs, and feelings.

The passage of Uranus and Neptune through first Capricorn and then Aquarius promises exciting developments in the field of astrology, particularly in the move toward professionalism. However, it does not, in my view, auger well for our organizations. The politics are likely to become more outrageous before they get saner. Many will be disillusioned with groups, and groups that do not meet the needs of their members will dissolve. The hope for sanity is the hope that more and more ACA members will come to recognize the syndrome in themselves and their groups. It would be helpful if some of the traditions the Twelve Step programs aspire to were adjusted for use in these groups. Just for starters, there is one that says, "Our leaders are but trusted servants; they do not govern."

How Current Conditions Intensify the Need for Recovery

Current world conditions, as signified astrologically by the passage of the outer planets through the universal signs, are intensifying the demands on all the service professions. People are extremely needy and confused, feeling helpless and powerless over the vast social changes just on the horizon. The forces of chaos are very strong just now. As a result, people are looking to astrologers and other service professions for guidance and answers. It would be easy to become burned out from clients' demands. Learning to set limits is becoming crucial. We will need to master limit-setting in order not to get so burned out that we stop the work.

We also need to learn to assess whether clients' demands are legitimate or not. Alcoholics and chronically dysfunctional people are able to project feelings of helplessness and "bottomless need" so powerfully that the psychically sensitive pick it up and react to it. To bolster low self-esteem, rescuers need to be needed. Thus, they often hook into the helplessness and keep people helpless by enabling them to continue dysfunctional patterns. Contemporary astrologers need to learn how crippling rescuing might be, so that we don't do it to clients. We cannot enable, rescue, or answer non-genuine needs for long.

However, when we function at the outer limits of our capabilities we stretch ourselves to a higher level of professionality. Stretching to serve others is stressful. If your limit was to run a mile a day and you ran a ten-mile marathon, you'd be tired. If you ran ten miles every day, you would not. As you stretch past your limits as service workers, new levels of functioning will ultimately become yours.

Even where the needs of your clients are legitimate and they really need guidance, you may grow weary from the work and tension of counseling. It's important to rest, relax, and take care of yourselves—emotionally, spiritually, physically, and fiscally. An important way of taking care of yourselves is to recognize and let go of codependency in your personal and professional lives. I hope this discussion has been a beginning of that recognition. If we astrologers who have the syndrome use the tools that are developing—the books, the groups, and other self-help aids—and if we tell our ACA and codependent clients about them as well, we'll all gradually get free.

CHAPTER SIX

Vocational Astrology–Updating the Tradition

To know how to use astrology for success in the workplace, we need to know more than vocational astrology: we need to know about careers themselves. We must assess such reality-based concerns as the practical demands of any given profession, the educational requirements, and the earning potentials. To advise clients well, we need answers to questions like the following: what is the shape of a particular vocation today? How are the traditional professions changing? What are the growth careers, and what careers are overcrowded or dying out? You may reply that we astrologers aren't counselors and that we are not trained to do vocational counseling. Yet, that is what a good proportion of our clients are going to pay us to do, and we must be able to apply our personal talents and our astrological intelligence to this extremely important specialization within our field.[1]

Of course, the birth chart is the beginning of the personal professional profile. Attitudes toward work, authority, and money do not readily show up in traditional vocational tests, yet they are clear in the horoscope. When these attitudes are clarified, it is easier for us to match job choices with temperament. In addition, astrology provides

---

[1]This chapter was originally printed in *How to Use Vocational Astrology for Success in the Workplace* and is reprinted with permission. Noel Tyl, editor, *How to Use Vocational Astrology for Success in the Workplace* (St. Paul, MN: Llewellyn Publications, 1992, Chapter One).

what no test instrument can, which is an indication of timing in career moves. Timing is everything, and though many clients seem to have excellent instincts in terms of such moves, others do not. Many are driven by frustration to make the right moves at the wrong times.

Where to Get Information on Careers

It would be wonderful if we could all go back to school and study counseling. However, if you were only able to take one or two courses, the most practical credits would be in the area of modern vocational realities and how to do vocational counseling. It would be an excellent investment in terms of increasing both your professional skills and your income. Courses of this nature are often included in M.B.A. programs or in the fields of personnel or vocational rehabilitation.

Short of taking classes, there are excellent reference books available which can help answer our special questions. See the career bibliography on pages 235–236 for several excellent career directories that get updated every year or two. Most of these publications have 800 numbers and will ship the directory to you. For the same price as still another astrology book, you could own one of these guidebooks and look up occupations clients are considering. For example, one called *OCCU-FACTS: Facts on over 565 Occupations* has information on working conditions, job duties, physical demands, temperament, aptitudes required, and earnings.[2] Short of owning one of these informative reference books, if you went to the library and checked out several up-to-date books about careers, you would immediately be better prepared to serve your clients.

Another listing which deserves special mention is Barry and Linda Gale's *Discover What You're Best At.*[3] Although not intended to replace full-scale testing and individual interpretation by a certified career counselor, this book contains a series of tests that measure vo-

[2]*OCCU-FACTS: Facts on over 565 Occupations*. Edited by Elizabeth Handville (Largo, FL: Careers, Inc., 1989).

[3]Linda and Barry Gale, *Discover What You're Best At* (New York: Simon & Schuster, 1982).

cational aptitudes. It sorts 1,100 vocations into 41 career clusters, identifies the clusters into which the person fits, and gives brief descriptions of the variety of lines of work in each cluster. The book is reasonably priced and could easily become part of your offerings to clients who are searching for a good career fit.

Even informally, you can make it your business to learn about different vocations. At a party or conference, when you ask the inevitable question, "What do you do," follow it up with questions about exactly what that line of work involves. Remember, you may have known what it was like to be a nurse ten years ago, but what it's like to be a nurse today is very different.

The Chart as Potential—Life as Reality

To give sound astrological advice, we must assess reality. We need information that the astrological chart does not give us. We must ask our clients important questions: What level of education have they reached? In what specific studies? What kinds of financial and environmental supports do they have? What has pleased them in their work experience? What other kinds of careers have they considered?

We must use our skills of observation to get an idea of the client's intelligence and verbal and social skills. When it comes to intelligence, however, it is important to distinguish between "Air smart" and "Earth smart." The person who is only Air smart may have brilliant ideas yet lack the practicality to make anything of them. The person who is Earth smart, on the other hand, may have only one original idea in a lifetime and yet have the business skills to parlay that idea into a fortune. (An Earth-smart individual would have strong Earth accents in the horoscope, involving Mercury and the Ascendant, for example. An Air-smart person would have much emphasis in the air signs, but not much going on in Earth.)

Suppose you do a reading for a woman in her early 30s whose chart indicates very fine counseling skills. She may have a strong and well-aspected Pluto and maybe the Moon or other placements in Libra. Before you suggest that she go for a Master's degree in social work or counseling, find out more about her situation. Suppose she only has a high school education: is she up to four years of college for a B.A. and two for a Master's? Is money for tuition and expenses available from savings, a mate, or family? Do you have any idea what tuition would amount to for the career you are recommending? Were her grades good enough to get a scholarship? With all the cutbacks in government funding, what is actually available now in terms of financial aid? Where would you find that out? Or, where would the woman herself find that out?

Suppose you discover that she is separated, has two little children, does not get child support and her family is poor. Are you still ready to recommend a Master's degree? What about the child-care concerns while the woman would be in class? Perhaps there are paraprofessional careers requiring only a two-year degree in which those same counseling skills would be an asset. If you look through a career directory (see bibliography), you might come up with some alternatives. My point is that there are many important dimensions of career counseling with which we need to become familiar in order for our astrological analysis to be practical.

Often, people have strong chart indicators for a creative talent—such as writing, music, or acting—and want to know if they are going to be famous for this gift that three or four astrologers and their own dear mother have recognized. When clients ask if I think they can make it big as a musician or a singer, I ask, "How many hours a day do you practice?" Of would-be actors, I ask, "How many auditions did you go on this week?" That's what it takes to make it in these kinds of careers—discipline, hard work, and getting out there. Even then they may or may not make it, depending on luck—but they cannot wait for luck to strike. Jupiter works *if you work it*—and working it is Saturn.

Finding Aptitudes *and* Attitudes in the Chart

In preparing for a reading, you might ask for three choices of careers the client has considered. Naturally, you are not limited to those choices, since the chart will surely suggest more possibilities, but the client's list shows you how that person thinks. Then analyze the chart to see how those choices fit. Traditionally, we have learned to look for some combination of the 2nd, 6th, and 10th houses; the planets placed in those houses weigh most heavily, and then you rate the signs.

In those houses, you can read not only the client's aptitudes for success but the attitudes toward work as well. Attitude often has more to do with success than aptitude. Many intelligent, competent, or talented people sabotage themselves in their work because of negative attitudes, such as believing they will fail or wearing a chip on their shoulder. On the other hand, a set of constructive work attitudes and habits can serve even a moderately talented individual in good stead. It is the old story of the tortoise and the hare: the hare had the aptitude for racing, but the tortoise had the winning attitude.

To illustrate how both attitude and aptitude contribute to vocational choice, let us suppose that someone has Uranus or Aquarius in the 6th house. The aptitudes suggested would be in modern, technical fields such as computers or offbeat, nontraditional professions such as astrology or biofeedback. However, the underlying attitudes could be that this person resents supervision and functions better unsupervised. When unsupervised, he or she could be highly independent and self-motivated, whereas when closely supervised, we might anticipate a rebellious, erratic, and somewhat contemptuous temperament. The ideal work might be self-employment, consulting, or in chaotic, rapidly changing lines of work where personal initiative pays off.

Let us suppose a client has Leo on the Midheaven or planets in Leo in the 10th house. The desire to shine and to "be somebody" is very strong and there is an aptitude for acting. Whether the person can, in fact, make it on stage depends a great deal on attitudes. The individual may remain a frustrated actor, given the Leonine wish to be loved and adored just because they are. Such beliefs need to be offset by attitudes that produce hard work, patience, and the willingness to expose oneself to auditions time after fruitless time. Without attitudes like these, people with Leo-emphasized Midheavens may be reduced to creating drama and uproar at the straight jobs they get while endlessly waiting "to be discovered."

It is important to distinguish between the 2nd, 6th, and 10th houses, however, even though the actual occupation may be found in any of them. The 2nd house shows skills and personal resources which the individual can draw on to earn a living. When the 2nd house (or the sign Taurus) is strong, while the 6th and 10th are unoccupied, then earning money is a primary concern, rather than a career path.

In the 2nd house, you will also discern attitudes toward money that can either enhance or block the career. Review the chosen vocation to see how financial attitudes or practices suggested by the client's 2nd house could affect success. For instance, with Neptune or Pisces in the 2nd, the individual may be very dedicated and work hard, but be self-sabotaging in terms of earnings. For a salaried employee, there is a degree of protection, but a self-employed person with Neptune in the 2nd could be courting disaster.

The 6th house shows work habits, attitudes toward the job, potential types of jobs, and what kind of employee the person would make. Look at the vocational choices to see how work habits and attitudes described by the 6th house match working conditions and job tasks required for the particular line of work. (Here, again, you could refer to a career directory for helpful information.) With the Sun or Moon in the 6th house, identification with a blue collar background may be a factor the upwardly-mobile would have to work through to allow success.

When the 6th house (or the sign Virgo) is strong, but the 2nd and 10th are not emphasized, then work for its own sake may be the motivation. Depending on the planets involved, these chart dimensions may show people who find work a primary gratification in itself—or, at the very least, a major focus of energy and concern. If there is little satisfaction at work, health could suffer. Some are workaholics.

The 10th house shows the long-term career path or the primary source of career recognition for that individual. As we will explore later, attitudes toward authority figures and toward becoming an authority can be seen here. These attitudes can be crucial in assessing the most suitable vocations and any barriers that can get in the way. When the 10th house (or the sign Capricorn) is strong and the 6th and 2nd are not, people are strongly motivated toward some vocation or calling. We are not looking at work for its own sake, nor is money the primary motivation; rather their drive toward significance is strong—they want to be somebody. The means may be less important than the ends.

In short, in vocational astrology we must assess attitudes and motivation as carefully as the aptitudes. Fortunately, both can be seen in the signs and planets in the vocational houses. When Gemini is involved in the 6th or 10th, for example, ask yourself what would be a Gemini modus operandi on the job? Specifically, how would Gemini operate in the current work situation or within the proposed change?

If Gemini would be bored, restless, and lonely, it's surely not a good match. What would be the Cancerian modus operandi? Or the Sagittarian one? By thinking through the things that motivate and satisfy the sign in question, you will come up with a strong vocational sense about the client. Then, discussing precisely how particular attitudes impact on vocational choice becomes enlightening and helpful.

Additional Vocational Indicators

Planets in aspect to the Midheaven color the career and show skills and resources the person can draw upon. Many astrologers do not have Uranus in the 10th house, but instead many have an *aspect* between Uranus and the Midheaven. The Gauquelin research showed that a planet within ten degrees of the Midheaven is the most powerful vocational significator—even and especially when it is in the 9th house.

The house the Sun is in is also an important indicator. Since the Sun is the center of one's being and an important source of self-discovery and self-expression, one might as well get paid for it. For example, in working in the health fields, I came across many health professionals with the Sun in the 6th house. Any house that has a stellium in it may also play a role in the career, either positively, or negatively, or both. Someone with a strong 3rd house emphasis will doubtlessly be a communicator, regardless of the actual career.

The strongly occupied houses are especially crucial when you find a chart where the 2nd, 6th, and 10th are all vacant. Usually, such people are basically only working to pay the rent and support whatever is really important to them—i.e., their avocation, as shown by the houses where they *do* have planets. If you can find a vocation which matches their avocation, they will be getting paid for doing what they really love.

There are occupations matching each of the twelve houses. If any area of life is outstandingly important, you can bet there is money in it. For instance, the 5th house generates hundreds of kinds of jobs dealing with children, recreation, or romance. The 9th house provides not only jobs in education but also in the travel industry and in law. And so on.

Fitting the Career to the Whole Person

Some people may have a 10th or 6th house that is somewhat favorable for the vocational choices given, but indications elsewhere in the chart make the selections questionable. You would then want to think of similar or related careers which do not have the difficulties suggested by the chart. The book, *Discover What You're Best At*, with its 41 career clusters, is especially helpful in this pursuit.

Looking at some mismatches shows you how to fine-tune career choices. Suppose you have a client with Gemini emphasized, a strong Mercury, or a strong 3rd house, but little Saturn or Pluto, who wants to be a writer. The client will undoubtedly have a gift for words, yet, as Julian Armistead has pointed out, may lack the Saturnian discipline to stay put long enough to complete anything major. Without a strong Saturn, this person could be eager for immediate gratification, whereas the rewards of writing are very long in coming. Pluto indicates an ability to spend time alone—needed for writing anything lengthy. In order to capitalize on verbal skills, such an individual can pursue other kinds of work involving communication, such as a teacher, speaker, salesperson, or even a journalist writing short pieces. The sign and house emphasized would help you pinpoint the possible focus of the writing or communicating. If it were Virgo, for instance, health education is a possible focus; in Leo it might focus on children, the theater, or romance.

On the other hand, let us consider someone who has strong Saturn, Capricorn, or 10th house placements, but has a remote Venus. (The way you can tell is to do the chart preparation and then go away and get busy with something else. Then ask yourself where Venus was in that chart and struggle to remember!) The individual wants to go into business management. Here, you would need to draw the distinction between administration and supervision. We know that Saturn-Capricorn focal points are good for administration, in that paper work would get handled and activities involving structure, order, and long-range planning would benefit. However, without a pervasive Venus, supervision would not be a good choice; the people skills—like the capacity to motivate others and resolve conflicts—might be lacking. This is not to say that supervisors automatically have the right people skills, but it is much harder on everyone when they do not. Fortunately, these skills are learnable to some extent through courses in management, supervision, and employee relations, so you might suggest some additional coursework or seminars to clients with this deficit.

A Chart Example of Whole-Person Vocational Astrology

Let's look at chart 9 (page 150). Pretend that this woman is your client. She has been a successful dancer, appearing in Broadway musicals and other shows, and comes to you for a reading. At 35, she feels she does not have many more years left as a dancer, so she wants to begin to prepare now for a career change. Her thought is that perhaps she should go for an M.B.A. and a career in business administration, as that would be lucrative. First, are there any chart features that would cause you to advise her *against* a career in business administration? What kinds of careers would you suggest as an alternative? Think about these questions: study the horoscope for a while, as though you were preparing for an actual consultation.

Despite the Capricorn Midheaven, her basic nature seems to mitigate against anything as dry as business administration. With the Gemini Moon and a mutable t-square involving Mars, Moon, and Mercury, I suspect she'd be easily bored with work that did not involve constant change and challenge, stimulation, quick reactions, and public contact. Additionally, the strong Jupiter-Uranus conjunction (which sat on her relocated New York City Ascendant) seemed to mitigate against anything so hierarchical as administration. This conjunction also suggested that excitement and frequent change are necessary for her well-being.

This woman came to me for a reading. Since she intended to go back to school, I suggested she consider a degree in Public Relations so she could become a publicist or manager for people in show business. She had a great deal of fire emphasis, with Aries rising and the Sun in Sagittarius. Therefore, the dynamism that had made her a successful entertainer could easily transfer to promoting others. In addition, the prominent Mercury and Jupiter highlighted the

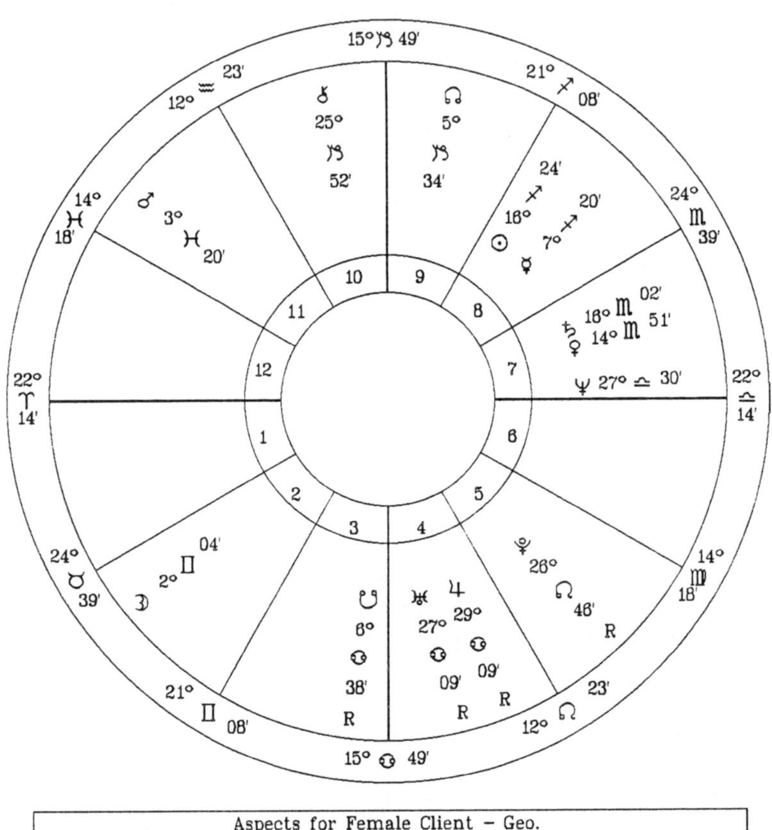

Aspects for Female Client – Geo.		
☉ ⚺ ♀ 1S33	☿ □ ♂ 4S00	♅ □ ♆ 0S21
☉ ⚺ ♄ 0S21	☿ ⚺ ☊ 1S46	♅ ⚺ ♇ 0A23
☉ △ As 5S51	☿ ⚼ As 0A06	♅ □ As 4A55
☉ ⚺ Mc 0A35	♀ ☌ ♄ 1A11	♅ ☍ ⚷ 1A17
☽ ☍ ☿ 5A16	♀ ⚹ Mc 0S58	♆ ⚹ ♇ 0S44
☽ □ ♂ 1A16	♂ ⚹ ☊ 2A15	♆ ☍ As 5A16
☽ ⚹ ♃ 2S55	♃ ☌ ♅ 2A00	♆ □ ⚷ 1A38
☽ ⚹ ♅ 4S55	♃ □ ♆ 1A39	♇ △ As 4A32
☽ □ ♇ 5S17	♃ ☍ ⚷ 3A16	♇ ⚻ ⚷ 0A54
☽ ⚼ Mc 1A15	♄ ⚹ Mc 0A14	As □ ⚷ 3A38

Chart 9. Female, born December 8, 1954, 2:32 P.M., AHST, 21N20; 158W04. Time from the birth certificate. Placidus Houses. Tropical Zodiac. North Node = True Node, South Node = Mean Node. Chart calculated by Astrolabe using Nova Printwheels.

3rd/9th house axis, important for publicity and information. The 7th house indicates business partnerships as well as more personal ones, and Venus, the ruler of her 7th, was in the 7th, conjunct Saturn, ruler of her Midheaven.

In any midlife career change, you would look to see if the client could transfer skills learned in the original career. All this woman's years of work in show business, plus her hard won connections could be put to good use in being a publicist. This recommendation was very pleasing to her, since she did not want to give up the glamour of show business, but was merely trying to be practical. The Capricorn Midheaven would be useful in managing creative performers, who are often disorganized.

Personal Liabilities Working against the Career

I have found it very important to look at the chart as a whole for character liabilities that might mitigate against career choice or performance. Let's pretend, again, that you are in an actual consultation. The young person in front of you wants to become a doctor. This is a bright individual who has plenty of money. The Sun and Mercury are in the 6th house and Virgo is rising, which would go along with a career in the health fields. However, you notice a Mars-Uranus conjunction in the 9th house, near the Midheaven. What *three* problems would you see in this placement that might make you advise the client against becoming a doctor? Take a moment and think this question through.

The three problems I see that conjunction presenting are as follows. The first is in getting *through* medical school. How would the person ever finish, when the degree requires approximately six to eight years of intensive postgraduate study in which all outside interests are put on hold? There might also be a strong tendency for rebelliousness to consider. When a career requires extensive education, look at the 9th house to see what's going on there!

Second, the rigid, conservative hierarchy involved in hospitals and other traditional medical settings would be extremely difficult for this individual to tolerate, both in school and after graduation. And, third, even if the person did complete school and begin to practice, there would be a strong propensity for malpractice suits due to unorthodox methods and a provocative bedside manner, all keyed to the intense Mars-Uranus conjunction.

What alternatives would you suggest? What about nursing? Although the education requirements are less arduous, there could be the same problem with the hierarchy, or even worse. A nurse has little power to take independent action, being subject to the physician's orders. Physical therapy, which could be an outlet for the physical side of the Mars energy, would hold similar problems in terms of the medical hierarchy. What about an alterative health career? The propensity to legal problems—like being accused of practicing medicine without a license—still exists. However, the curriculum in alternative school settings may be more acceptable and thus more likely to be completed. What type of alternative health career would you suggest? Possibly energy-oriented work like Reiki or acupuncture would be a place to channel the Mars-Uranus conjunction. Maybe the inventiveness of the Uranus factor could be turned to medical equipment, and the result would be a medical engineer.

With the strong 9th house emphasis, rather than being sued for malpractice, perhaps this person could become a malpractice attorney for the downtrodden. Other possibilities include becoming a lobbyist, activist, or educator for health concerns—like AIDS, health hazards in the workplace, or toxic waste. The 9th house conjunction is then addressed and channeled very well into political action, although rash activity won't go away. However, the conjunction also strongly suggests the need to get free of anger toward authority based on childhood experiences—probably from the early school years. Otherwise, there would be the propensity to act in explosive and rebellious ways that would be damaging personally and also damaging to the cause.

With a Uranian client like this one, the astrologer needs to discuss the desirability of healing the rage. Address it in a detached, logical manner. You are not doing it to pry into early childhood and emotions, which the client would surely resent; rather, you are pointing out exactly how the temperament could interfere with a current, stated concern, which is choosing a career. Sermonizing and generally acting like a disapproving parent will only provoke this client to rebel, possibly very angrily. In less extreme reactions, the client might automatically reject what you have to say. In order to be effective, you will probably have to listen to—and maybe even draw out—the anger against educators and other authority figures. You need to accept the anger, perhaps agreeing with how terribly unfair it all was. Do not justify or rationalize the authority's actions. You would want to examine any difficulties of your own about conflict, such as a fear of anger and a need to suppress it in yourself and others.

You would be on particularly shaky ground if you attempted to bring in sweet reason, the karmic necessity for forgiveness, or the spiritual lessons to be learned with this client. ("After all, you chose this set of parents.") As an authority figure with Divine overtones, your *acceptance* of the anger can, in itself, be healing. It allows the person to move on from there and finish school so the things that really bother him (or her) can be changed.

The example we have been looking at is extreme, of course, but this is the kind of reasoning that takes place in any vocational reading. While the traditional career houses are your starting point, you do need to scan the chart as a whole. Are there any character traits that contraindicate the fields the client is considering? Does the work rely heavily on logic, for instance, and yet the person has a stellium in Pisces in the 3rd house and a Mercury-Neptune conjunction? Your analysis would not only include the astrological factors but also the specific kinds of tasks involved. If you don't know what those tasks are, check the vocational reference books. If you are beginning to think this is complex, you are correct, and yet the choice of a career is such a serious matter that it merits a complex and thoughtful analysis.

Why a Vocational Reading Is Not Psychotherapy

It is important to understand that a vocational reading is not psychoanalysis. That statement may sound strange from an astrologer who is also a psychotherapist, but consider where clients who ask for vocational advice are coming from. They are in a business frame of mind, a bottom-line mood, even a Saturn sensibility. They are probably having Saturn transits or transits to the Midheaven or they would not be coming for this particular session in the first place. They are future-oriented and want to get on with their lives, not rummage around in the garbage of the past. They are not paying you for that, so any rummaging you do had better be relevant to the question at hand. You need to be able to demonstrate, clearly and logically, just how any emotional and historical questions impinge on their potentials for success.

To do otherwise would be intrusive. I believe strongly in a non-intrusive approach to the chart analysis, one in which you focus on clients' concerns and, in other matters, respect their right to privacy. If you can show precisely why a problem with Mom or Dad causes the client to do self-defeating things on the job, then you are providing useful information. If you are skillful in this, you can go a long way toward motivating the client to seek help with the problem. The client now would have a practical reason to spend all that money on therapy, healing, or investing precious time in a self-help group.

Proving the relevancy of the past to the present is not even that hard to do. Consider that the 10th house (which shows the parents as authority figures) is related to how people handle authority figures as adults. Suppose the client is having a difficult relationship with the boss or, especially, a pattern of difficulties with supervisors. You can delineate with a good deal of accuracy what the primary authority figure at home was like. It is then easy to lead the client to make connections between reactions to that authority figure and habitual reactions to bosses.

Incidentally, that tired old 4th/10th house debate about which house represents the mother and which is the father is a false one, to my way of thinking. The 10th is the primary authority figure, but also depicts both parents in their authority function, while the 4th is the nurturing function. The Moon at the Midheaven suggests a mother-dominated home, but also generally describes the father as a lunar type. (You can usually tell whether astrologers come from a mother-dominated or a father-dominated home by which parent they espouse as representing the 10th house.)

The father's influence is shown in several ways—in the Sun and its aspects, Saturn and its aspects, the Midheaven and any 10th house planets, and even, at times, in Mars. You might think that men more than women would derive their identity and self-worth from the father, thus from the Sun. However, difficult Sun aspects are devastating to the self-esteem regardless of gender. When I delve into the causes of self-esteem problems related to difficult Sun aspects, the relationship with the father is nearly alway implicated.

Surprisingly, in doing vocational counseling for women, both the Midheaven and the Sun are often signficant in showing identification with the father and his impact as a role model in terms of career. This is particularly true when the mother filled the more traditional roles and did not work oputside the home. Thus, when dealing with career issues, I am careful to find out about the woman's father, his vocational history, and his success or failure in following his dreams.

Saturn and its aspects are only partially related to the father, although he often shows up in chart readings as Saturn. Here, the authority functions of both parents are indicated, as well as the discipline, structure, and consistency they provide. Astrologers in some European countries delineate the mother's influence as Saturn, rather than the Moon. This no doubt reflects profound differences in child rearing patterns and family roles. The Midheaven and 10th house plans also show the parents as authority figures.

Mars and its aspects have to do with the images of masculinity which both boys and girls take in. They also show such Mars-related issues as how we deal with anger, how we go after the things we desire, and how able we are to assert ourselves. While we do not exclusively learn these things from our fathers, he is generally the earliest role model and thus perhaps the most influential. When there are difficult Mars aspects in a chart, there are almost always obstacles to overcome in these areas. When I delve into such problems the cause is nearly always the father and how he treated the child or how he acted as a role nodel in dealing with these issues.

In showing how issues with parents get transferred to supervisors, it is also powerful to point out that the expectations and needs that the inner child is still trying to have met are *not appropriate to the workplace*. Bosses are not parents, and it is no use being mad because they are not taking care of you. Speaking as one who has supervised, when you hire an employee, you are not looking to adopt a child, you just want to get the job done. And, yet, it is very common for residues of unmet or frustrated needs to be transferred onto the employer—especially where parents have been dysfunctional. Even when the boss is different by nature than the parent was, the behaviors and attitudes of the employee can re-create family dynamics, setting up conflict. For instance, with the Moon on the Midheaven, there may have been a strong codependency with the mother. By being highly responsive and sensitive to the supervisor's emotions and needs, the employee may set up codependent relationships at work, time after time.

An examination of the 10th house and parental authority is also relevant at another stage of the career. That is when the person crosses the line into supervision or management—from *having* a boss to *being* a boss. This is an important developmental stage in the career, and one which is fraught with potential stumbling blocks. If you cannot master this task, you limit your success potential. Even if you are in business for yourself, you can only go so far without eventually having to hire some employees.

Parental modeling is likely to creep in at this stage, without conscious awareness, as a model for now becoming an authority. Or, people in this position may bend over backwards *not* to be like their parents were and thus to avoid the boundary issues that being a boss entails. Similarly, people who function well as single adults or even in marriage get tripped into acting like their parents when they become parents themselves. We live what we learn. Thus, in order to be successful in an administrative or supervisory capacity, the person may well need to resolve any remaining authority problems.

How Personal History Affects Vocation

Chart 10 (page 157), is of a man who came for a reading in the midst of a career crisis, having recently been demoted out of a management position. He was a conservative businessman who did "benefits consulting," i.e., he planned benefits, such as insurance and pension plans for major corporations. At the same time, his wife was thinking of leaving their long, committed marriage.

You might like to take a look at the transits for the original consultation, which took place late June, 1989, and the follow-up in February, 1991. The most important transits were that Neptune and

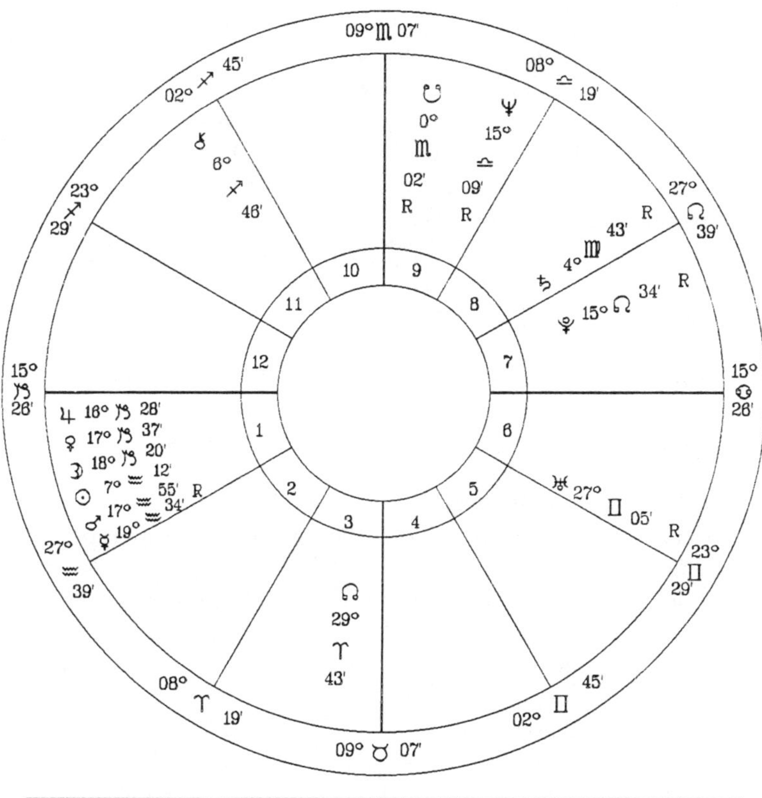

Aspects for Vocational #2 – Geo.		
☉ □ Mc 1S55	☿ ☌ ♂ 1A39	♃ □ ♆ 1S19
☉ ✶ ⚷ 0S26	☿ △ ♆ 4A25	♃ ⚻ ♇ 0S54
☽ ⚺ ☿ 1A13	☿ ☍ ♇ 4A00	♃ ☌ As 1S02
☽ ☌ ♀ 0A44	♀ ⚺ ♂ 0A18	♄ △ ☊ 4A59
☽ ∠ ♂ 0S26	♀ ☌ ♃ 1A09	♄ ✶ Mc 4S25
☽ ☌ ♃ 1A53	♀ □ ♆ 2S28	♄ □ ⚷ 2S03
☽ ⚼ ♄ 1A22	♀ ☌ As 2S11	♅ ✶ ☊ 2S38
☽ □ ♆ 3S12	♂ ⚺ ♃ 1S27	♆ ✶ ♇ 0A25
☽ ☌ As 2S55	♂ △ ♆ 2S46	♆ □ As 0S17
☿ ⚺ ♀ 1A57	♂ ☍ ♇ 2S21	♇ ⚻ As 0A08

Chart 10. This is the chart of a male client who came for vocational advice, reproduced here with his permission. According to his birth certificate, he was born January 27, 1949, 6:02 A.M., EST, 39N27, 75W10. Placidus Houses. Tropical Zodiac. North Node = True Node; South Node = Mean Node. Chart calculated by Astrolabe using Nova Printwheels.

Saturn in Capricorn were beginning to set off his Capricorn Ascendant and planets, while squaring natal Neptune. This repeated a natal Neptune square to his Capricorn Ascendant, Jupiter, Venus, and Moon. In addition, transiting Pluto in the 10th was beginning to set off the natal opposition between Pluto and Mars-Mercury. The transits of Pluto square natal Pluto and Neptune square natal Neptune are part of the midlife crisis for all of us. Here, they were doubly difficult due to their strength in the birth chart.

My feeling, in looking at the chart, was that his mother was an alcoholic and that codependency was at the root of both his marital and professional problems. I was led to this deduction by squares from Neptune to the Moon, Venus (ruler of the 4th), and the Ascendant/Descendant axis. With transiting Neptune repeating the natal aspects, the pattern was reaching a critical point, a breakdown in functioning. These suppositions proved to be correct. Not only was his mother an alcoholic, a steady, daily drinker, but his father was a problem as well, coming home drunk and disruptive at least once a week.

Having just read extensively on codependency, I was at that point crusading for people with this pattern to read the books, watch Bradshaw marathons, go to therapy, and attend Codependency Anonymous meetings. How would this hard-nosed businessman—who had never considered therapy in his life—come to see the need for it? Suffice it to say that my own recent acquisition of the material and my zeal to help others get free of codependency rendered me both knowledgeable and eloquent. I was able to show specific ways this history affected both his functioning in his career and his shaky relationship with his wife. He was also beaten and ready to listen. He was at a crisis point in the two areas of life that had the most meaning for him—his career and his marriage. He had suffered what had to be unbearable for one with so much Capricorn energy—the humiliation of demotion and the possibility of losing the job altogether. I had his ear!

In February, 1991, he returned for a repeat reading—or, for what he called, in his inimitably Capricornian fashion, a "midcourse correction." He had just re-listened to the tape of our original session. Thus, all the material we had discussed was fresh in his mind, and he could see that he had made substantial progress in that year and a half. He had not gone to therapy—that was just too much for him to contemplate—but he had read a variety of books about codependency and adult children of alcoholics.

With Sun, Mars, and Mercury in Aquarius, he had to put the books down as simplistic, of course. Yet he seemed to have fully absorbed the ideas and worked hard at applying them. This was shown by marked changes in behavior, with a tougher approach to conflict—direct and honest. He had recently taken some very assertive, courageous, and effective stances with his bosses and his wife. Future transits by Neptune to his Capricorn planets, followed by Uranus, suggested that he was far from out of the woods. He had faced the fact that both the job and the marriage might end. However, he was prepared to continue growing and felt he could not go back to the old patterns at work and home.

In this example, we see how *psychological interpretations need to be couched in career-relevant terms* when you are doing a vocational astrology reading. The same critical issues will doubtlessly have come up if the client had come for a psychologically-oriented reading, yet the focus is very different. You would endeavor to show exactly how long-standing emotional and behavioral patterns affect the client's success. In doing so, you are more likely to be heard with less resistance and to be able to motivate the client to change.

The ACA Astrologer and Vocational Advice

In the last chapter, we discussed the reasons so many astrologers—and so many of our clients—are Adult Children of Alcoholics (ACAs) or members of dysfunctional families. This background has an especially strong impact on the area of career and relationships to authority figures. Where the alcoholic parent (and often the sober parent as well) has been erratic or destructive, the child's reaction pattern to authority may be carried over into adulthood. Since much of our conditioning about authority happens before age 5, the now-adult offspring may react to bosses with the same resentment, codependency or intimidation that went on in relationship to the parent(s).

Given that at least 25 percent of the population is affected by alcoholics, then at least one in four of the clients who come for vocational advice are struggling with this syndrome. In order to make sense of what is happening to sabotage the client's career, the astrologer would do well to be familiar with the aftereffects of alcoholic and other dysfunctional backgrounds. Not all express it in the way the client in the example above did. There are a number of well-established roles children in alcoholic families fall into, such as The Family Hero, The Lost Child, and the Scapegoat. Until awareness and de-conditioning is achieved, these roles often get played out over and over in adult life, *including on the job*. Other primary characteristics of alcoholics and many of their offspring which carry over to vocation are grandiosity and defiance—Neptune and Uranus. Due to modeling the parent's lack of grounding and dysfunctional behavior, even a completely sober ACA can lack certain survival skills needed for success.

Astrologers who are ACAs may mirror the grandiosity, defiance, lack of grounding, and low self-esteem of their ACA clients. This may affect the soundness of vocational advice they give—possibly egging clients on in grandiose schemes, unsound financial practices, or unrealistic career choices. For the sake of clients, as well as ourselves, we astrologers who come from dysfunctional backgrounds like these would do well to soak up all the recovery literature we can, to belong to groups for ACAs, and in other ways do everything possible to deprogram ourselves and our clients from our upbringing.

Outer Planet People and Careers

The clients for whom we can have the most difficult time finding a satisfactory career match are what I call "Outer Planet People." The individual with outer planet emphasis in the 10th house is often reduced to earning a living through the 2nd house and the skills and resources shown there. Our society does not tend to validate or reward the callings denoted by the outer planets. (OPPs are likely to regard their true vocation as a calling—not as something *they* chose but as something which chose them.) They are otherworldly rather than worldly, visionary rather than practical. These would include nontraditional careers like New Age practitioners, creative artists, or political or environmental activitists—alternate life styles. Traditional vocational testing is likely to be useless—probably 90 percent would register as poets or artists.

Briefly, Uranian fields of work might involve any state of the art or leading-edge endeavor, such as those in science and technology, computers and other electronic media, astrology, working with groups or adolescents, political activism and social change. Neptunian careers could be in the creative arts, performing, work in service agencies such as prisons, hospitals, chronic care, or addictions. Plutonian fields include counseling, healing work of various sorts, work with death and dying, investigation, research, financial services. Within any one of the areas given for an outer planet, there are a large variety of jobs, at various levels of skill and education. Again, a vocational directory would help you sort out where within a given field a client might fit.

OPPs tend to meander and have a history of false career starts until the Saturn return or later. They often feel like miserable failures and wonder why they are not as well-established as their contemporaries. There is good reason for this, in that it takes well-seasoned, mature individuals to handle these planets' energies well. Finally, after years of meandering, some transit sets off their 10th or 6th house or the Midheaven, and they find their calling. This transit often coincides with a re-evaluation of the life path, in which the individual changes to a nontraditional career.

You may find rather extreme examples of authority problems with people who have outer planet emphasis in the 10th house. This is especially true when these planets fall into the Gauquelin sector (ten degrees from the Midheaven on either side, even in the 9th). These people come by this authority complex honestly, based on a history with a seriously dysfunctional or highly unusual parent, or some unfortunate loss of a parent. When these planets are emphasized in the 6th house, a similar line of work is indicated, but authority problems are not so clear, except when Uranus is involved. Instead, you may be looking at how low self-esteem gets in the way.

Often the parents were also OPPs who never got to do anything with their personal gifts or visions of achievement. This is especially true with Neptune, in that a parent's failed dream may have important consequences for the career of the offspring. On the one hand, the person struggles to live out the parent's dream for the child, so the parent can have vicarious achievement. On the other hand, it would not do to succeed, which would be showing up the parent. Thus, the person tends to do and not do—for instance, to be the artist, musician, or writer the parent wanted to be, while living from hand to mouth.

None of this needs to operate on the conscious level—with Neptune, what is? The parent may appear to be proud, supportive, and sympathetic. Yet, I see this dynamic so often that I am forced to conclude that it is a rare child who dares to live out the parent's failed dream and succeed at it. Part of my work, then, is in making this dynamic conscious and in giving the client permission to succeed. This permission, coming from a seemingly divine source, can have a powerful impact.

Looking at Uranus or Pluto in the 10th or in hard aspect to the Midheaven, you may say that such people are better off working for themselves, and that is probably so. However, unresolved authority problems continue to operate even when you do not have a boss. When you are self-employed, your client is your boss, if only for the hour or two that they hire you. As most astrologers fit into this category, it would be worthwhile to notice how authority issues play themselves out in your sessions and how attached you are to being considered an authority or guru by your clients.

Fairly often, the conflicts simply get projected onto *them*. The visual artist with Neptune in the 10th feels victimized by The Art Establishment, the musician by Show Biz. (For Neptune in the 10th, also read Pisces on the Midheaven, Neptune aspects to the Midheaven, and so on.) The astrologer with Uranus in the 10th rebels against the constraints of society and The Astrological Community in particular. The sometimes gnarly 10th-house-Pluto healer can be resentful and paranoid against a variety of *thems*, but especially the all-powerful AMA.

Vocational Counseling with an OPP

Let's look at an example of a career reading for an Outer Planet Person. See chart 11 on page 163. The man came for a reading the week of his Saturn return, in April 1990. He was a salesman of pharmaceuticals and was doing fine at it, but he had begun to feel he wanted more out of himself than that. He had a longstanding interest in yoga and other spiritual practices.

The client qualified as an OPP: Pluto in Virgo was on the Ascendant, part of a Grand Trine including his Sun. Neptune and Pisces were prominent, with the Moon and Mars in Pisces and Neptune op-

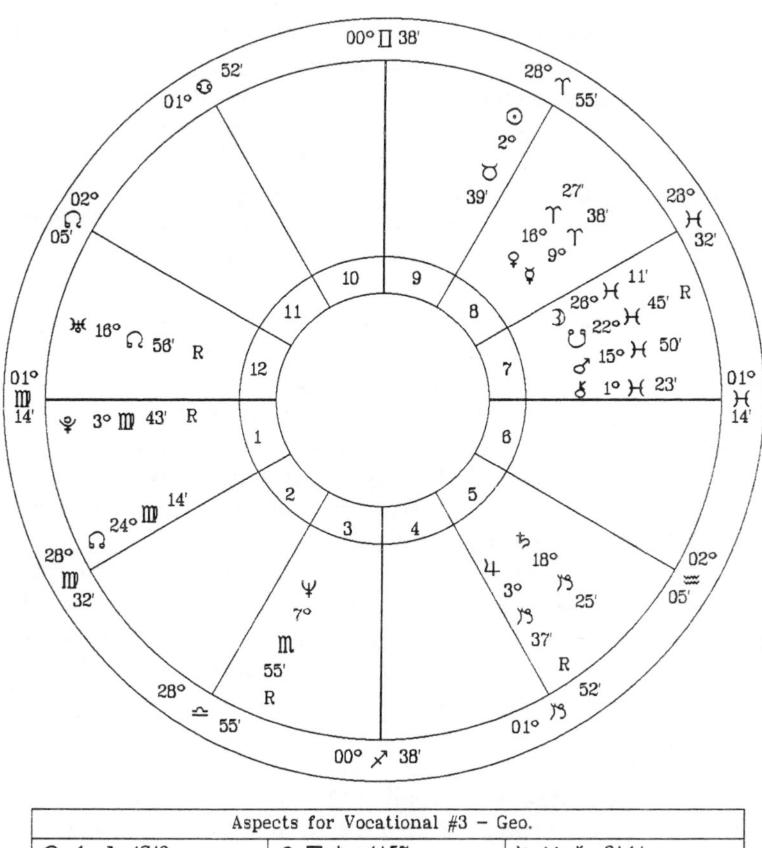

Aspects for Vocational #3 – Geo.					
☉ ∠ ♂	1S49	♀ □ ♄	1A57	♃ ⚹ ⚷	2A14
☉ △ ♃	0A58	♀ △ ♅	0A29	♄ ⚻ ♅	1S29
☉ ☍ ♆	5A16	♀ ⚼ As	0A14	♄ ⚼ ♇	0A18
☉ △ ♇	1A03	♀ ∠ Mc	0A49	♆ ∠ ☊	1S19
☉ △ As	1A25	♀ ∠ ⚷	0S05	♇ ☌ As	2S29
☉ ⚹ ⚷	1S16	♂ ⚹ ♄	2A35	♇ □ Mc	3A04
☽ ☍ ☊	1S57	♂ ⚻ ♅	1A06	♇ ☍ ⚷	2A20
☽ ⚹ Mc	4S27	♃ ⚼ ♅	1A41	As □ Mc	0A36
☿·⚻ ♆	1S43	♃ △ ♇	0A06	As ☍ ⚷	0A09
♀ ⚺ ♂	0S37	♃ △ As	2A23	Mc □ ⚷	0A45

Chart 11. Male, born April 22, 1960, 2:20 P.M. EST, 23N08; 82W22. Time from the birth certificate. Placidus Houses. Tropical Zodiac. North Node = True Node; South Node = Mean Node. Chart calculated by Astrolabe using Nova Printwheels.

posing his Sun, Uranus, in the 12th, was the apex of a Yod configuration (Uranus-Mars-Saturn). As an outer planet person, the likelihood of an unusual or nontraditional profession seemed likely. Healing work of some kind seemed indicated by the Pluto rising and the strong 8th house. With Virgo on the Ascendant, a physical or body work approach rather than counseling seemed likely. While the Gemini Midheaven did show his ability at sales, it could also indicate working with his hands. Having done the charts of many chiropractors, I often find this form of health care represented by Gemini or Mercury.

As we discussed his chart, he responded very positively to the idea of studying body work. Both chiropractic and acupuncture had an appeal for him, but he did not know which would suit him better. I suggested he visit a chiropractor in the neighborhood who had an acupuncturist on staff. That way he could talk with both, observe, and get more of an idea of which appealed. I also suggested he request catalogs from chiropractic colleges and schools of acupuncture to see what the course work entailed.

After the initial reading, our work together involved monthly sessions with flower remedies for slightly more than a year. He followed up on my suggestions and ultimately decided that acupuncture was both more appealing and required less in the way of science prerequisites. As you might imagine from the 9th house Sun opposite Neptune, we needed to address self-esteem issues and past educational barriers in order for him to succeed in school. He registered for science classes and did well. He applied to various acupuncture schools and was accepted. Eventually, given the 9th house Sun, he may incorporate some form of teaching or health education into his career.

The OPP at the Midlife Crisis

When Uranus, Neptune, or Pluto is connected with the vocational houses natally, the midlife crisis discussed in chapter Three is likely to result in a midlife career change. Many with outer planets in these houses have failed to find a true vocation due to a lack of opportunity to express these planets constructively and creatively earlier. Perhaps society was not ready for it when they entered the work force. The opportunities for such vocations were limited, or careers involving such abilities are only now developing. Or, perhaps, the need to please a parent—or family responsibilities—kept them from pursuing their true path. Many outer-planet vocations are not easy to manifest or to do well at until one is a more seasoned individual with some experience in the real world.

With outer planets in the vocational houses, the yearning for a true vocation may emerge sharply at midlife. The person may contemplate a new career. With any such major change, there is great resistance. It may seem easier, safer, and more secure to continue to follow the same old path. Yet, the outer planets repeat natal aspects over the course of two years or longer. The pain of resisting change grows until the individual virtually has no choice but to pursue a new path. The alternative is stagnation—merely marking time for the rest of one's life.

By this time the individual has had to pay some dues, so some of the original barriers may be gone. The children may be grown. The disapproving parent may have died. The Outer Planet Person who has been dysfunctional may have sobered up or grown up. Or, for the female client, maybe society accepts women doing the particular job now, when it was unthinkable in her youth. Over the years, the person may have saved up enough money to go back to school. Even better, some of the newer careers may match the person's original life purpose and abilities—careers that were unheard of when he or she first went out into the world. Not just love, but *many* things are better the second time around.

How World Changes Affect Vocational Guidance

As the outer planets pass through the universal signs, the rate of change in the world is accelerating. Economic and vocational realities are shifting quickly and continuously. Under such circumstances, confused and uncertain people will come to us for vocational advice. It is all too easy for us to peddle Neptunian wish fulfillment or satisfy clients fantasies rather than dealing with vocational realities. We would do well to get as real as possible by becoming informed about what is actually happening to various professions. The vocational directories discussed earlier can be used to keep up to date on various occupations. See the Career Bibliography on p. 232.

The other consideration is that individual careers are very likely to be affected by rapidly-changing world conditions. The price of oil in Kuwait, the shrinking rain forest, or the changes in Russia may well have a direct impact on the career of the client in question. Global uncertainties may affect choices and potentials so it is important to know what is going on in the world. It's also important to question the client about precisely what connection world conditions may have with his or her business.

With so much rapid, confusing change everywhere, it is much harder now to make definite predictions about a client's future. Although we will continue to predict—and although clients' demands for predictions are likely to increase—we would do well to be cautious and conservative in our prognostications.

CHAPTER SEVEN

Reading the Charts of Children and Teens

Most of us are familiar with the legend of prince Oedipus. When he was born, a fortune-teller said he would grow up to slay his father and marry his mother. To prevent this tragedy, his parents ordered the baby killed, but a kind servant spared his life and gave him to someone else to raise. He grew up and set off into the world to seek adventure and fortune. Sure enough, he unknowingly met his father, the king, on the road; they got into it, and Oedipus killed him. Then he arrived in the capital city, fell in love with the queen, not knowing it was his mother, and married her. When he found out what he'd done, he was so guilt-stricken that he put his eyes out, and they made his life into a TV movie.

My question is, WHOSE FAULT WAS IT THAT THIS HAPPENED? I THINK IT WAS THE FORTUNE-TELLER'S FAULT. No doubt her reputation was enhanced by this predictive coup, but I personally hold her responsible. Would Oedipus still have killed his father and married his mother without the soothsayer's prediction? Didn't the prophecy—and the parents' actions to avoid the seemingly inevitable—actually create the tragedy? If little Oeddy had grown up with his mother nagging him about his homework and the mess in his room, she wouldn't have been so glamorous. Besides, he would have had the family structure and taboos to guide him. The *National Enquirer* notwithstanding, you just don't bump off your dad to marry your mom. *Because* the parents took the fortune-teller so seriously and Oeddy got shipped out, he didn't know this beguiling damsel was his mother, and he and his father didn't recognize each other.

Keeping the legend of Oedipus in mind, how do you read children's charts? Verrrry gently! Given your seemingly omniscient set of tools, it is important not to give negative and fatalistic interpretations, as there is too much power in them. Prophecy by authority figures has immense influence over a child's life. Time and again, it's been seen how compelling negative parental prophecy is: "You'll never amount to anything." "You're going to grow up to be an alcoholic just like your father." "You'll never find anyone to marry you."

I call statements like these "The Curse," since too many people obey them unconsciously, and spend their lives proving the parent right. Sometimes my therapeutic work involves finding these curses and taking them off. It even happens sometimes during chart readings, if "The Curse" becomes obvious as a thought form barrier to fulfillment. I use the power inherent in our work to dispel that thought form, sometimes by taking on a mock-gypsy fortune-teller persona. The client giggles (nervously) and yet unconsciously heeds.

You don't want to be the negative gypsy fortune-teller archetype and create Curses (i.e., limiting thought forms) by making fatalistic predictions. "Your child will never marry." "I'm afraid he's in danger of growing up to be a drug addict." "She's doomed to failure in her career." Maybe you wouldn't say things like these, but be vigilant about what you do say. Otherwise, you may influence the parent to think negatively about the child, who could then live out the parent's prediction. Am I too tentative in dealing with difficult chart placements in readings for children? Perhaps so, but out of respect for the power of suggestion.

Who Is Your Client in this Session?

We also need to be aware that the client is not actually the child but the parents, who are there out of concern for their offspring. Parents who come for readings are vulnerable people, worried about whether they are doing a good job. They can project a great deal of power into your assessment, coming from the seemingly omniscient and even supernatural point of view astrology gives. Nothing gets better if you take on a judgmental role.

Put yourself in the parent's shoes. Parents react strongly when outsiders criticize their kids—even though they are ostensibly asking you to do so. They also are very sensitive to any hint of faultfinding about their parenting skills. One woman tracked me down by long distance phone to tell me in a huff that she had read my book, *Moon Signs*. She wanted me to know that her son had Moon in Scorpio and she's not at all like I said she was. How dare I criticize her, when she was a good mother! (Considering some of the things I've said about that Moon sign, I'm lucky she didn't start a class action against me.)

Another time, a sweet young woman took me aside after a seminar in Norway. She confided that when she read what I said about her daughter's Moon sign, she cried for two days. When I expressed my chagrin, she said that afterward it was helpful, because she changed the way she did things with her daughter. Still, I would have wanted my writing to be more sensitive. We never know how the things we say will wound a parent.

If you've never had children, it may be hard to fathom this vulnerability. If you've ever had a poem or article rejected by a magazine, you have a hint of how fragile the ego is when it comes to the 5th house. If you do have children, you may have forgotten the fear that parents have of doing something wrong, especially the anxious, first-time parent. It is so painful, you may have defended yourself by becoming convinced you did it right. If parents would only listen to you, they, too, could do it right. The young parent is already bombarded with shoulds. There used to be just the ones the grandparents and other relatives laid on them. Now there is all the advice they get on talk shows, in magazines, and in how-to-parent books. Do you want to add a layer of astrologically-derived shoulds?

Adjusting to parenthood is a difficult process. It entails a year or longer of major and deep-seated change. Often the new parent is deeply ambivalent about the responsibilities and the total self-sacrifice involved. Cultural myths about how woooonnnnderful it is to have a baby don't prepare them for the less positive feelings. The reactions often include depression, a sense of loss of freedom, resentment, and even rage. When everyone around them is telling them how incredible it all is, it helps to have one person who doesn't judge the ambivalent feelings. When you're seeing the mother, her Moon sign, aspects, and transits can give you more specific information about her adjustment process.

Parents carry around tremendous guilt if anything goes wrong. When I did a reading for two hyperactive brothers, their intelligent, educated mother expressed concern that c-section births might have been responsible for their hyperactivity. She seriously deliberated over whether she should have done it another way, when in reality neither she or the babies would have survived the delivery without it. I've worked in many medical settings, and parents who have children with birth defects inevitably feel very guilty and responsible for the handicap.

Remember that new parents, in particular, are presenting this product of their union and the marrow of their selves to you. How devastating it can be to hear that there is something WRONG with that child. Discussing the chart's flaws is almost like pointing out a birth defect—not to the fingers or toes, but to their Venus or Moon. Parents are likely to react to a negative interpretation with still another layer of guilt.

The following additional questions are presented to mull over in sorting out who your actual client is. Are you seeing both the mother and the father? Which parent is asking for the consultation? What is the position of the mate regarding either the reading, itself, or astrology in general? Answers to these questions can give you additional understanding of the relationship between the parents and of the parents to the child. It would be better to proceed as though both are present, as the other parent will doubtlessly hear the tape sometime—probably as soon as he or she gets home!

Assessing Parental Motivation—Why Is the Reading Being Done?

Love and joy at having a new baby can, of course, prompt the consultation, just as it does the photography sessions. The parents may come to celebrate and to find out just who this new individual is. The birth of the first child, in particular, may prompt a reading—the New Age version of bronzed baby shoes. It's typical for parents to record first children's early years in detail in the big album of baby pictures and the baby book with locks of hair and every milestone noted. (Second children may get a few pictures in the family album, and the third and thereafter are lucky to get recorded in the family bible.)

Narcissism is often a motive of the first-time parent in doing the chart of a newborn. At that stage, many parents see the child as little more than an extension of themselves. Any talents reflect positively on them, and any deficits make them look bad. This is natural in infancy, when little of the true self has emerged. If the astrologer raves too much about potential talents, the parent may fantasize that this will be a famous performer or a genius in the fine arts. Offspring may be pressured to pursue these gifts at the expense of balanced development. Too bad Stage Mothers Anonymous doesn't exist yet.

When kids are a little older, parents often request an appointment because the kids are already having problems. Some will say they are just curious or want to actualize the child's abilities. In asking what areas they wish to discuss, you may sense underlying concerns. Some are tuned into the child's spirit or sense past life connections, not all happy ones. It is interesting to draw out their fantasies and projections. Who do they think the child is going to be like—mother, father, a favorite brother or a hated one? (Later we'll talk about teenagers.)

Astrology students who come for a consultation are a special case. Again, consider who your client is. Students know enough astrology to be freaked out by what they see. Imagine yourself in such a position, worried about the horoscope of your baby or grandchild. How can this little being who has been entrusted to you possibly cope with difficult aspects? It is hard to imagine such a fragile creature handling a strong Saturn or Pluto when she can't even handle pabulum yet! Draw out their concerns and interpretations of what they see. You can't gloss over the concerns and give only a glowingly positive reading. Students of astrology may need help so they won't take the worst possible view of the outer planet aspects.

Should the Child Be Present for the Reading?

Sometimes, the parent will want to bring the child to the reading. You may want to consider how old the youngster is and why he or she is there. Can the child understand what you are saying? I've done charts for babies who were very much alert and present, seeming to take it all in. Maybe it's just imagination, but many of those being born today seem to be very old souls, and I'm not so sure they don't understand.

Remember when you were a kid and heard adults talking about you—how humiliating and painful it was? What small children may get from being present while adults discuss them is that they are somehow bad. It is like being at a conference with the teacher or a doctor, where all the worst traits get trotted out and discussed. To return to the question of motivation, some parents bring older children in the hope that you will magically straighten them out. Even though that wish is unrealistic, it hangs, unspoken, in the atmosphere of the consultation room, and the child picks it up.

For attunement purposes, it can be useful to see the child or a picture. I'm not sure it's wise to talk extensively about the child—even a seemingly preverbal one—in his or her presence. Few little people can verbalize that this experience is distressing. Often, if you are alert, you can read distress in body language or behavior. For instance, they may begin crying, becoming hostile, or demanding attention. Sure, kids get restless during a reading and find it hard to be still for an hour or longer—but exactly *when* they get restless is a telling clue.

Discuss with the parent beforehand how vulnerable children are when you talk about them, and that it's not a good idea to bring them along. In doing so, you are modeling more sensitive parenting behavior. Funds may be tight, but if you bring up the need for a baby-sitter in advance, it can be planned for in the cost of the session, or parents can ask a friend or relative to take care of the children so you can really have a valuable session with the parent.

The Astrologer's Relationship to the Parent and Child

How does the parent regard you and your seemingly supernatural insights? You would be surprised what projections and magical thinking lurk under even the most rational of facades. In dealing with a child's chart, you tap into a very primal level of thinking. You become the court soothsayer, here to tell the parents what will become of their little prince or princess. This is true even when you know the parent from other contexts, even when they have seen you, warts and all, in more rational endeavors for years.

When you know the parents in another context, there are a few questions to ask yourself about that relationship. Past connections can complicate the reading immensely. How hard does that relationship make it to read objectively? Could past history contaminate the reading? Should you refer these parents to another astrologer? Some astrologers would say you should not do the reading. A therapist would never take a friend or relative into treatment because of the difficulty in remaining detached. With astrology, it's an individual decision, based on the people involved, but the issue is worth careful consideration.

For instance, are these long-term clients whom you've seen through many stages? You saw them when they were single and lonely, did the synastry when they were dating, and then chose a wedding chart. Now they are bringing their firstborn for your blessing. By this time, you've doubtlessly grown fond of them and want only the best for them. It may be hard to be objective. [Or, is this a good friend or relative? If you read charts for close relatives, it is even more difficult to be objective. Your projections or needs easily get in the way. You may see things as unrealistically bad or good—with rose colored glasses or dark glasses.]

How Your Own Childhood May Get Played Out in the Reading

Consider how unresolved history with your own parents might get in the way of objectivity when reading for children. Therapists are trained to watch for countertransference. That is, their clinical supervisors are constantly making them aware of ways unresolved difficulties with their parents contaminate their reactions to clients. These unconsciously get projected onto clients, who are then assumed to be just like the parent was. Since few astrologers go for clinical supervision, we also need to be vigilant about countertransference. Nowhere is this more true than with a child's chart, as the Inner Child readily gets activated. Be sure you're not using the session to get out your anger about your parents' mistakes.

To assess how childhood experiences could influence your readings, look at your Moon, which represents the nurturing you received. Suppose you have Moon in Aries and received hostile caretaking in childhood. There may be leftover anger about unmet dependency needs, which you then project onto the child's parents. You decide that they aren't taking care of this child properly and become protective. With Moon in Virgo, your mother may have been overcritical. Thus, you interpret the parent's concerns as being overcritical of the child—and you may be overcritical of the parent's handling of the child. Or, with Moon in Pisces, you might have had to be your mother's caretaker because of illness or inadequacy, so you're convinced this parent is incompetent.

Nurturing patterns and attitudes toward children, as shown by the Moon, may also be played out in the reading. Often, they mirror our mother's expectations of how a child should behave. We live what we learn, and unless we are alert, we can act out the attitudes and parenting behaviors we experienced as children. For instance, one student who had Moon in Capricorn recalled that her mother would always say, "I'm not raising children, I'm raising adults." When pressed, she admitted that her reactions to children were not so different from her mother's.

Think through your Moon's sign and aspects and how that illustrates your early years. Also think about the things your mother did that were the most upsetting, as anticipation of those behaviors is likely to be an undercurrent in the session. By becoming aware of any leftover baggage, you can avoid carrying those issues into the consultation. Lunar experiences and responses are very early ones. They tend to be less conscious than issues related to the Sun. They may also manifest as a general feeling tone in the reading. It is also useful to know the Moon sign and aspects of the parent who is coming for the reading, to pick up on their nurturing and child-rearing patterns.

The Need for Knowledge of Child Development

When done by a sensitive individual who is knowledgeable about children, pediatric astrology could be a valid and valuable specialization, as much so as mundane or medical astrology. However, just studying astrology isn't enough. If you decide pediatric astrology is your niche, don't just study charts, study children. Learn about child development, so you know what is normal at various ages and you have an understanding of the special developmental tasks of each stage.

Read about learning theory, so you can talk to the parents about the best learning conditions or what might be going wrong in school. For example, "L.D."—learning disorder—is a hot diagnosis now. You might want to know about it and about methods that are helping children with this problem.

Study child psychology to learn what may be going on in a problem child's behavior. You need not master these subjects to the extent of being able to do therapy or remedial education. However, you need to know what may be going on, to recommend where parents might go for help. The public library is a rich and free source of books about childhood problems, all the more readable because they are written for parents rather than professional educators or therapists.

Books aren't enough. If you have raised children or are around them a great deal, you already have a wealth of practical experience in their behavior and phases. If you haven't been around children much, volunteer work, such as at a nursery school or with the scouts would provide more intimate acquaintance with children. Such exposure also quickly cures the arrogance of the non-parent who judges those inevitable parental lapses into less than loving and enlightened handling of their offspring.

It would be well to know about new family life-styles and the relationship complexities involved, as many of your clients will be involved in them. Between 1986 and 1989, there were more than a million divorces in the USA each year. The number of children living in single parent households has doubled over the last twenty years. The step-family is another increasing phenomenon. Of all the marriages in 1987, only half were first marriages for both the bride and groom.[1] Read about divorce, single parenthood, and step-fami-

---

[1]These statistics came from three reports by the U.S. Census Bureau: Arlene F. Saulter, "Marital Status and Living Arrangements." *Current Population Reports* #445, 6/90. U.S. Department of Commerce, Bureau of the Census; *National Center for Health Statistics*. Monthly Vital Statistics Report, v.38:12, 4/3/90, "Advance Report of Final Marriage Statistics, 1987"; and in the same issue, "Births, Marriages, Divorces, and Deaths, for 1989."

lies, so you know about typical emotional reactions and consequences of such changes in the family structure.

Introducing Parent to Child

My recommendation would be to give a very general impression of what sort of being the parents are dealing with. Helping them become acquainted with the nature of the child can be especially useful where there are astrological incompatibilities. These would be revealed in comparing the charts of parent and child. Many differences that parents take personally are not deliberate challenges to their authority, but fundamental differences between two people. It really helps to know what they are in astrological terms!

For example, a Pisces Moon mother who values gentle, sensitive men may give birth to a macho fireball with Sun and Moon in Aries and Sagittarius rising. She will never turn that child into a poet or a mystic, no matter how hard she tries. Stress that blame is not to be assigned—it is not her failing, but the child's inherent makeup. Contrarily, a macho Aries father with a son who wants to study music can be helped to see that the child's sensitivity is a gift and not a reflection on the father's manhood.

A highly sensitive Cancerian parent may come to see that a Virgo child criticizes because it is in her nature and not because of the parent's inadequacies. Youngsters with Aquarius rising and a strong Uranus may go through an especially rebellious and stormy adolescence. They need to become independent, self-sufficient adults who are not intimidated by social pressure as they pursue their unique, preselected life path. The rebellious period is not so much a challenge to parental authority as it is a necessity in becoming who they are intended to be. It's also a part of growing up.

Recognizing the child's inherent nature eases conflict. For instance, if you match a quick-moving Aries parent with a slow-moving Taurus child, this is a setup for friction. Understanding that pokey pace as natural to the bull and not merely bullheadedness, parents can make allowances. For starters, it might be wise to wake that particular child up a half hour before the others. This strategy would give the youngster time to come back to life and complete those routines Taureans find so comforting. In short, when parents understand that children behave in certain ways due to their astrological makeup and not out of a deliberate desire to upset, the maddening qualities can be taken less personally.

Also survey the chart for positive qualities which parents can foster. Trines, sextiles, and especially quintiles show gifts to encourage. The quintile, a 72° aspect, is well worth looking for, as it can show the individual's own personal genius. Understand that not every person who has a quintile is going to score over 140 on an IQ test. It is quite possible to be brilliant in a single area of life. The quintile is your personal genius, which you may or may not develop, and which you may or may not use in a socially constructive manner. A Sun-Jupiter quintile might show a gift for teaching and uplifting others by using one's own experience or personal charisma. A Mars-Uranus quintile could suggest leadership in avant-garde situations or social causes, or might indicate technical and mechanical brilliance. A quintile between Mercury and Neptune could mean creative writing or psychic abilities. What would you speculate would be the talent represented by a quintile between the Moon and Venus or between Saturn and Pluto?

The biquintile (144°) is similar to the quintile and yet is also apparently connected to the quincunx (150°) aspect. A 3° orb seems to work in these aspects. Thus, the quincunx would still be in effect when two planets are 147° apart, while the biquintile would also be in orb at 147°. In that overlapping area, the irreconcilable impulses that the quincunx represents make the individual stretch to find a creative solution. Here, personal genius arises out of the necessity to reconcile the irreconcilable.

Should You Tell the Child's Future?

In doing children's charts, I just don't focus that much on the future, period, nor do I do transits for babies or young children. It is important to note that natal outer planet aspects will repeat themselves as transits for the first two or three years of life. Suppose Pluto is 7 or 8° before a conjunction or opposition to the Sun. This aspect will repeat by transit several times in the first years of life, because it is a slow-moving planet. Yes, that may signify a major, life-shaping event or condition.

In one way, it is useful to consider the future: it provides a perspective on childhood versus adult expressions of the same astrological placements. What is difficult in a young child or teenager's chart may be an asset in an adult's chart. Those qualities that represent a problem today may be necessary for the future adult to develop to meet the life purpose. The same strong Uranus that makes Johnny such a problem in school and so challenging to authority can make him an inventive, independent, self-starting innovator.

As children, Capricorns can be serious, perfectionistic and hard on themselves. They often blossom as adults, having paid some dues and accomplished some of what they set out to do. Strong Virgo or 6th house placements have little venue in the life of a child and may result in low self-esteem. They are happier and have better self-esteem when they grow up and find fulfilling work. Youngsters like these would develop more confidence by having a little job like a paper route. Children with a strong 2nd house or Taurus emphasis might be also be happier with a little job, so that they can earn money of their own.

Houses that are full of planets show areas which will be important in adulthood. Parents might want to enrich the child's experience by planning special opportunities and activities in those areas. For instance, when a child has a strong and especially a positive 11th house, friends are going to be very important, maybe even more important than family. The parent might want to put the child into a play group or nursery school early, and encourage associations with youngsters who would have a positive influence.

Concerning the less desirable qualities shown in the chart, Joanna Shannon, an excellent New York based astrologer, has suggested keeping what you say to parents on a need-to-know basis. She feels too much intimate detail gives the parent ammunition to use against the child in the inevitable parent-child battles. Keep in mind that what you say may be thrown up in the child's face some day, probably in a much-distorted form.

When you discuss qualities or future life-styles that parents may consider less positive, their need to control can come up. Disapproving of future directions, they may strive to suppress the very qualities the child has come here to develop. We do not have to know all, see all, and tell all—we can use discretion in what we say. Aren't there things about your adult life that you wouldn't have wanted an astrologer to tell your parents when you were a baby?

For example, one of my students told a father that his young son had far more yin than yang in his chart. Apparently that's what they're calling the signs now rather than masculine and feminine. The next step is to label such individuals testosterone challenged. Unimpressed by euphemisms, the father growled, "Are you trying to tell me my son is going to be a faggot?" She asked me how she should have replied. My question was, why did she feel she had to say that in the first place? Wasn't she herself questioning the boy's masculinity, in an abstrusely metaphysical way?

If the son is indeed going to be gay—and you wouldn't conclude that on the basis of a single factor—it's none of his father's business. The prediction of homosexuality can create serious relationship problems with the parents, with all sorts of adverse reactions. Furthermore, the interpretation may be wrong, and homosexuality can't be prevented, any more than heterosexuality can. Any child's future sex life, regardless of proclivity, is absolutely none of the parents' business.

In the horoscope, you can see the talents and gifts, you can see the issues, but you cannot know the outcome—how that child will use those gifts or resolve the issues. It is presumptuous to think you know how the being will use those energies. Many children are born on a given day with the same chart—twins and astrotwins—but the souls who incarnate are not identical in their development. For instance, I have a young friend who is always going on about how she wants to be a famous performer, although she hasn't a shred of talent along that line. She particularly wishes she could be Madonna. Only when I looked up Madonna's birth information did we discover that my friend had the same birthdate and year as Madonna!

To illustrate how the soul incarnating determines the expression of the planets, take the wide spectrum of uses and abuses of the planet Neptune. When you survey the charts of alcoholics, psychics, and saints—all possible manifestations of Neptune—there is little difference between them. Probably if we had access to enough birth data, we'd find many pairs of astrotwins, one saint and one sinner. Some psychics become alcoholics in order to escape the psychic bombardment. Many recovering alcoholics become spiritually beautiful people—not saints, but with great wisdom and love to give.

Knowing and encouraging the constructive uses of planetary placements, on the other hand, can help the parent give the child a head start on optimal emotional and spiritual development. For instance, the child who has a strong Neptune can be exposed to spiritual teachings, given opportunities for creative expression, and watched for psychic abilities.

Throwing Light on the Child's World

Rather than looking too far into the future, it is more useful to discuss those areas of a child's world that a reading can appropriately clarify. A child's world mainly consists of parents, siblings, school, and friends, so it is most useful to help the parent understand these areas. Explain in advance that this is your focus, so that the parents aren't disappointed by not getting the child's total future. Here, again, it may be useful to clarify the motivation for the reading.

A particular contribution you can make is to analyze Mercury and the 3rd house for learning and communication styles. It is helpful to explain that there are at least twelve styles, rather than the single, standard way most public schools expect. Parents can then work to provide the best set of circumstances for study. Even if the school can't individualize instruction, parents can supplement at home.

For instance, how Mercury in Taurus assimilates new material is similar to the way a cow digests its food. The cow has four stomachs, and it chews the food over in each of those stomachs before it finally gets all the possible nourishment out of it. The Mercury in Taurus individual chews over every new bit of knowledge in a similar way, until it is digested and assimilated. They aren't fast, but once they have it, they keep it. Mercury in Gemini, on the other hand, picks up the vocabulary and appears to catch on very quickly, but possibly in a glib and superficial way. Natural mimics, they often skip past the basics and acquire the vocabulary but may not acquire as deep an understanding of the subject as their slower-moving Taurean brothers and sisters. While Mercury in Aries children also have quick, sharp minds, it is hard for them to sit still long without contemplating mischief. They learn better by doing and also tend to thrive on competition.

Another part of the child's world that a reading can throw light on is relationships with brothers and sisters, again a 3rd house or Mercury question. (As the 3rd house shows both communication and siblings, siblings play an influential role in the way we learn to communicate.) Mars in the 3rd can show competition and conflict. With Pluto in the 3rd, there can be sibling rivalry with a vengeance. The parents should not play on this for they could unconsciously foster rivalry or jealousy. With either Mars or Pluto, there may also need to be intervention to prevent one of the siblings from being abusive to the other.

Those with Neptune in the 3rd may exhibit the tendency to rescue or make sacrifices for a brother or sister, sometimes because that sibling has special problems. It is important that parents take care not to make too much of a handicapped or problem child at the expense of the youngster in question. This intimate exposure to a sibling's problems may ultimately help the individual develop such admirable qualities as compassion and a desire to serve. However, it is important that these qualities not be overdeveloped at the expense of self-esteem or other important areas of life.

Preventive Aspects of Reading Children's Charts

Instead of delineating the child's entire adult life, focus on what parents can do to develop the child's gifts and to prevent problems seen in the chart—not necessarily spelling out all the grim possibilities. I try to give practical suggestions on how to avoid whatever possible in the way of parenting mistakes, based on knowledge of child development. We won't know how this works out for twenty years or more, but it's the best we can do. These are just my own methods and clinical decisions, and you may find me overly cautious. However, we can't be too careful in reading children's charts. You are shaping a vulnerable little life.

For example, I talked with a black divorcée who was raising her young son alone. The boy's chart had a Moon-Neptune conjunction in the 2nd house, a quality I called Magic Mommy. She'd had a hard time financially when she was growing up and wanted to make sure her son didn't have the same experience. She shielded him from the money problems a single parent inevitably has by not talking about them and by giving him everything he wanted. I recommended she be more realistic about money, teaching him now that it doesn't grow on trees. Otherwise, he could grow up with the expectation that women would always take care of the money problems and magically provide all his needs without it being his responsibility.

And, yet, is it possible to prevent the problems seen in the chart—or does it just become another expression of that same combination? For instance, recall the example given earlier of the Virgo child whom I'd advise to have a paper route. It would be important to caution balance between work and play, so you don't just wind up creating a workaholic whose self-esteem depends on being productive. We don't have much power over the major conditions children are going to meet that will shape their character and lives. We *can* help the parent avoid some of the glaring mistakes of child rearing.

It would be a missed opportunity for prevention if I didn't mention how much the Bach and other flower remedies can do to keep a child's undesirable qualities from crystallizing into an adult's hard defenses. As the Bach remedies are available in many health food stores or New Age bookstores, I will confine myself to them here. The child who wants to be the center of attention, even getting it through negative behavior, can change this pattern with the help of Chicory. In cases of sibling rivalry, Holly and Chicory may be good for both children. Where there has been trauma, even birth trauma, early administration of Rescue Remedy, in the acute phase, or Star of Bethlehem, for the aftereffects, can alleviate fearfulness. Timid children can be helped by Mimulus, which is also good for specific phobias, and youngsters who lack self-confidence can be given Larch. For more information, see my *Flower Remedies Handbook*.[2]

Trouble in the Child's Chart

Many times, from the child's chart, you can see trouble coming, such as parental divorce or losing a parent. Such possibilities might be suggested by Uranus in the 4th or by difficult aspects between the Sun and Moon, especially when combined with the outer planets. Should

[2]Sterling Publishing, New York, 1992.

you predict divorce? No, that's not what the parents are asking about—and it's a lead balloon—creating an unnecessary fear overload on the child's reading. This interpretation could also be wrong—an unconventional home life may be suggested, rather than a divorce. Instead, ask how the parents are getting along and recommend counseling if the marriage is in trouble. Emphasize that it is important not to involve the child in the conflict or ask him or her to choose sides.

What would you do if the chart suggested health problems? For example, what if you saw Saturn or Capricorn in the 1st house or some very difficult placements in the 6th or 12th? Ask about the child's health and caution the parent about regular medical checkups. You would not want to alarm the parent, of course. You don't know for sure the health problems would show up in childhood and you don't know for sure that the effects of the planets would be physical. In the 1st house, for instance, tough placements might show difficulty in putting oneself forward in the world and in getting along with others. In the 12th house, an emotional issue could be indicated. In the 6th house, such placements could be more directly related to the life work. Having noted that a Virgo Ascendant or Moon can show an allergic constitution, I sometimes caution parents to be on the alert for this. Moon afflictions sometimes show an adverse reaction to dairy products.

What about future horrors, such as the chart that looks like a possible drug addict or a promiscuous type. Here, we particularly don't want to create an Oedipus through our predictions. When Neptune or Pisces are strong, focus on the need to encourage development of the higher sides of Neptune—spirituality, creativity, and service. On the other hand, it would not do to push spirituality too hard. Children will rebel against New Age teachings when overdone, just as they might if you pushed the church too hard.

One very knotty ethical question is what to do when the child's chart looks like physical or sexual abuse is a possibility. In most states, laws mandate various professions to report child abuse. Astrologers are only exempt because we are not accepted as a profession. I would have no hesitation in questioning the parent about physical abuse, which is generally out in the open. I would phrase it gently, asking if one of the parents is a harsh disciplinarian. If the answer is yes, ask for details on their brand of discipline.

The question of sexual abuse is likely to appear if you are doing many children's charts—statistics show that one little girl in three suffers from sexual abuse of some degree. As openness about such experiences grows, more and more men are revealing they were sexually abused or molested in childhood. There is enough evidence to conclude that nearly as many boys as girls may be victims. In my experience, if either parent has been sexually abused or molested as a child, the chances of it repeating in the current generation are much higher. It is not always the former victim who does the victimizing. Uncannily often, the former victim is magnetically drawn to a mate who turns out to be a child molester.

When the signatures for sexual abuse show up in a child's chart, I have no hard and fast answers to offer. It is an individual matter, based on how serious the possibility of abuse and on your assessment of the parent. One might create literal Oepiduses—or, most likely Electras—by such discussions.

Suppose that you tell the mother of a girl with Pluto rising to watch out that she doesn't get molested or become the victim of incest. The mother watches the girl like a hawk, constantly casting dark suspicions on the entire male race and on the males in the family in particular. The men around her finally react to being treated like monsters by becoming monsters, taking revenge on the little girl for her mother's behavior. Or, saved from incest by her mother's watchfulness, but having grown up in such a warped atmosphere, the young woman develops twisted relationships and magnetizes men who wind up abusing her. The question is not an easy one to resolve.

Relationship Charts for Parent-Child Connection

The child's chart is a frozen slice of the transits the mother and father were having at the time of the delivery. From outer planet connections between the child's chart and the parents', you may even get a sense of why this being was born. You may be able to deduce what the mother and the father hoped to accomplish by the pregnancy and what was going on in the marriage. Not all motives for having a baby are as pure as the driven snow. Particularly where the offspring's chart strongly emphasizes Pluto, pregnancy may be a ploy in a marital power struggle.

Generally, the baby's chart will form strong outer planet connections to the parents' charts. In consequence, throughout life, that child will tend to activate the same issues that arose at that time. For example, a child born on the parent's Saturn return will always be a Saturn experience for the parent. The child's very presence forces the parent to grow up. I read a quote somewhere once that said, "The miracle is not that adults produce children, but that children produce adults."

For another child, born on a transit of Pluto to mother's Moon, the relationship will always carry a Plutonian tinge. Apart from the possible power struggle mentioned above, such pregnancies are sometimes part of the aftermath of grief. (Even when the baby is born before the loved one dies, the pregnancy may have begun in anticipation of the loss. The baby is still strongly affected by the atmosphere of mourning.) The newborn may, at some level, be seen as a replacement for the loss of a key figure in the mother or father's life.

How can an astrology reading help? The effects can be mitigated by pointing out the results of unresolved grief and discussing what resources are available—for instance, bereavement groups. You can show how this atmosphere may affect the child. A needy infant cannot meet the parent's needs, be a clone of the lost loved one, or fill those shoes.

All too often, in the child's chart you can see a difficult relationship with one or both parents. (Chart comparisons or composite charts give even more information.) It always seems to be the gentler parent who comes for the reading and who reports that the other is a harsh disciplinarian. When the parent who is difficult is not present, how do you handle it? Is that absent parent going to listen to the tape? Even though you may not think he or she will, there is little privacy in a family. Not only that, but the worried parent is likely to cite you as an authority at some point and play the tape to the other. You might want to speak on tape as though both parents were present, so the absent parent can listen without becoming defensive and rejecting all this astrology garbage.

Working with Teenagers and Their Charts

A different set of considerations comes into effect when parents ask you to look at the chart of a teenager. As a profession, astrologers are ruled by Uranus, the same planet most strongly connected with the adolescent period and its turmoil, so astrologers naturally have something to offer this age group. Looking at the horoscope as the blueprint of the individual, you can help identify the young person's true self, as opposed to peer, family, and societal pressures to conform. Thus, an astrology reading, given by a sensitive, supportive, positive, and constructive adult, can be very helpful to any teenager trying to find out who he or she is. No doubt, you and I could have used a reading like that when we were young!

Before you do this type of reading, it is important to confront your own attitudes about adolescence. Some astrologers are especially gifted with teenagers. These are often people who have raised children and enjoyed them, or who have worked with them in other contexts, like in school or recreational settings. On the other hand, if you are currently raising teenagers, conflicts, wishes and fears about your own offspring may also interfere. Others, because their own adolescence was difficult and remains green in their minds, have a special empathy for this age group. If you are uncomfortable with teens or dislike them, however, this will come through and contaminate the session. You are better off referring them to someone who just thinks teens are the best thing God ever made.

If you have unresolved issues from your own adolescence, be aware that working with this age group may trigger them. For instance, you may over-identify with the teen against the parent, thereby inflaming their conflicts. Or, you may be overeager to suppress their natural rebelliousness if you had to suppress your own in youth. To discover what your personal issues might be, spend some time remembering those years, how you were, and how you got along with your parents. Your natal Uranus and its aspects may give you some clues, as well as the transits and progressions for that period.

When Parents Ask You to Look at a Teen's Chart

Sometimes parents ask you to look at teenagers' charts during their own reading. This is an instance where, to my way of thinking, astrology skates perilously close to being an invasion of privacy. That's an interesting question, isn't it? Could an astrologer be sued for violation of the constitutional right to privacy? If we were taken more seriously, we'd be enjoined from looking at a person's chart without written consent. (If we were taken seriously as a profession, we'd probably need malpractice insurance!)

You are looking at the chart of an emerging individual, so be respectful of that person's search for an identity. Ask yourself this question: What if this teenager were listening to the tape? (You can bet they probably will, somehow, some time.) What would they want you to tell the parent and what would they not? What would they want to hear about themselves? You might do well to act as though the young person were present.

Attention to the parent's motivation in asking is merited. If it comes from a genuine and heartfelt wish to help, you will sense it and act accordingly. If you sense that control is a primary issue—and you might already know that from the parent's horoscope and your interactions—caution is in order. Be circumspect and think about how your words would sound quoted out of context. Parents may well use your pronouncements as ammunition against the young person. "You'd better watch your step, young lady. That astrologer said you'd probably get pregnant before you marry."

Assessing Parents' Motivation and Expectations

Sometimes—especially after you've commented on a teenager's chart—the parents will ask you to see their son or daughter. Since parents are usually paying for the session, attention to their motivation in sending the child is important. Sometimes parents ask out of genuine feeling that the reading will help this young person make the right choices in terms of schooling and vocation. When young people are earnestly searching for a vocation, astrology can be an excellent tool. Or, parents may feel the son or daughter suffering from low self-esteem might discover personal gifts and potentials, and the chart does this well, too.

Occasionally, however, clients who've been well-impressed with your work will ask you to see their difficult teenager. This is tricky—really tricky. You might start by talking with these parents about what they hope the session will accomplish. The intimate understanding astrology lends doubtlessly has given you an aura of divine wisdom. Consciously or unconsciously, they may be saying, "Here, you fix my problem child."

Suppose you discuss the expectations and what you find is that the parents hope you will talk some sense into Jason or Jennifer. Where control is the motivation, caution is warranted. You need to clarify what astrology can and cannot do. You cannot sic Saturn onto this young person and straighten him or her out. A reading of this sort is not a substitute for therapy when there are serious conflicts or behavior problems. It cannot scare a young person out of a drug problem. It is not a birth control method. You would do well to talk parents who are having serious problems with their children into going for family counseling or to a parent group—which you just happen to have the phone number for. Otherwise you may be caught in the middle in a most unpleasant way.

The Question of Confidentiality and Your Teenage Client

When you talk with the parent beforehand, you also need to stress that the reading will be absolutely confidential. What is said will be just between you and the young person. You will not be sharing with the parents the information gained in the session. Unless you can agree on this issue, don't proceed. And you need to honor that commitment. Otherwise, there's no hope of any real communication between you and troubled or rebellious youngsters.

How would you deal with the subject once you have the teenager in front of you? As with any other client, you will want to assure teenage astrological clients that what is said in the chart reading is held as confidential. With this ground rule, they are more likely to be honest about what's going on than if you're seen as a potential snitch. In addition, adolescents are generally so painfully self-conscious and so desperate for acceptance that the very idea of adults talking about them is horrifying and humiliating. Can you remember how important privacy was to you in those turbulent years?

Suppose, however, that the teenager tells you something that is potentially life-threatening and therefore crucial for the parent to know? Suppose the youngster is shooting hard drugs like cocaine or is planning on running away or committing suicide? Or, suppose the youngster is being molested by another adult or family member?

In cases like these, even a licensed therapist cannot guarantee confidentiality. The parent has a legal right and even the necessity to know such things, and the therapist could be sued for not reporting it. While you couldn't be sued for malpractice, you are still potentially liable and have to take action. You would need to explain to the teenager that you must discuss this with the parent and why. You might offer to sit with the teenager while he or she tells the parent what is going on. You also need to have emergency numbers, like suicide or drug hot lines.

Is it fair, though, to swear that everything is confidential and then go back on it? In order to maintain integrity within the discussion of confidentiality, then, perhaps it is better to add a disclaimer. You might say something like, "Of course, if you told me you were shooting drugs or planning on doing away with yourself, then your parents would have to know. Anything else is between you and me." Pregnancy, incidentally, is not a life-threatening condition and will sooner or later reveal itself. In my opinion, the young woman who tells you she is pregnant should retain the right to confidentiality. You would do well, however, to suggest that she talk to a health professional who would help her discuss it with her parents.

Given the complexity of confidentiality with an adolescent, the routine discussion you would have with any client of whether to tape the session becomes serious. You might want to ask whether the young person feels privacy would be respected with regard to the tape. Bringing it up and discussing it in an understanding way shows that you respect their need for privacy.

You need to know, however, that there's no reciprocity in this agreement. In the heat of a future battle with the parent, the teenager can and will throw up in the parent's face anything and everything you said—or could conceivably have been construed as saying—or didn't say but felt. "That astrologer you sent me to said I didn't need to go to college." Choose your words carefully—with all teens, not just the troubled ones—with an ear to how they could sound quoted out of context.

The Actual Session with a Teenager

Self-awareness and honest self-examination of where you stand with teens is as crucial in preparing for the reading as finding all the aspects and transits. Teens are particularly acute in seeing through adult hypocracy—it's their job. Whenever you are anything but honest with them—or yourself—they will catch it immediately and let you know in no uncertain terms. Straight speaking, albeit in a gentle and respectful way, is probably your best shot with this age group. If you don't know something, say so. Don't try to fake anything.

Establishing rapport is likely to be different from establishing rapport with an adult and not always easy. Remembering yourself and your confusion in that phase can give you empathy and understanding of young people's struggles. Reading about teenagers, looking at their books and magazines, and listening to their music will remind you of what that time of life is like, as well as giving you a base for communication. (Recall, however, that any slang you may pick up has a life cycle of about three months.)

In order to start off well, you need to discover and align yourself behind what teens would see as a need the consultation could meet. Most teens have never had a chart done before and thus won't know what is possible. You might start by mentioning typical adolescent concerns it could shed light on—like friends, school, and dating. Focus on those concerns without a hidden agenda of your own. The microcosm of the adolescent's world will lead you naturally into any problem you may see in the chart. However, you are unlikely to get anywhere unless you listen seriously and respectfully to the matters that interest and trouble them. Remember how dramatic the teen years are, where a pimple can be a major social catastrophe, and don't minimize their concerns.

If the reading was arranged because the parent consciously or unconsciously expects you to straighten their son or daughter out, you are probably in for it. Adolescents rebel against adult authority—again, that's their job. The more controlling the parent, the more rebellious the child is likely to be. Potentially strong defiance will show up in the chart as a strong Uranus influence, natally or by transit. You will doubtlessly have to contend with some degree of defiance even if the preparation for this reading has been flawless. If you are seen as an adult authority figure aligned with the parent, a troubled teen is going to be just about as thrilled to see you as if the parents sent him or her to a shrink. In these instances, the work of establishing rapport and of focusing the reading around the young person's own concerns is even more important and even more difficult.

Sex and the Teenage Years

Sex is a specific issue that may come up in the reading and one to handle delicately. Detailed discussion of sexuality exceeds our province as astrologers, unless we also have other qualifications. I am not in any way meaning to imply that this is a subject we should take it upon ourselves to raise in the reading. If one did so consistently, it might even be suggested that it was for prurient interest. The reason for this segment, however, is that the topic is bound to come up if teenagers feel safe in confiding in you. Foot soldiers don't need to be demolition experts, but they'd better know what to do with the mines that are directly in their path.

Parents, by and large, are terrified that their teenagers might be having sex. It is hard for them to even contemplate. For instance, one of my students brought in the chart of her 16-year-old daughter, who had Scorpio rising and Pluto crossing it by transit. The woman was freaked out about the transit, convinced that her daughter was going to die, just as her elderly mother did when Pluto crossed her Ascendant. My student was a staunch and very ladylike Catholic. She didn't know whether to be more relieved or alarmed when I pointed out gently that a more realistic concern at age 16 would be whether the girl was having her first sexual experiences.

Teenagers are likely to be thinking about sex, even if they are not actively engaging in it. How do you talk about it to either parent or teen if it comes up? How comfortable are you in talking about sex, in general? How comfortable would you be discussing birth control?

If these topics are hard for you, perhaps it would be helpful to practice discussing them out loud with a friend or on a tape. It might also be helpful to read some books for parents on sex education.

As with any deeply personal subject, your own feelings, judgments, and blind spots are likely to interfere unless you practice self-awareness and self-discipline. This would be equally true whether you were inhibited about sex or whether it was your favorite sport. Put your own feelings and judgments, pro or con, aside in favor of empathic understanding of the adolescent. If the area is too embarrassing, the best practice might be to suggest that the teen talk to the parent or, if that is too difficult, to a guidance counselor, nurse, or other professional.

Teenagers could find it both embarrassing and invasive for a stranger to introduce the topic. Let the question come from them, although you may subtly let them know that the door is open for such discussion. If the young woman with Pluto crossing her Ascendant had come to me for a reading, for instance, I might have asked whether her relationships with guys were becoming more intense and if she was having difficulty handling them.

Remember that there are major controversies in many cities and towns about sex education. Parents have been known to throw huge demonstrations at school over the issue. We are not talking about a rational subject, even when the parent is otherwise a rational and even liberal-minded individual. Thus, phrase anything you say with great delicacy, as it is very likely to get back to the parent. In the heat of battle, a teen is likely to say, "The astrologer said it's normal for me to be experimenting with sex at this age."

Today young people face some new and painful questions—are you ready for them? It was heartbreaking when a cute young college student in my astrology class came for a reading to ask whether her boyfriend, whom she was sleeping with, had AIDS, due to some symptoms she had observed. It certainly was one possibility, as she also had a Scorpio Ascendant, a strong Pluto natally, and transiting Pluto crossing the Ascendant. Most people who die of AIDS are in their early to middle 20s, and it is spreading rapidly among heterosexual youth. Since the disease appears to take several years to reach a critical stage, many of the victims got it when they were teenagers. How well informed are you about AIDS? In such an instance, could you talk comfortably and knowledgeably about safe sex? If not, perhaps you should read about it and practice discussing it with a friend.

Adolescence—The Age of Identity Formation

Even after you negotiate the possible stumbling blocks we've discussed, the session should be different from a reading for an adult. Teens are—and need to be—very focused on the present and on themselves, because this is the age of self-discovery and the formation of an identity. They are insatiably curious about themselves and all their possibilities, almost obsessed with the question of "Who am I?" Because the natal chart is a map of the self and its potentialities, a natal reading can be exciting for both of you.

This age is a major one in terms of defining one's identity. Thus, the things you tell young people about themselves could easily become fixed features in their self-concept. You would want to focus heavily on the strengths and abilities shown in the chart, and on the constructive expressions of any difficult placement. Focus on talents, gifts, and assets—remember to look for quintiles. Downplay limitations—they will, after all improve with age—and keep any assessments conditional. Your interpretations may well stay with them and form part of their identity. Thirty years from now, they'll still be saying, "I went to an astrologer when I was young, and he said I'd never be any good at business."

Should You Tell a Teenager's Future?

Too much prognostication about the distant future is ill-advised, even if the teen is asking for it. Here again, you don't want to be Oedipus' soothsayer and create a self-fulfilling prophecy. Given teens' notorious propensity for drama, they might find it interesting to act out your worst predictions, sooner rather than later.

Teens are not that focused on the future, except in very romantic and unrealistic ways—like believing that they'll be a movie star or marry someone rich and gorgeous. It can be devastating to put too much attention on the unlikely prognosis of these adolescent dreams. We all outgrow them, but only in our own time, and they serve a purpose while they are with us. Nor should you give too much attention to the difficult areas of the chart as they relate to adulthood rather than the now. Extreme gentleness is in order. Imagine how you would have felt if you were 15 and an astrologer told you something negative and fatalistic.

For example, you would not tell a hopelessly romantic teenage girl with burgeoning hormones and Pluto in the 7th that she might marry a real bastard who wouldn't let her out of the house. Talk, instead, about how she might be attracted to passionate and possessive fellows, but that as romantic as that might seem in the beginning, she might wind up feeling suffocated by that possessiveness. You might engage her in a discussion of boyfriends she's already had who were like that and what went wrong in those relationships. You are planting a seed that may take hold and make her think twice, but you're not coming down like the Oracle of Doom. Again, like poor Oeddy, if you were too negative, her life might be rearranged to avoid your prophecy. She decides never to marry because she can't trust men—another interpretation of Pluto in the 7th!

Likewise, you wouldn't tell a motherly little Cancer with Saturn in the 5th that she might never have kids. What you might say instead would be that her own family might be small or come later in life, but that a career involving children would be highly rewarding to her. Stress that with her strong sense of responsibility she could make a fine contribution in that field.

By focusing on current situations that are forerunners of adulthood, you may be able to help the teen learn to use difficult chart positions more consciously. That way, the most negative potentials of those placements can be avoided. Almost any situation that is currently important to the teen has its adult equivalent. Dating issues can be similar to problems they will meet in marriage, problems with parents may be similar to those they may encounter with bosses, and concerns about acceptance by peers can be similar to those they would meet in adult social life. If teens can use the session to gain the insight to handle today's problems intelligently, they will have tools to approach adult difficulties intelligently as well. That outcome is all you can hope for in reading charts at any age, and it is service well done.

A Final Word

Given all the cautions mentioned in this chapter, and all the issues involved in reading for underage clients, you must by now wonder if it should be done at all. It can be very helpful if done well—and very harmful if done by Oeddy's astrologer. The self-watchfulness we need to exercise in any chart reading should be doubled and tripled when we are dealing with the chart of a young person still in the formative stages. Still, done well, there is room for the development of pediatric astrology as a specialization within the field.

CHAPTER EIGHT

Building Your Astrological Practice

In order to succeed as an astrologer, you have to get comfortable with selling. How comfortable were you with selling cookies or candy bars for your scout troop or parochial school? Have you been procrastinating about advertising? Perhaps you feel funny promoting yourself. Knowing and *accepting* the basic principles of sales and promotion can make the difference between being a successful professional astrologer and just surviving.

Yes, advertising *is* sales. Unless you can get past that emotional hurdle, you may not be able to reach the people who could benefit from your services—the very people you studied so hard to be able to help. Examining and working through resistances to promoting your services, as we will do in this chapter, may well be a prerequisite to building a practice. We will explore your barriers to self-promotion and to charging a fee for your work. We will also look at some marketing ideas, including how to compose effective ads and bios.

"What do you charge?" Did that question throw you for a loop? The most painful topic for the beginning astrologer—or even many an experienced one—to discuss with clients is the fee. We are not immune to grappling with issues about money, even doing such "enlightened and spiritual" work as astrology. Discomfort over setting a price for your services unnecessarily clouds the issue of going professional. It creates additional stress when you're trying to make that transition. Concerns about fees are distinct from the issue of whether you happen to be a good astrologer. Yet, your comfortability with charging for your services affects your success. If you feel you don't deserve an adequate fee, then you're going to have difficulty in building a practice. For that reason, let's start this chapter with a substantial discussion of feelings and attitudes about money.

There are many reasons for your discomfort. You don't come to the question, "What do you charge for an astrology reading?" in a vacuum. You come to it with the total of your own experiences with money, your emotionally-charged family programming, and the mixed messages society gives. (On one hand, it's the root of all evil, but on the other hand, you're nobody if you don't wear Reeboks.) There are even factors peculiar to the astrological world which influence us, like our group poverty consciousness.

Furthermore, the better the handle we have on our own money issues, the better we will be able to help clients with theirs. Many clients ask about money problems—mainly couched in future-oriented questions like, "When are my finances going to improve?" Many will come in a chronic financial mess, due to 2nd and 8th house complexes. We need to get comfortable talking about financial attitudes and practices. Statistics show that money worries are far and away the most common cause of marital disagreements. Since a high proportion of clients come about relationship problems, you need to be comfortable asking whether money strains are contributing to these as well.

If you heal your own prosperity issues, then you have suggestions for clients who come with similar issues. You can make recommendations out of the confidence of having used them successfully. Otherwise, it's like a blind healer telling a blind client, "Just do this and you'll be able to see."

The Psychology of Money in Our Culture

Money is a convoluted and emotionally charged issue, and we assign tremendous power to it. We're ambivalent and receive mixed messages. You have to have it to be socially acceptable, but it's not socially acceptable to be too eager to make it—then you're a money grubber. Talking about money is a taboo with strong emotion attached. What do you think of someone who is so bold as to ask personal questions about what you earn, what you have in the bank, what you owe, or what your car cost? You, too, may hesitate to bring up such a loaded topic.

When someone asks what you charge, that's not a comfortable question either. It's like making a public declaration of what you think you're worth. It's not just a question we face once in a while, but each time we talk to a prospective client. We have to desensitize ourselves, or this inevitable question will be a stumbling block. Work on getting comfortable with saying it, perhaps by role playing it over and over with friends or fellow students.

You're also dealing with clients and their values, which are essentially not your problem. One of my therapy clients would come sporting a fur coat, designer boots, and a Gucci bag, and she insisted she could only pay the minimum. In certain California communities, people with diamonds on their false fingernails and vanity plates on their big cars say they just couldn't afford more than $5 for an evening astrology lecture. There are New Yorkers who spend $100 on a dinner for two and pay $500 a month for therapy who think we shouldn't charge more than $50 for a consultation. Part of the answer may be to do a better job of selling people on the value of astrology.

Money and the Helping Fields

It is an additional point of sensitivity when someone is coming for help and then you have to talk about how much it will cost them. We're not alone in being uncomfortable. Therapists are not immune, even those who do not conceive of their work as being spiritual. Part of their training is in how to deal with money issues. Whole therapy sessions are spent on fees—especially when the therapist has had the nerve to raise the rate a big $5 after several years of sessions. Clients might have to pay $75 to talk about how they feel about paying $75. So you're not alone in the discomfort—you're in some very good company!

Nobody wants to pay for getting help. It's a leftover Moon thing—Mommy should just take care of us and not ask for anything in return. Every human being at some level has this desire and expectation, but astrologers hook into it and say, "Oh, they're right. We shouldn't charge." It is an unfortunate fact of life that as adults we have to pay Mommy, but we can resent it. While you may perceive the neediness or the resentment and take it personally, you have as much right to payment for being Mommy as any other professional.

Therapists get ulcers over the same questions. However, they have strong professional associations and a legitimate status that says they are entitled to a certain fee, while we do not. They also have networks of supervisors and colleagues who will say, "Oh, clients are like that. They always complain about the fee. But we're worth it."

Beliefs and Attitudes that Get in the Way

The most typical reasons beginning astrologers give for why they don't charge more than a minimum are things like: "I'm not good enough. I don't know enough. I can't predict 100 percent." Doctors, lawyers, economists and other prognosticators can't predict anywhere near 100 percent either, but they charge plenty for their educated guesses.

When people ask, "What do you charge?" it comes down to a question of, "What am I worth?" When you tell them and then people say no, in effect, it's like they are saying, "No, you're not worth that." On some level, however rational we try to be, it's a rejection. When you sell a product—even one you didn't make—it's hard enough to take the *no*s and keep on selling. When what you're selling is yourself—your knowledge, your wisdom, your intuition, your heart—rejections become much harder to take.

Part of the solution to the discomfort is to work on self-esteem. Even when your self-esteem is decent, however, public attitudes about astrology and about seeking help of any kind affect us. We are still often viewed as fortune-tellers. Astrology is not held in the same respect as other professions. It is okay for a doctor or a lawyer to charge a lot of money, even though no one likes to pay it, but people think we should not!

It is also self-sabotage not to get paid the right amount. It can affect your confidence, and then prospective clients pick up on it. They may think, "Well, she obviously doesn't think she's very good, so she must not be very good. Let me go to someone else." Even if they do come, your lack of confidence, as reflected in how you deal with money, can make clients less confident in your work.

It also ultimately affects how you feel about doing readings. If you resent working so hard for so little, that response can bleed through into the consultation. Clients think everything you do relates to their chart. They might think your anger means that their chart reveals that they are loathsome people. Or, suppose a wealthy client is asking about stock holdings while you can barely pay the rent. It would be hard not to let some degree of envy spill over into the reading.

There are also a variety of spiritual traditions that reinforce not being paid enough—or paid at all—for service work and especially for work like ours with some divine dimension. Many of us come from long and dimly remembered incarnational histories in cloisters, convents, and ashrams where physical needs were met in exchange for hard labor, but money was not involved. People with Neptune in the 2nd, 6th, or 10th may be strongly influenced by such histories. Many of us during those lifetimes took vows of poverty which we may need to consciously release ourselves from. (A simple written statement will do it.)

Even where we are not still affected, the culture dimly remembers and expects us to continue in unpaid service. We need to be aware of such undercurrents during the discussion of fees so that we aren't tempted to charge less than we are worth. Once again the New Age and the "old" age dovetail, for there is a great deal of guilt and ambivalence among New Age practitioners about charging for their work, even though the expressed reasons may be different. Those of us with Flower Child fallout may also find that the 60s left an imprint that we need to address.

I'm not suggesting that astrological practice should be a path to riches, just that we deserve to be paid for our hard work, as much as anyone else. When someone genuinely needs a reading and doesn't have my fee, there are a variety of ways I handle it. Sometimes I trade, provided the person has a skill that I need, and sometimes I refer a person to a good but less experienced astrologer who charges less. Few people place a high value on freebies.

How Cultural Programming Affects Women Astrologers

We women astrologers also got the programming about how women were just supposed to take care of people, and we feel guilty for charging. We are socialized into the Mommy role, even if we never have children, and it comes up when someone needs us. This may be particularly true of the homemaker. She may be a very fine astrologer who has studied for years. She may give clients a grounded wisdom gained from her rich life experience in raising a family. However, she has had plenty of practice at being Mommy and has learned to meet all needs unselfishly and without asking for anything in return. Her clients often get away with murder, calling her for advice at any time of the day or night without a charge.

Generally speaking, her prices are low—and it unfortunately depresses the rate for the rest of us. She may rationalize that her husband brings in most of the income. She may feel she doesn't have "a real job," after all, just something to bring in a little extra. She also may not need to charge as much as someone does whose sole income is from astrology. If you are a housewife/astrologer, please learn to value your worth correctly.

Despite all the progress in career options, the women in any given profession are still underpaid in comparison to the men. No matter how enlightened we would like to think we are, this can even be true in astrology. In any given astrology organization, there are generally no more than four or five men to a hundred women, but the men are more likely to be officers. The men who are professionals do better in income and recognition, by and large, than the women. The majority of clients are women. They carry the old and far from eradicated cultural beliefs that men know more and are more capable. Many of these same clients might hesitate to go to a female doctor. So, like women in all the professions, women astrologers have to work a little harder to show their competence and also work on themselves to overcome the programming.

Ironically, the Women's Movement itself may have added another layer of ambivalence on women astrologers about fees. We who have some feminist sympathies are prone to guilt about charging our "sisters" who are having a bad time of it financially. If we charge what we are worth, we may be subjected to pressure and shaming from the women's community. We may even be subjected to the ultimate shame—being told we are politically incorrect!

Don't single mothers and other disadvantaged women deserve a break? Of course they do, but there needs to be some balance. When a practice consists mainly of disadvantaged women, the astrologer herself winds up being still another disadvantaged woman. In such situations, I prefer to trade my work for an amount of work of equivalent value, as this preserves the dignity of the other person. It empowers the client to be able to use work to gain something of value.

Low self-esteem is a perennial theme in consultations with women clients. Women don't gain self-esteem through being objects of charity. When we women astrologers undervalue our work, it sends a message to women clients that they should undervalue both our work and their own. We may be talking about self-worth, but demonstrating the opposite. Rest assured, behavior has a greater impact than words, so if you want to teach self-esteem, practice it!

Dysfunctional Backgrounds and Money

As discussed earlier, people from alcoholic or dysfunctional backgrounds may be drawn to practice astrology because it is typical for them to want to rescue and save others. We tried hard but were never able to fix our families. No one can fix another person, but we may carry that unrealistic expectation over to our work with clients. Then, we feel we aren't any good when we don't succeed in fixing them.

Many students of astrology from backgrounds like these have a particularly painful problem with self-worth. They may find it especially difficult to feel entitled to charge a decent amount for their services. John Bradshaw has identified toxic shame as a major result of such backgrounds. Work on shame can be crucial in overcoming self-esteem problems that make potential astrologers feel that they are not good enough to be paid for their work.

People from addictive homes—alcohol, gambling, whatever—also tend to have dysfunctional attitudes about money, which they picked up from their parents. Addicted people tend to have grandiose ideas and are not well-grounded. Their children may either take on these ungrounded attitudes, even if they do not have an addiction, or they may be overly cautious and over-striving in order to feel safe.

What Should You Charge?

Now that we've examined some of the barriers, let's get back to the question of fees. When you are starting out, there is a place for an apprenticeship period when you charge small fees or you read for friends free just for practice. You can't learn enough astrology from books. You really begin to see how it works when you do charts—or pieces of charts—for live people. Medical students do years and years of unpaid work before they become doctors. You wouldn't expect to pay a medical student the same as you would a brain surgeon. Trading readings with other advanced students is one way to get practice—and you can learn more about your own chart.

When doing charts for free goes on too long, you might begin to suspect that the motive comes from issues around money or self-worth. Still, at a certain point you will undoubtedly feel you now know enough to charge something. For paid readings, you may also be starting with people you know—like friends or co-workers. If so, the relationship may also create discomfort when setting a price.

In a sense, *you need to charge what makes you comfortable*, even if there is a standard rate. No one can tell you what your fee ought to be, whether it is more or less than the going rate. The astrological world is affected with a poverty consciousness, so many astrologers and even students tend to disapprove of people who charge high rates.

There's also a point at which it's helpful to raise your prices. In other lines of work, for every year or so of experience, you get a raise. When you work for yourself, you also need to declare periodic raises. Not only will the client take you more seriously, but you will, too. Like most people, we judge our worth partially by how much we make. If we charge more, we tend to think we're worth more. Strangely enough, we may work harder and expect more from ourselves after a raise. Just like salaried employees who are given a merit increase, we may stretch ourselves to be worth the new price. In going from $125 to $150, I felt I had to stretch myself to be just that much better. I experienced anxiety during readings for a while, but, lo and behold, my readings did get better. Your work may also get better if you charge a little more.

Talking to Clients about Fees

It is stressful to talk about what you charge, no two ways about it. It's stressful to me, even after doing it for twenty-four years. Salaried employees only have to talk about salaries on job interviews or when negotiating for the occasional raise. As astrologers, we have to negotiate fees as a condition for our employment whenever a potential client calls. Doctors and lawyers also get fees for each client. How do they handle discussing their prices? They have their receptionist or billing department take care of those tacky transactions!

You need to get comfortable with saying what you charge. Practice saying it out loud. Say it in the shower. Have your friends telephone pretending to be possible clients. Once, when raising my prices to a level that wasn't comfortable, I wrote the amount on a pad by the phone. Then, if I couldn't get the words out any other way, I would just pick up the pad and read: "I charge . . . "

Do you ever find yourself justifying what you charge? Justifying it to yourself is okay—that's part of the inner process. You may tell yourself how much time it takes you, how long you've been studying. You may even talk it out with friends and colleagues as part of getting comfortable. For me, the justification is that the client is going to get much more out of this session than from several with a psychiatrist. So, I find out what the going rate is for a psychiatric visit—then I double it.

You are better off not justifying it to the client, though. It destroys confidence and respect—your own in yourself, the client's in you. It betrays a lack of sureness that you're worth it, and clients will manipulate around that. It is an entirely different thing to *explain* your fee to a client, yet there's a fine line. Suppose the client asks for a rectification, and you say, "That's $100." The client says, "Why so much?" So, you explain exactly what you do when you—or any astrologer—rectify a chart. Or, let's say it's a relationship chart.

You explain that it is necessary to calculate and interpret both charts, then see how the charts fit together, and then do the composite. You could say exactly the same words, and if the feeling behind it was defensive, then it would be justification rather than explanation.

How do you handle it when the first question callers ask is, "What do you charge?" It feels like they're going to accept or reject you on the basis of your reply. Pass on answering that question the first time around, because otherwise you are going to have a very short conversation. You might say, "That depends on what you want." Then explore what they need, as described in chapter One. From that discussion, clients get a sense that you can offer something that they need. So, you've already shown your worth, and the question of fees takes on a different tone. Also, many astrologers have a menu of services, with different prices for different kinds of work.

A second question clients may ask is, "What does that include?" (Translation: "What am I getting for my money?") Some astrologers have things they give the client, like premiums. Some write out a few things for clients or use beautiful graphics so that the chart is practically frameable. Some buy a computerized chart interpretation program and do a printout for the client as part of the package. I always use the tape as a selling point, and all clients get a copy of the chart.

Many callers want to bargain. It's almost a ritual with them—they feel like they haven't been smart shoppers unless they bargained. There are cultures, too, where bargaining is an expected part of doing business. Some clients ask you to knock off something if they provide a computer chart they already have. Do it if you want to, but don't do it with hand-calculated charts, because you never know about the accuracy. (Also, over the years many clients give differing birth times to different astrologers.) It's just important to detach and know that the bargaining has nothing to do with your worth.

Some callers want free samples. Some demonstration of the astrologer's abilities is not amiss, but the free samples type is rarely serious about coming for an appointment. They are usually the ones who ask you to guess their sign and want to know how that sign goes with their newest flame's sign.

GROUP EXERCISE

The group forms a circle, pairs facing each other. One person in the pair is to be the astrologer, the other is the potential client, and they discuss fees. The client gives the astrologer somewhat of a hard time. When this is complete, the client of the pair passes to the astrologer of the next pair, and they do it again. After a few such changes, the client becomes the astrologer. This helps you practice saying what you charge, and also gives you an idea of what others charge and how they handle their discussion of fees.

Confronting Another S Word—Sales

Now that you've decided on a fee, it's time to look at some marketing ideas. One way to get more comfortable is to understand that you aren't selling *yourself*, you're selling services. Put yourself and your self-consciousness aside and focus on the prospective client, just as you would during a reading. Remember, people primarily want to know WIIFM—"What's in it for me?" Whether they articulate it or not, that will be the question in back of their minds. If you don't answer it quickly, you lose them. I've heard it said that, when it is a product, people make the actual decision to buy within 20 seconds, even though the sale may take longer. Most commercials aren't much longer than that. Even though we would hope it takes longer to decide about a service, be aware that you need to prove your usefulness in very short order.

Put potential clients first by finding out right away what they need. Chapter One suggested that you begin by asking, "What do you need to get from a reading now?" That way, clients get the message that you can put *their* needs first. When you have the answer, your pitch is focused in on exactly what they are looking for. You tell them what you can do that will fill that need. This will be more effective than raving about how uplifting and spiritual astrology is and how you ought to know your signs.

Sell yourself only when you have thoroughly sold the need for your services. As a rule of thumb, spend less than a third of the encounter or ad space talking about yourself and two-thirds about the client. Spend most of the time talking about how astrology could help them in their situation. Only when you've thoroughly sold them on that, go to why you're the right person. Go easy on that. Mention your credentials by all means—we'll talk later about how to make up a bio or ad—but don't make this an ego trip. The potential client will lose interest very quickly if you talk too much about yourself.

Another point of view is that sales is communication. Mercury was the god of commerce, after all. In order to determine how astrology could help prospective clients, you have to ask them. In your willingness to listen and to explain astrology to them, they will see that you are a good source of understandable information. They will not respond well to incomprehensible and mystifying jargon about aspects and midpoints and solar arc.

Is It Selling or Is It Education?

One helpful way to look at encounters with potential clients is that many times you aren't so much selling them as you are educating them about what astrology can do. Wouldn't that encounter feel different if you felt you were teaching something—sharing your knowledge—than if you saw it only as selling? It will feel different to them, too—more human and helpful.

To that end, ask if they've had readings before or studied any astrology. That way you identify astrological virgins and devote more energy to educating them. You've been in astrology for so long that you may have forgotten your first experiences. Put yourself for a few moments in the shoes of people who have never had a chart done. In talking to them, it would be helpful to restore those memories—maybe of your first reading and how stunning it was if it was done well.

Do you remember how exciting astrology was that first year you studied it? Remember that heady feeling of being in touch with something special? Try to recall the joy of self-discovery that came from getting to know your chart. Recapture that excitement and convey it to the person you are talking to. Possibly you could retrieve those memories through a meditation where you regressed yourself year by year to that time of discovery. Capturing and storing that excitement and then tapping into it will convey to potential clients the worth and fun of this method. You're not going to be full of enthusiasm all the time, especially if the clients come with serious problems, but it does help in putting yourself across.

Those who've had readings before are what salespeople call "qualified prospects." In other words, they are the best prospects because they are already receptive and sincerely interested in astrology. They just need to justify why another reading would be a good thing to have now. They already know something about astrology and what it can do. However, they may or may not have a grasp of the additional possibilities,depending on how good that astrologer was at educating them.

For example, maybe they had a natal reading with transits. Do they understand why periodic updates are a good idea? You would want to find out how long ago the reading was. Give them some idea of how the planetary picture has changed—for instance, what signs Saturn and Jupiter are in now as opposed to then. From asking the exact birthdate, you would know the approximate degree of the Sun. You would know whether any of the outer planets are likely to transit the Sun this year—or last. Not that you give people detailed readings, but you can give enough to let them see whether a reading is in order.

You might also mention any current major configurations that may be affecting them. If you get people talking about their lives, you'll hear Uranus or Neptune or Pluto in what they say. For instance, you're sitting with someone at a party, and they're saying, "I want to change my job, but I really don't know what else I'd want to do. I just know that there's got to be more than this." Chances are, Neptune is in one of the career houses or aspecting the Midheaven. Tell them it sounds like Neptune, but that you couldn't know for sure if it was that or when it would change without seeing their complete chart.

Suppose they had a natal reading some time ago, but they're thinking of moving to Seattle. (Nowadays, everyone's thinking of moving to Seattle. I'm considering giving group rates.) Talk to them about a relocation chart, or about an Astro*Carto*Graphy map, which you could order for them. With these tools, you would be able to show them the influences in effect there and also the optimal timing for the move. Especially when people move under a Neptune transit to the Moon or MC-IC axis, they're not moving *to* something they're moving *away from* something. Such people have the fantasy that all their problems will be solved by the move. They may relocate and then spin their wheels for six months or longer without finding a job. Talk about how essential timing is and how getting this reading can save them time, money, and stress. Incidentally, I've found that it's rather difficult to keep a mailing list current. So many clients come under strong Uranus transits—Uranus being the ruler of astrology. And, what else do people do under Uranus transits but move?

Suppose they've met someone—explain about composites or synastry as a way of understanding the other party and the relationship. It may also be time to look at their own horoscopes for relationship patterns they would need to change to make this one work. A birthday coming up? Why, you can't have a birthday without a solar return chart! That is, if you like doing solar returns—if you don't like them, don't sell them. Many people want to take stock of their lives around their birthday, so they may be ready for a transit reading. (Some astrologers send birthday cards to their clients as a reminder.)

Suppose they're thinking of going into business. You *never, ever* start a business without finding the astrologically correct moment. Astrology is one tool, but it has endless applications. It has something to offer in practically any situation. There's always something more astrology can do for you—that's why it holds our interest as students for so long. The trick is in identifying exactly what the client wants and then selling the technique that fits it.

The Fine Line Between Promotion and Hype

When you read the ads of New Age entrepreneurs, many sound like snake oil salesmen. "Just take our green algae sixteen times a day, at a mere $200 a month, and you'll have perfect health, more money, a better sex life, and you need not ever die." If you see the three catch words *money*, *love*, and *health* in one ad, you can be sure it's hype. Pick up New Age newspapers and magazines and read through the ads, noticing which ones don't convince you or turn you off, as opposed to the ones which make you feel like calling. If you keep reading ads, you'll develop a sense of what's genuine and effective, so that you can model your ads and promotional literature on them.

Although we can learn from the world of advertising, ads for New Age media have special requirements. We want to present a clear, accurate, honest picture of our services. There's a very delicate task to accomplish. You need to promote yourself and your services, and yet, you do not want to go into hype. Spiritual hype is repellent. Friends and acquaintances especially despise being hustled. You can share what you're into now—friends do that. Don't pressure people to have a consultation or to refer people, or you've lost both a customer and a friend.

The important thing to understand is that if it's hype, prospective clients will know it and be turned off. If you're convinced that the current planetary lineup has relevance and that knowing about it will help them, then that conviction will come across. If you don't believe you can help, they will intuit that as well. Understand that you don't have to be able to *solve* the problem, only throw light on it. Sometimes just knowing that there really is something happening, that they're not going crazy, and that it will pass is a relief. It gives them a perspective on the pain.

Where is that fine line between selling and hype? How can you avoid crossing it? First, never claim to do what you cannot. Suppose clients ask questions about the stock market and you don't know a bull from a bear. Say so and refer them to someone who does. They will respect you for the honesty. It was a great relief to recognize that I had my limits and wasn't good at every area of astrology—and that it was all right. It pays to know your strengths and deficits and get to work on the deficits. Be honest with yourself about what they are, as the lack of real knowledge will come through.

Second, avoid hype by listening to clients and focusing on what they need, rather than jumping in every chance you get to tell them how great you are. Relate to what they are saying by explaining how your service can help with that problem or need. It boils down to coming out of the heart center—from caring—rather than the solar plexus—which is ego.

The Myths of Scarcity and Competition

The idea that competition is a threat is based on the myth of scarcity. There is no scarcity of potential clients, only a scarcity of astrologers with the imagination, courage, and know-how to go out and find them. There are new astrology clients born every day. According to the National Center for Health Statistics, over 4 million babies were born in the United States in 1989. (The year 1989 is simply the year for which the most complete statistics are available as this is written. In most respects, we would assume the year in which you are reading this would be similar.)

Did you know that there were almost two-and-a-half million weddings in the U.S. in 1989? An astonishing number of these couples got married on the last two Saturdays in June. By looking at the charts for those days, any astrologer could have told them they were making a big mistake! They could either have used a chart comparison before they got married or an electional chart to choose a better day. Among them are a big group who might have had natal readings earlier but who are now entering a partnership that astrology could shed some light on.[1]

Did you know that 682,000 new businesses incorporated in the USA during 1988? Eight out of ten businesses fail in the first year. Electional charts and advice about timing for advertising and other activities could help many of them. Did you know that 17 percent of the population in the USA moved in the two year period 1987–1988, with 2.7 percent moving to a different state? That's four million people who moved, and 650,000 who moved to a different state. That's a lot of relocation charts and Astro*Carto*Graphy interpretations.[2]

Granted, not all these people believe in astrology—although we could do a better job of reaching skeptics and could learn skills for dealing with them. However, 65 percent believe at least enough to read their daily horoscopes. Therefore, there are many potential clients. We just need the confidence to reach out and the verbal skills to sell our services. We can't sit back and wait for them and, when they do not come, complain about how bad business is and how nobody appreciates astrology. Most don't even know where to look for us or how we could help.

---

[1]Birth and marriage statistics come from the National Center for Health Statistics, *Monthly Vital Statistics Report*, V. 38:12, from two articles: "Advance Report of Final Marriage Statistics, 1987," and "Births, Marriages, Divorces, and Deaths for 1989."
[2]The statistics on business and relocation come from *Statistical Abstract of the United States*, 1990 edition. Business statistics appeared on p. 530, and moving statistics on p. 19.

The biggest mistake astrologers make is in not tapping new markets like the ones just discussed. Instead, they tend to compete for the same old ones—the people who are already involved in the New Age and have already had a few chart readings. In her workshops and books, movie star Shirley MacLaine did us a favor by introducing New Age teachings to millions who never paid attention to them before. Many of those people would now be receptive to chart readings.

Success may well mean establishing a new beachhead for yourself. Reach out and educate more people who will want to know about themselves through astrology. You might give talks, even free ones, to business luncheons, at libraries, the PTA, or to your club or social group. Over lunch, show your coworkers what a chart looks like. Explain why they're not just their Sun sign, that there's a Moon sign and a rising sign and more. Perhaps you could have informal evenings where you give a talk about astrology and do sample readings. If you have a talent for it, write articles for your local newspaper or go on the radio. There are many ways to reach out, wherever you live and whatever your level of knowledge.

Finding Your Niche

Astrologers who fear competition are off base, because we each can create our own niche and therefore our own market. We each know a different circle of people, with potential referrals rippling off from that. For instance, you may begin to find clients through coworkers, your circle of friends, neighbors, and relatives, a social club, or a political or environmental action group. Except in a small town, no two astrologers know exactly the same people. We begin to establish a clientele by word of mouth from our own friends, relatives, and coworkers to the friends of friends, relatives, and coworkers, and so on from there.

Toothpaste is toothpaste, but advertising creates a market for dozens of brands, all new and improved. Astrology is essentially the same everywhere—there's a variety of asteroids and techniques—but astrologers are different. When you go to a major conference, there are bound to be twenty-five speakers with twenty-five different points of view and twenty-five specialties. Uranus, the ruler of astrology, has to do with discovering and expressing our uniqueness. Each astrologer brings a unique history, background, and set of skills to the profession. We each have a curriculum vita in its literal sense, which has nothing to do with college credits. It's useful to think about your life history to find out what is unique about you. Digest those life circumstances that make you special.

First, what jobs have you had? Suppose your background is in sales. You may not want to do that any more, but you are several steps ahead of the astrologer who has no sales training. This important skill can be turned to marketing yourself and also gives you an expertise that you can use to advise business people. If you worked in business, use that background to help clients who want to start a business, or help young people looking to have a business career. If you were a teacher, you have valuable information about children and education. Your niche might be working with parents of children who are having school problems.

You say you have no experience? Unless you've been in suspended animation since birth, that cannot be so. All our life history has potential value—nothing we did before astrology was a waste of time. Wisdom gained of experience is an asset to an astrologer. Think about what your particular circumstances have been and what you've learned that you can teach others. Suppose that you devoted the last fifteen years to being a wife and raising children. Your skills give you much to offer younger wives and mothers. Suppose you took care of an elderly parent? You have something to offer the great number of middle-aged people who are confronting the stresses involved with aging parents.

Difficult events can also leave you with something to teach others with similar problems. Quite a few recovering alcoholics become astrologers who are helping others in recovery. They convey the higher side of Neptune in a way that is impossible for someone who's never had that problem. They can tell a fellow alcoholic that meditation and spiritual pursuits are a better high than booze, and the alcoholic will believe them. Astrologers who've barely touched a glass of wine much less gotten soused day after endless day come across as preaching and as not knowing what they're talking about. The alcoholic or addict will listen more readily to someone who can say, "Look, I've been there."

If you've lost someone important, you can understand bereaved people, and can listen to clients' pain. You can also teach them about the nature and probable course of grief—if you've done your own grief work, rather than burying the feelings. Even battered wives or survivors of incest or child abuse can use their history to help the growing number of people who are working to overcome those experiences. That is, you can help if you've worked the experience through, done some healing work, and at least partially recovered from its effects.

What do I mean by recovery? Well, I don't mean "getting over it," and doing a phony forgiveness number. I mean actually working on it in therapy, self-help groups, body work, and reading the literature. If you were unrecovered and in denial, all you'd teach would be how to suppress and deny. There are a large number of ACA astrologers who've never done any work on that issue. As we saw in chapter Five, denial and acting out of unresolved feelings about that family background can seriously affect their approach to clients in general and to ACA clients in particular.

The problem you've worked hard on and mostly overcome gives you something to offer. You wouldn't reveal the gory details of your past—it's not *your* session. If you can share one telling detail that lets them know you know, that can be powerful. Then you're not some expert pontificating, you're coming from authentic experience. For instance, when talking to bereaved clients, I might briefly share part of my own grief process: "After a while it fades, but something like a holiday brings it all back." However, the solution that worked for you may not be correct for your clients, so don't push them to adopt it.

Shared experience creates a bond that is in itself healing. The success of various self-help groups is based on this truth. I read one of those studies that get done now and then about the effectiveness of therapy. The conclusion was that what helps is *accurate, empathic understanding*. With astrology you can be devastatingly accurate, but if you're not empathic, it is destructive. Clients feel stripped, treated as a case rather than a person. Shared experience—being heard and understood—is healing in a way that no mere delineation of aspects or progressions can replace.

Think through your experiences to find out who you are, what you've done, and what you have to offer. Once you identify your niche, your special slant, or point of view, you can go after that market—if that's what you want. You may find, however, that you have a *potential* specialty, but you're not there yet. In order to be good in that identified area, you may need to do more reading or research, take related courses or workshops, and work on developing the material—or, recover some more. Take what you know and work with it until you know it thoroughly and can articulate it. Then slant your ad or brochure so others will be drawn to that knowledge.

Another part of identifying your astrological niche is finding out what you're good at—or what you most enjoy doing—and specializing in it. Chances are, that's what you'll feel most comfortable selling because the confidence and enthusiasm will come through. If you're gifted at synastry, let it become your specialty. Maybe you just love love, and you love to listen to people who are in love. You love to help them see how they could work out their relationship problems.

If you have a flair for natal interpretation, capitalize on that—some astrologers do nothing but natal charts. Some are talented at horary, or mundane astrology. Your specialty may even be unusual—say, Vedic astrology—but then you'd have to do an even better job of educating the caller about how that technique helps. However, jaded astrology clients who've gone for many readings may well be intrigued by the thought of having their chart done a whole new way.

Do what you do well and enjoy, but concentrate on getting even better at it. You will get better over time anyway, but it's worthwhile to do it to death. Grab every example you can and work it over. Read everything you can get your hands on. Work with famous people's charts like those in the four books by Lois Rodden and track their transits or progressions through biographies. If you're interested in relocation charts, collect them. Do a mini-research project on your subject. If it's composites, collect data on every couple you can get your hands on and follow that relationship by transit through every phase. Interview both parties to see what the various chart aspects meant from both sides of the picture.

Just studying astrology isn't enough. You may have an encyclopedic knowledge of astrology, but if you don't understand people and how to reach them, you won't be a good astrologer. If you decide, for instance, that vocational astrology is going to be your niche, you don't just study charts, you study careers. Whatever your astrological specialty, there are real life experts who've observed and explored that area and who can teach you more about it. You need the concepts in order to know what the difficulty may be and what solutions are available, so you can recommend where they might go for help.

I'm not talking about going back to college and getting another degree. You will be better prepared than you are today if you go to the library or a bookstore and get four or five books in your chosen field. Even if you already have a degree in your specialty, you would want to survey the literature from time to time. The knowledge base, technology, and philosophy may change. If you want to be a good astrologer, you need to know more than astrology—you need to know life.

Paying Attention to the Law of Supply and Demand

Now that I've told you to identify what is unique about yourself and build a practice around it, I'm going to contradict myself and recommend that you pay attention to the law of supply and demand. What does supply and demand mean when you apply it to an astrological practice? It means that if you are offering a service that people want, you are more likely to get clients.

We all have our own niche, but you also need to learn those skills that clients are asking for, at least at a sound, basic level. You need to be capable of all the major techniques at a certain level. Attend a workshop on Astro*Carto*Graphy, take a course on chart comparison, and so on. Still another benefit of asking prospective clients what they need is that you ultimately find out what clients do want. At least 75 percent of the time, in major cities anyway, people want to know about career and relationships. (In California, it was relationships and spiritual development!)

On a certain level, self-confidence comes with knowing your stuff. Take inventory of what you do and don't know, promote what you do know for now, and concentrate on building your practice around that. At the same time, make up the deficits. Take courses or read books, both in astrology *and* outside it, to learn more about areas where you lack information. That way you need not continue to feel inadequate.

Clients' needs change from time to time, as the outer planets change signs and fall into different configurations. No one ever asked me about incest before Pluto went into Scorpio, and now people bring up that question all the time. Pluto in Scorpio brought many secrets out into the open. As the astrological configurations change, you need to keep on top of them and their implications. Conferences where a variety of colleagues share their insights are the best way to avoid astrological tunnel vision—i.e., opinions based only on your own experience.

Dealing with the Client's Objections

One of the most important factors in sales is understanding and dealing with potential clients' objections. People who are inexperienced and uncomfortable often try to sidestep the objection and smooth it over. Listen carefully to the caller's reservations. Work with the objections, bringing them out and grappling with them rather than trying to push them aside. If the potential client goes away with an unanswered objection, you've lost the reading.

Listen carefully to clients' responses when you talk about a reading. ("I tried that, and . . . " or, "I couldn't do that because . . . ") Otherwise, they will conclude that you're too bound up in your own pet answers to hear what they have to say. Successful salespeople regard the objection as a buying signal—that is, when prospective clients care enough to object rather than just shutting you off, you know they have a degree of interest. You may be wise to ask about objections, as some clients will not bring them up. "I hear that you're hesitant. What troubles you about it?" Take the objection seriously. You're there for the client, you're listening, and you're getting their experience.

"Well, I went to an astrologer one time, and this woman was so negative, I was depressed for six weeks." Unfortunately, many people have had bad experiences with astrologers—or read negative interpretations in books. Even if you sold the client on a reading, you would want to know about that experience before your session anyway. That way, you can rectify the damage and avoid making the same mistakes. By listening to the bad experience, maybe even reacting to it, you learn a great deal. (Sometimes, when the client is disturbed, you can pick that up and conjecture that that would be what they'd say about you afterward, too! It may be part of your screening process.)

Another typical objection is that of the self-fulfilling prophecy. "I'm afraid that if I have a chart done, and you say that such and such is going to happen, I'll make it happen." Take that statement very seriously. You have an intelligent person on your hands who deserves to be given an intelligent response.

You might reply, "You know, that's an idea I've heard a lot, and there is some truth in it. You'd want to keep it in mind with any kind of forecasting—even, let's say, with what a doctor says when you ask for a prognosis. That's not quite how I work, though. I don't believe anything is written in stone. By seeing the coming trends you can prevent the worst outcomes, and you can also use your energies the best way. How you use those energies is up to you."

Other prospective clients say that they do not want to know the future. Here you correct the impression that astrology is fortune telling. You might tell such people, "We don't have to discuss the future at all. We can get a sense of today and the areas that need improvement or ways that you might be sabotaging yourself. If we come up with new insights or suggestions that help you change the way you operate, then the future is going to change for the better."

If the objection is financial, it is important not to automatically back off. Some people simply do not have the money for a consultation, and nothing you say can alter that reality. You would tend to hear the truth in what they're saying. For others, it's a matter of priorities, and you need to convince them that a chart is a smart investment. Show how this reading is valuable and would save them money. For example, if the person is in therapy, talk about how the insights gained will save therapeutic time and money. By discovering which issues can be most fruitfully addressed in the coming year, the work with their therapist can be even more effective. Suppose they are thinking of moving to another state, and they need to save money for the move. Explain relocation charts and Astro*Carto*Graphy. Compare the cost of the reading to what it would cost to move and then find out it's not the right place.

How do you know the difference between the potential client and the "Yes, but . . . " types who are just playing games and wasting your time? Game players have their own agenda, so they're not listening. If you have a counter to their objection, they don't even hear you out before they pose the next objection. There's a kind of *gotcha* look on their face when they do pose it. The sincere individual will listen to what you say and engage you in a dialogue.

As you listen, you may hear that the objection is the truth and thus a signal that it's not worthwhile to pursue the matter. Or, perhaps it's something you have a valid answer for and can work through. The real key is listening to people and not getting all bound up in a sales pitch. When you're presenting a canned rap, clients are likely to lose interest. That would be true of anything you were selling. When what you're selling is your understanding of the client, listening to objections shows that you will listen in the session, too.

Composing Appealing Ads—What You Need to Know

The question of whether to advertise or not is one that many astrologers debate. Similarly, lawyers, doctors, and other helping professionals had taboos on advertising for decades. Now, however, you even see their ads on television. Many well-established astrologers say that they do not need to advertise, because all their business comes from repeat clients, referrals, and word-of-mouth. That's lovely for them, but astrologers who are just starting out in practice, or who have relocated, need to get the word out that they are available. Judiciously placed ads or flyers can bring in clients who will be the start of a practice.

What is a judiciously placed ad? My own experience, in moving from one coast to another, was that ads in the New Age newspapers brought spiritually inclined clients who were a pleasure to work with. Annual directories, with their expensive ads, brought virtually no result. Advertisements in the regular media like local newspapers produced some unwelcome callers and no serious clients. I have not placed an ad or listing in the yellow pages, but colleagues who have done so report that it brings them calls. You would want to experiment for yourself, as media conditions are different in different areas.

How would you compose an effective ad? As a start, consult a book or tape on sales or borrow a book on advertising or public relations from the library. You don't always have to reinvent the wheel—you can learn from the pros. You can also learn by becoming aware of media advertising, because the principles for advertising services are not necessarily so different. Notice what ads appeal to you in the media and analyze what makes them successful. Your own ad should be interesting, polished, and eye-catching.

To remind you of a few of the crucial points made earlier, remember that you aren't selling *yourself*, you're selling services. Put yourself and your self-consciousness aside and focus on the reader. Put the potential client first in the ad. Sell yourself only when you have thoroughly sold the need for your services. As a rule of thumb, spend less than a third of the ad space talking about yourself and two-thirds about the client.

The more specific the ad is, the better the response. If you've identified a niche for yourself, base the ad on it. Pick a target group—who is the ad aimed at? What kinds of clients are you especially good with or interested in? Write as though you were talking to them. What would their concerns, issues, and needs be? How can working with you meet those needs? How is your work different from others using similar methods or approaches to the same issues?

Again we run into that ethical fine line. You don't want to climb on a bandwagon like ACAs, codependency, or eating disorders unless you have something to offer. You can—and should—read up on these hot topics, because clients will ask about them. Don't pretend to know more than you do, because clients will sense that and be turned off.

One element in the ad could be a short bio. We'll be working on a bio in the next section, and what you learn about yourself in that process can also help in composing ads. The short version of the bio can be used, but the client isn't interested in all those workshops you took or who you studied with. They just want to know you do have credentials and experience. When you mention no credentials, the buyer will beware.

In preparing this chapter, I scanned ads in *Free Spirit*, New York's foremost New Age newspaper. Many were hopelessly dull; others made outrageous claims, like the man I'd never heard of who claimed to be the world's greatest living astrologer. (I have to say, though, that

that one was tempting! What if it were true?) One appealing ad showed a little girl's picture, taken in the 1940s, which read: "Missing Person: Have you lost the little child in you? Out of fear, we bury the child in us at a tragically early age, losing our true selves and leaving a painful wound. I can help you heal yourself by letting your little child resurface and enrich your life." That's a good ad—striking, specific, and sensitive. A fun ad by a massage therapist who did house calls was headlined: HAVE HANDS, WILL TRAVEL.

Although we don't know how well those particular ads worked, here are leads from two ads which have consistently worked well, so you can get a sense of what clients might be looking for. I've had hundreds of responses to this first one.

> WHY GET YOUR CHART DONE AGAIN?
>
> You'd get a second opinion on surgery, so it's smart to get one on your life. Astrologers, like doctors, vary in approach, qualifications, and experience. Periodic chart updates, like annual physicals, clarify what's happening in your life. Focus readings throw light on specific difficulties and your contribution to them.

Here's one for August, New York's most dreaded month:

> WHILE YOUR THERAPIST IS AWAY . . .
>
> Rather than regret the hiatus in your work together, use this time to take stock of your progress and set new goals. Periodic astrological readings highlight issues you can productively address in therapy in the coming year. They can also throw light on an emotional morass.

In both cases, a brief bio of my qualifications followed the text.

Be creative in writing the ad, with the lead being the primary hook. Your ad deserves time and thought. Read it as though a stranger wrote it. Would you be drawn to it? Don't be discouraged if there's no immediate response. Often people have to see a name for a while before they call. However, if months go by with no result, rethink your ad and possibly get a professional opinion from someone who does promotion or advertising copy.

Just Send Us a Bio . . .

You've practiced a few years, feel good about your work, and have a special approach you want to share with others. You decide it's time to do a workshop. You call the local New Age center, and they love the idea.

"Great!" the coordinator says. "Now, just send us a bio."

Feeling warm and good, you hang up and sit down to write. Three months later, the bio is still not done, so the workshop is not happening, and your stomach churns every time you think about it.

Here's another version of the same story. Friends, colleagues, and appreciative clients are urging you to do a brochure so you can promote yourself more widely. You have something special to offer, a unique combination of services that fills a gap. You sit down to write the bio . . . Two years later, there's still no brochure. No ad, either, since for the ad, you'd need to write . . . guess what?

Granted, a certain amount of writing skill is helpful, and a bit of promotional savvy would come in handy. However, it's really not these things that stop us. Most of us have the required basic communication skills or we wouldn't be able to talk to clients. We've watched enough commercials and read enough ads to have a sense of what's appealing.

The real reasons are emotional—with self-esteem often the major barrier. When we sit down to compose a bio or ad, feelings of inadequacy may loom. "Am I really any good? Maybe I'm fooling myself. Maybe I don't know all that much." Tackling self-doubting statements is the first step. Co-existing with low self-esteem may be a New Age variety of egotism. "My work is so special and so unique, not to mention so divinely inspired, that I shouldn't have to prove myself to anyone. They should just sense how good I am and come to me."

The work we do feeds into self-doubt. The public has subjected astrology to intense ridicule, and many of us have faced skepticism and putdowns from friends, family, and acquaintances. The fear of looking foolish and of being invalidated can come up strongly when we think of going public. Networking with other astrologers and New Age professionals can provide a much-needed support system when you begin to do promotion.

Apart from its usefulness to your career, writing a bio can be a healing experience—an affirmation of self. You come away from it with a new understanding of who you are and what you've accomplished. In summarizing your life work, you may even discern unsuspected themes in the variety of experiences—a new picture of where all your efforts have led. The process can validate your capabilities and accomplishments. There is often a joyful sense of, "Yes, that is who I am!" You may also share the all-too-human tendency to believe something more strongly when you see it on paper. Thus, a bio can be a legitimization of your curriculum vita. I've helped many colleagues and clients write bios, and it's common for them to finish by saying, "You know what? I'm impressed with myself!"

Finally, a powerful barrier is that many of us have suffered from persecution for speaking out about our beliefs in past lives. It would be surprising if this were the first time you've entertained heretical notions! If the idea strikes a responsive chord, it might be helpful to have past life therapy or at least a reading. Past lives need not have been traumatic to have an impact. A few modest, peaceful lives in a cloister or ashram could make one spiritually reluctant to take center stage.

We can't deal with all possible obstacles here, but you may want to spend time identifying exactly what yours are. Be your own most beloved client for a while so you can move forward and take your special skills and knowledge to a wider audience.

The Nuts and Bolts of Writing a Bio

A bio is a compact summary of your life path as it pertains to your work. A resume is one place to look for material to include, but our goal is something more than a "Reader's Digest Condensed Version" of your resume. Although not all the answers may go into the finished product, ask yourself the following questions:

1) Exactly what is it that you do? For how many years?

2) How did you learn to do it? (Teachers, programs, classes?)

3) What kinds of clients are you especially good with or interested in appealing to?

4) How is your approach different from others using similar methods?

5) Have you had achievements related to the field—courses taught, workshops, publications, media appearances, awards?

6) What life experiences or educational background contributed to your special approach or to your beliefs about service?

7) Is your work affected by any particular philosophy or spiritual teaching?

Based on these questions and others you may think of, make a list of skills and experiences that have made you who you are. Keep the complete list, as it can have more than one use.

Often less is more. We who have been on the path for a while and who are devoted to self-improvement tend to accumulate a variety of skills. They don't all need to go into one bio. When you include long lists, you won't impress the reader. Rather, that tends to have the opposite effect of making you look like a dilettante or jack-of-all-trades, not taking time to master any of them.

Choose only those that are relevant to the purpose of this particular bio. When the item is unrelated to readers' needs, you lose them. The inclusion of irrelevant details makes them wonder if you can focus on them. A bio is not an excuse for an ego trip. Who cares that you were in a theater group, unless your work involves astrodrama? The reader doesn't care that you volunteered at a halfway house for drug addicted teens—unless you're specializing in people in recovery. However, if you're leading an evening about networking, it could be important that you spent a year in Israel in a kibbutz.

Let's say that in thinking about the questions above, you came up with eight items. Next, rank them in order of their importance and also, to some degree, how impressive they are. Put the most important or impressive near the top, rather than in chronological order. Recent accomplishments are likely to be more skilled and more pertinent to what you're doing now. What you do and what your qualifications are would usually go first.

Now summarize the list, blending it into complete and readable sentences. Keep polishing and cutting out repetitious or unnecessary phrases. Pretend you're sending a telegram and have to pay per word. (If it goes into an ad, you will!) Remember that your audience has a limited attention span—someone else's bio gets boring after about twenty-five words. Pretend that you're reading about a complete stranger—what would you think of that person? Give it to friends and colleagues and get their honest feedback. Make sure the grammar and spelling are perfect before you send it out.

If you've followed all these steps and still feel stuck, why not hire someone to help? Writing may be a block that you needn't overcome in order to make a worthwhile contribution to your clients' lives. You don't have to heal all your self-esteem issues in order to have something valuable to offer. A public relations specialist can help you over the hurdle. They have special training and experience in how to present you in the best possible light. A one-time consultation need not be prohibitive—the PR person may even be willing to trade for services.

An outsider may see you in a better light than you see yourself. The expert also has a more detached view of exactly what is—and what is not—impressive about you! Remember, however, that public relations people may have little understanding of astrology. You need to be firm about presenting yourself accurately. Still, explaining your work intelligibly to an outsider may be a valuable part of the process.

Tailoring the Bio to Different Situations

Once completed, the bio isn't written in stone for all time. The items on your list that weren't appropriate to your current plans may still be useful in the future. I have separate writeups for astrology, flower essences, writing, and social work. The most important facts, like qualifications and educational background, may appear in all of them, but the emphasis and order is different.

It is also useful to have long and short versions. For example, a conference coordinator may need to see a comprehensive summary to decide if you should be a speaker. However, the listing that goes in the program may be only four or five lines. (Incidentally, the current trend in choosing speakers is to ask candidates to submit lecture tapes, so hang on to tapes of your classes or lectures.)

The bio you send out when you want to speak to professional colleagues will differ from what you include on a flyer about a public lecture. For peers, you'd want more specific details about who you studied with, where you've worked or lectured, and what techniques or theoretical orientations you espouse. The public will not understand such technical details or even bother to read them. They just want to know how your lecture or service will benefit them. They don't want to know your whole life history, just that you are qualified and that you have something they need.

Financial Options to Consider for Your Clients

As you advertise or give public lectures, you will attract many kinds of clients. To return to the subject of money briefly, there may be people you'd find it rewarding to work with who are genuinely unable to afford your services. A few astrologers work on a sliding scale, although not too many. Therapists do it because they feel no one should be disqualified from getting help for financial reasons. If a sliding scale comes out of a genuine desire to serve the less fortunate—rather than merely relieving guilt about charging—by all means do it. However, be sure that the bottom of the scale is comfortable, because many of your clients are going to slide right down to it. If it's too low, you are going to be unhappy and that attitude will bleed through into the reading itself.

Some astrologers give discounts for various kinds of people, like repeat clients or their students. People in recovery programs sometimes give discounts to others in recovery. Many extend professional courtesy to other astrologers or other kinds of helping people. You'd need to think policies like this through, sometimes on a case by case basis, to see if there's any of the rescuer motivation. If you ever become uncomfortable, that is a clue that you should not be doing it.

To me, once you have reached a certain level of skill and are charging, a trade is better than doing a reading for free, because that's too much like charity. It's not a good idea to do a reading because you feel sorry for someone. Even though consciously grateful, on some level, the person may feel you are condescending. People may well dislike the position of being rescued, which does not honor their ability to help themselves. Letting them do something for you, too, preserves their dignity. Even if you're just starting out and you're doing a consultation for a friend, you may want to let your friend do something for you in return. Clients often get less from readings if they don't have to pay, at least in kind, because they value the advice less. You will probably also work harder at the reading when people pay you than if you're doing it free. So, maybe clients *are* right and it's not worth as much as if they paid for it.

Trades can be gratifying, but only if you want what you're trading for. The best trade is when both parties think they got the better end of the deal. If clients come for advice about a career change because they are doing work they hate, you're better off not trading them for that hated line of work! I have made many wonderful trades. I've been rolfed and acupressured, had my apartment painted, gotten a beautiful one-of-a kind quilt, and had stationery and brochures designed. I get many services that I might not feel I could—or at least should—afford.

Letting clients owe you or pay in installments is quite like letting a friend owe you money. It creates problems—especially with people you already know from other contexts. You would especially want to avoid doing this with clients whose 8th house has outer planet complications. They would simply be playing out with you the same money games they've been playing all their lives. When clients say they'll pay in installments, you usually wind up getting exactly what they've paid by the end of the session. However, it hasn't been a problem when clients give me a postdated check.

Should You Give Up Your Straight Job?

Finally, there's the question of how much you can expect to earn as an astrologer. Where does the public get the idea that astrologers make scads of money? Or, that we spend all our time counseling movie stars on whether they should get their hair done today? (Or presidents on whether this is a good day to drop the bomb?) My advice is, don't give up your straight job, at least not right away. Let the practice build. That also takes off the pressure in terms of giving yourself time to learn and grow in the work. It's a good second income in the early years.

The more dependent you are on astrology for your total livelihood, the more difficult it can become to handle money questions calmly with clients. A second or third way of earning money helps out in the bleak times. Many astrologers find that the months of August and mid-November to early January are slow. People are spending money on vacations and school clothes in August. During December, many people don't have much money to spend on themselves or gifts, so I often run a holiday special with a reduction in price. If you decide to go into astrology full time, start in a month like October or February rather than in a month when the nation is on vacation.

It's different when you work for yourself than when you are paid a salary. Being on salary provides security and protection, no matter what its disadvantages. Working for yourself is like looking for a job every day of your life—not easy. Something like 80 percent of businesses fail in their first year—and astrology is a business. Some astrologers do well, but they are either very good at astrology or very good at business—usually both. You can be an excellent astrologer and be broke unless you learn to promote yourself. Developing businesslike attitudes, promotional skills, and an eye to marketability can make the difference between just surviving and having a successful practice. I hope the ideas in this chapter will be helpful to you, but you may also want to take a trip to your local business library. The books in the reading list on pages 231–232 are general suggestions to further your understanding of the principles I've discussed.

A Last Wish

Dear Readers,

So many of you have written me wonderful and touching letters over the years that a letter seemed a fitting way to close. I hope you have found the various chapters and topics helpful. If you're just starting out, perhaps some of the principles discussed here will help you avoid some of the mistakes many of us made as fledgling astrologers. Even after years of practice, giving readings can still sometimes be challenging, but the early years are often full of painful self-doubt. An internship or mentor relationship would be the ideal solution, but until that institution develops in our field, this book is my attempt to give some wisdom and counsel born of my own experience.

If you've already been practicing a while, perhaps these counseling techniques will help make your practice even better. If the focus of your work is very different from mine, you may be stimulated to write curriculum materials from that perspective. We need all the input we can get from seasoned professionals to help the newer members of our field, as well as for each of us to get sharper in our practice.

Because my time is increasingly spent in the world of flower remedies, I suspect this will be my last astrology book and doubtlessly my most valuable legacy to the field. (If it's not the last book, then we can all have a good giggle at my expense!) My books have given me many gifts over the years, including traveling all over the world and meeting astrology lovers from many cultures. The most special gift has been feedback from readers like yourself about the ways my words have touched you and contributed to your lives and your study of astrology. If my earlier books stimulated you to study astrology more deeply and ultimately to go into practice, then I hope this book helps you successfully bridge the gap between student and professional. Each new generation of astrologers uses the experience of the previous generations to become even better, and I am sure that the generations that follow will be the best of all! My fondest wishes go with you.

Donna Cunningham
Port Townsend, Washington

Suggested Reading

America's Top 300 Jobs: A Complete Career Handbook. Indianapolis, IN: Jist Works, 1990.

Andrews, Phyllis, ed. *The Source Book: Social and Health Services in the Greater New York Area.* Phoenix, AZ: Onyx Press, 1989.

Beatty, Melody. *Codependent No More*. New York: Harper/Hazelden, 1987.

Bradshaw, John. *Healing the Shame that Binds You* (Deerfield Beach, FL: Health Communications, 1988).

Cermak, Timmen L., MD. *A Primer for Adult Children of Alcoholics.* Deerfield Beach, FL: Health Publications, 1989.

Cunningham, Donna. *Flower Remedies Handbook*. New York: Sterling Publishing, 1992.

———. *Healing Pluto Problems*. York Beach, ME: Samuel Weiser, 1986.

Fairfield, Gail. *Choice-Centered Astrology*. Smithville, IN: Ramp Creek Publishing, 1990.

Falwell, Jerry. *Strength for the Journey: An Autobiography*. Simon & Schuster, 1987.

Gale, Barry and Linda. *Discover What You're Best At: The National Career Aptitude Test*. New York: Simon & Schuster, 1982.

Handville, Elizabeth, ed. *OCCU-FACTS: Facts on over 565 Occupations*. Largo, FL: Careers, Inc., 1989.

Harkavy, Michael. *101 Careers: A Guide to the Fastest Growing Opportunities*. New York: John Wiley & Sons, 1990.

LeShan, Lawrence. *The Medium, the Mystic, and the Physicist.* New York: Ballantine, 1982.

McEvers, Joan, ed. *Astrological Counseling*. St. Paul, MN: Llewellyn, 1990.

Miller, Alice. *The Drama of the Gifted Child: The Search for the True Self*. New York: Basic Books, 1981.

Park, Jeannie, and Robin Micheli. "Falling Down and Getting Back Up Again," in *People Magazine* (1/29/90).

Petrucelli, Alan W. *Liza! Liza! An Unauthorized Biography of Liza Minnelli*. Walled Lake, MI: Karz-Cohl Publishing, 1983.

Press, Nona. *New Insights into Astrology*. San Diego, CA: ACS, 1991.

Ray, Sondra. *I Deserve Love*. Berkeley, CA: Celestial Arts, 1987.

———. *The Only Diet There Is*. Berkeley, CA: Celestial Arts, 1981.

Sheehy, Gail. *Passages: Predictable Crises of Adult Life*. New York: Bantam, 1976.

Shneidman, E. S. and N. I. Faberow. *Clues to Suicide*. New York: McGraw-Hill, 1957.

Somers, Suzanne, *Keeping Secrets*. New York: Warner, 1988.

Statistical Abstract of the United States, 1990, the National Data Book. Washington, DC: United States Printing Office, 1990.

Strieber, Whitley, *Communion*. New York: Avon, 1988.

Tyl, Noel, ed. *How to Use Vocational Astrology for Success in the Workplace.* St. Paul, MN: Llewellyn Publications, 1992.

U.S. Department of Labor, Bureau of Labor Statistics. *Occupational Outlook Handbook*. Orange, CA: Career Publishing, 1990–1991 edition.

A Career Bibliography for Vocational Astrology

I. A Do-It-Yourself Vocational Test

Gale, Barry and Linda. *Discover What You're Best At.* New York: Simon & Schuster, 1982.

An excellent self-test, designed by two vocational counselors, that clients can use to determine which types of careers suit them best. Order from (201) 767-5937.

II. Career Directories

The following directories are paperbacks and are relatively inexpensive. They are essential tools for vocational readings and good desk references. (They are udpated every other year.) Check your public library under 331.702, perhaps in the reference section, to see which you would like to own.

Harkavy, Michael. *101 Careers: A Guide to the Fastest Growing Opportunities*. New York: John Wiley & Sons, 1990.

A big, readable, excellent book at 350 pages. Order from 1-800-225-5945.

Jist Works, Inc. *America's Top 300 Jobs: A Complete Career Handbook*. Indianapolis, IN: Jist Works, Inc., 1990.

Here is detailed information on each of the careers, including the nature of the work, training and education required, working conditions, employment trends, job outlook, and earning potential. Order from 1-800-648-JIST.

OCCUFACTS: *Facts on over 565 Career Occupations*. Largo, FL: Careers Inc., 1989–90.

An excellent directory that breaks down career information into many categories, including duties, working conditions, physical demands, temperament, aptitudes required, and earnings. Order from Careers Inc., Box 135, Largo, FL 34649-0135.

U.S. Department of Labor, Bureau of Labor Statistics. *Occupational Outlook Handbook*. Orange, CA: Career Publishing, Inc. 1990–91 Edition.

About as dry as they come, but with the true statistics on what's happening to 250 major careers. The books listed earlier were based on this one, but they tend to be more readable. Order from 1-800-854-4014.

INDEX

About the Author

Donna Cunningham received a Master's degree in social work from Columbia University. With over 25 years of counseling experience as a certified psychotherapist she uses various healing tools—such as flower essences, guided meditation, and visualizations in her work. In 1969 she began her astrological practice, and received certification by Professional Astrologers, Inc. and the American Federation of Astrologers. She has been speaking at national and international astrological conferences since 1970 and has written hundreds of articles. She is the author of *An Astrological Guide to Self-Awareness, Healing Pluto Problems,* and *Being the Lunar Type in a Solar World,* among many other books. Donna currently lives in Port Townsend, WA where she has her practice and is the advice columnist for *Horoscope.*